# FOWL LANGUAGE

## THE STRUGGLE IS REAL

### BRIAN GORDON

Andrews McMeel
PUBLISHING®

# INTRODUCTION

When I became a parent, I was sure I was going to ruin my kids at any moment and lived in constant fear of making a single mistake. Unfortunately, my mistakes began in the delivery room and have persisted ever since.

I'm happy to report, however, that my kids are way more resilient than I give them credit for. Despite their fragile appearance, evolution has seemingly hardened small children against numbskull parents like myself.

If anything, I'm the one who's taken a beating.

The sleepless nights, the constant worry, and the endless bickering have all taken a toll on my body and mind. I'm almost positive there was a time when my hair wasn't graying at an alarming pace and my ever-deepening wrinkles could still euphemistically be called "smile lines." But my memory's shot, too, so maybe I've always looked this haggard?

In spite of all this, people still ask me from time to time if I have any advice about parenting. Raising two precocious kids hasn't killed me (yet), so I guess I do have some grounds to spread the little bit of wisdom I've gained through trial and error. Mostly error.

So, by way of analogy, here it is, the one piece of wisdom I can say I've learned:

When you board a plane, they give you a safety talk about possible emer-gencies. If something bad happens, you're supposed to put your own oxygen mask on first, before you put your kids' on. This seems antithetical, as we parents tend to instinctively protect our kids above all else. But the reason they tell you to do this is that if you wait to put on your own mask, you're likely to pass out. And then you'll be of no use to your kids or anyone else.

That kinda sums up parenting for me.

If you forget to prioritize care for yourself, it's gonna bite you in the ass one way or another. Whether it's your mental or physical health, or the health of your grown-up relationships, you gotta put your metaphorical mask on first, or you're gonna metaphorically pass the hell out.

Other tips:
- If your kid will tolerate it, swaddle the crap out of them. It totally helped my son calm down as a baby. I'd still do it, but he's in fourth grade now, and evidently that's frowned upon.

- If you have the opportunity to take a nap, you take that damn nap. Laundry can wait.

- If all else fails, try the cathartic act of bitching about your children by drawing them as ducks. Works for me.

— Brian Gordon, October 2017

For my ducklings, Max and Phoebe

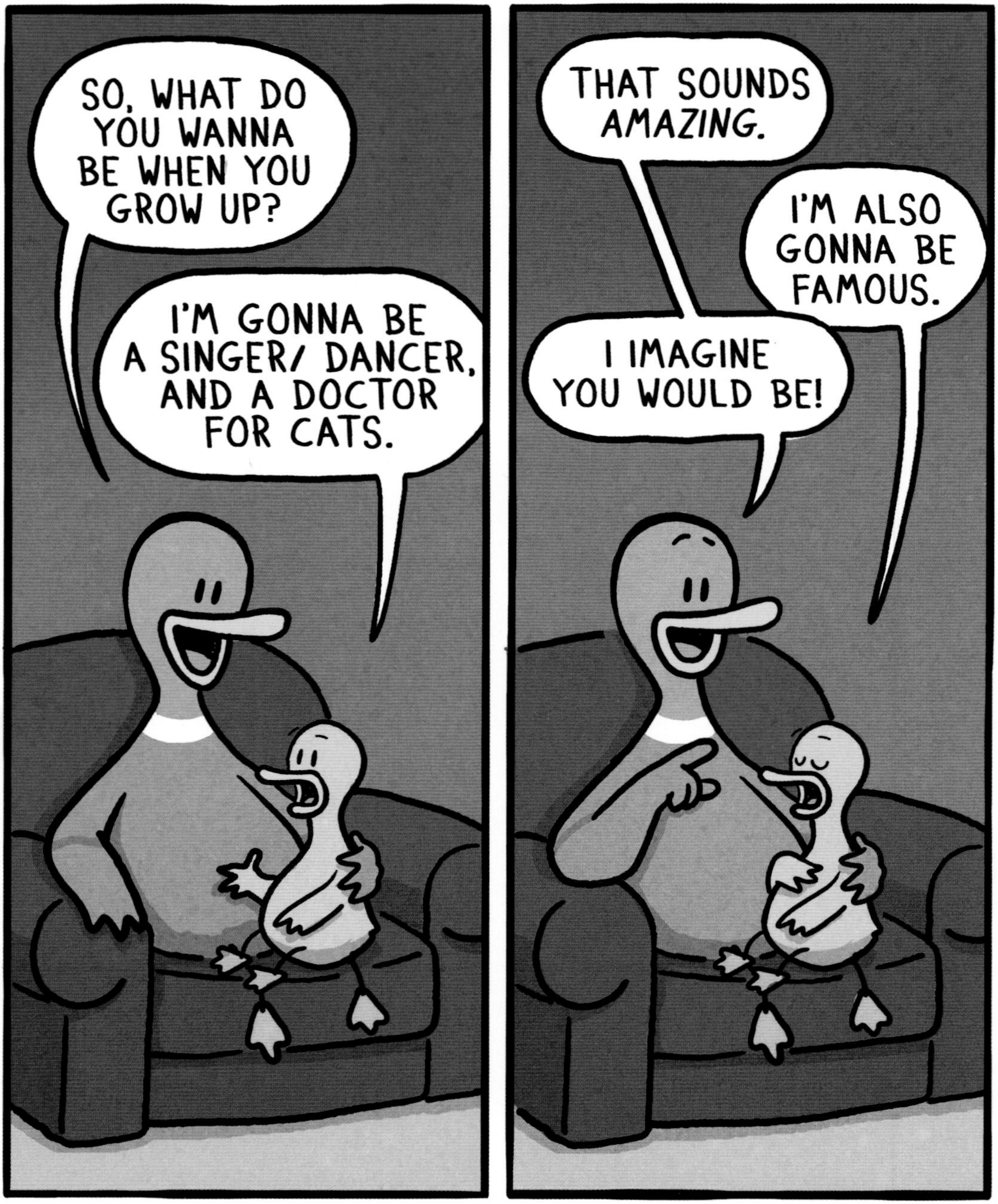
SO, WHAT DO YOU WANNA BE WHEN YOU GROW UP?
I'M GONNA BE A SINGER/ DANCER, AND A DOCTOR FOR CATS.
THAT SOUNDS AMAZING.
I'M ALSO GONNA BE FAMOUS.
I IMAGINE YOU WOULD BE!

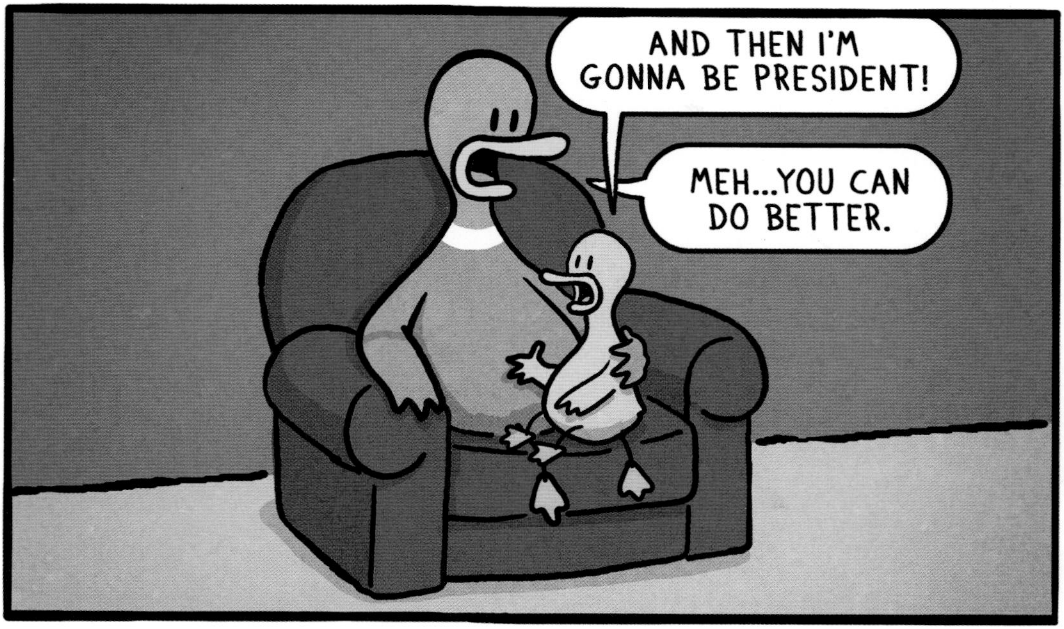
AND THEN I'M GONNA BE PRESIDENT!
MEH...YOU CAN DO BETTER.

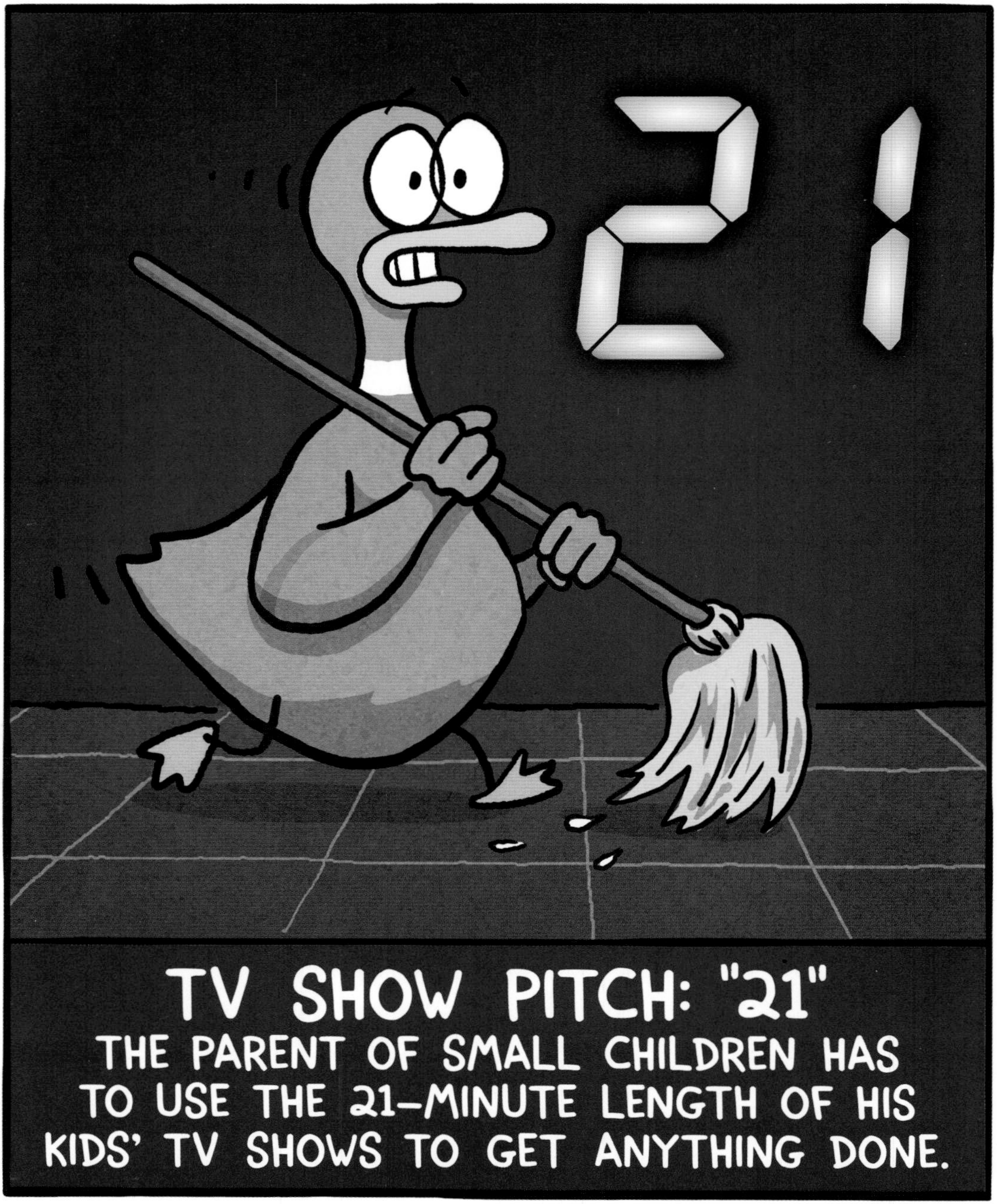
21

## TV SHOW PITCH: "21"

THE PARENT OF SMALL CHILDREN HAS TO USE THE 21-MINUTE LENGTH OF HIS KIDS' TV SHOWS TO GET ANYTHING DONE.

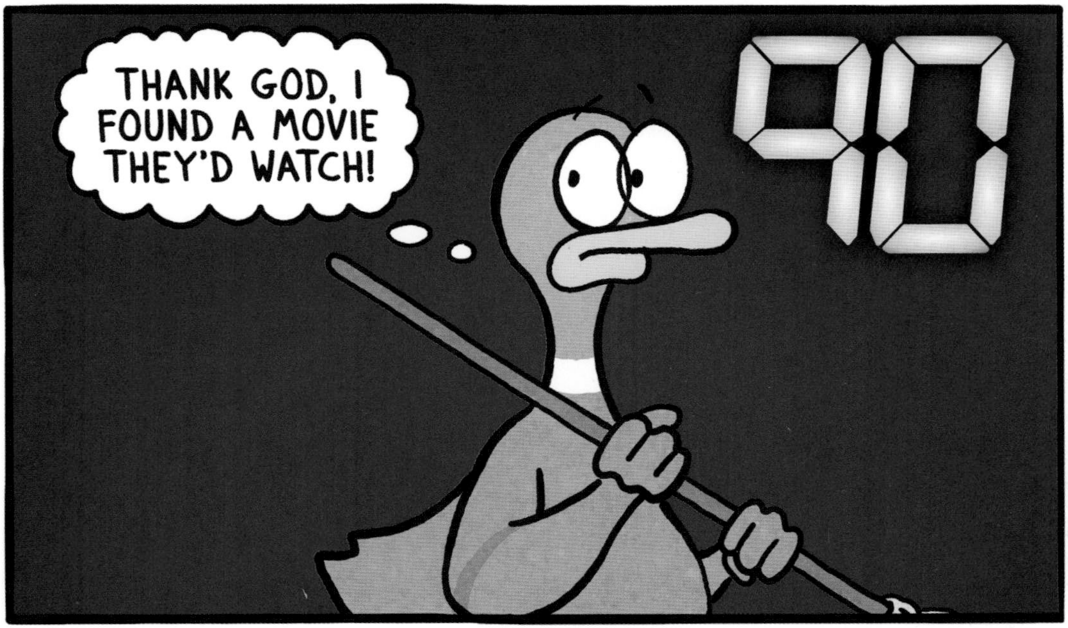
THANK GOD, I FOUND A MOVIE THEY'D WATCH!
90

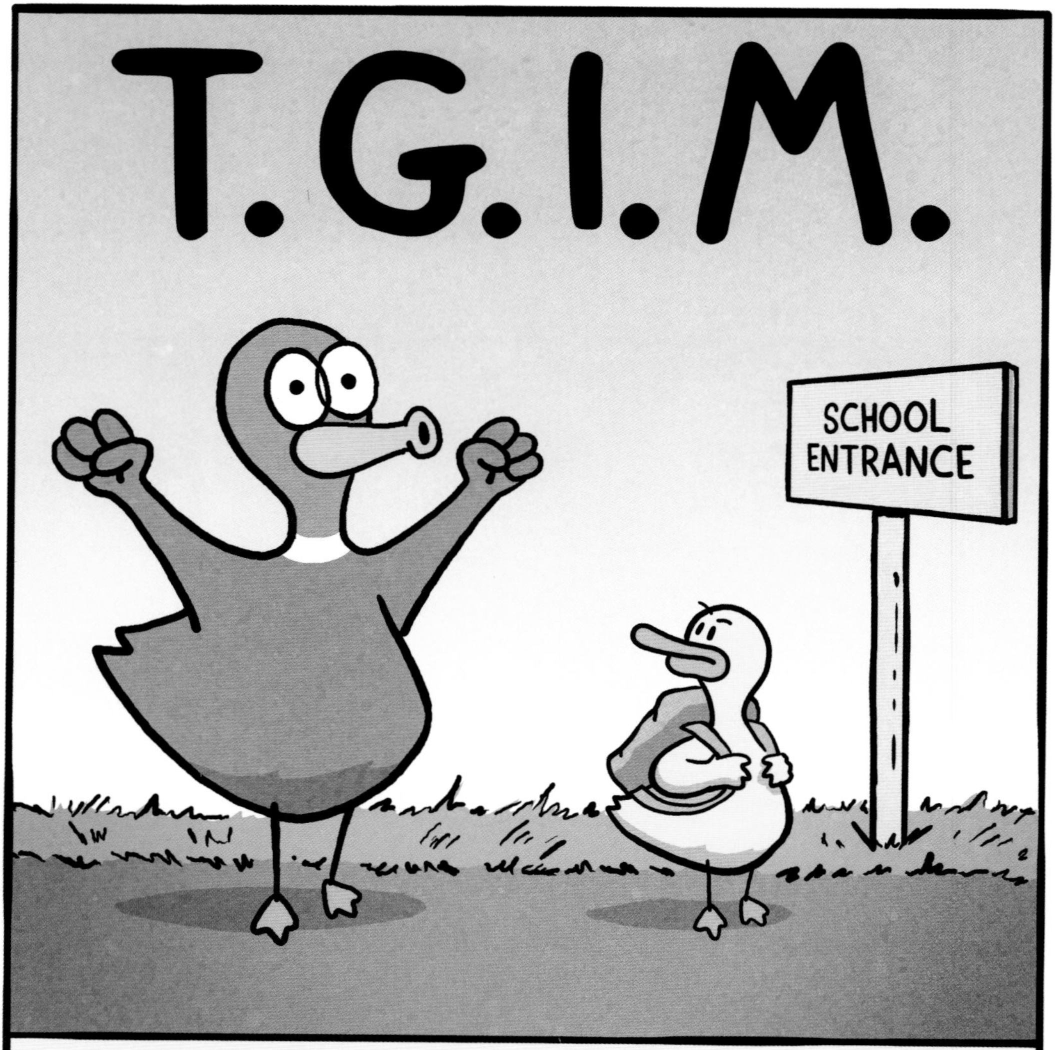
T.G.I.M.
SCHOOL ENTRANCE

THE RALLYING CRY OF EVERY PARENT WHO BARELY SURVIVED AN ESPECIALLY SHITTY WEEKEND WITH THE KIDS.

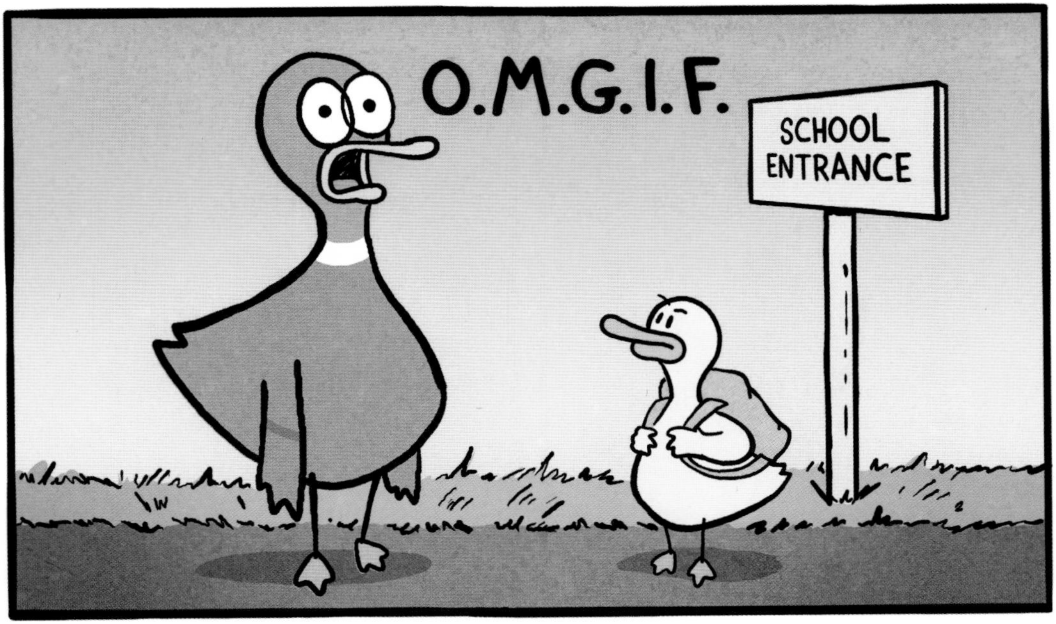
O.M.G.I.F.
SCHOOL
ENTRANCE

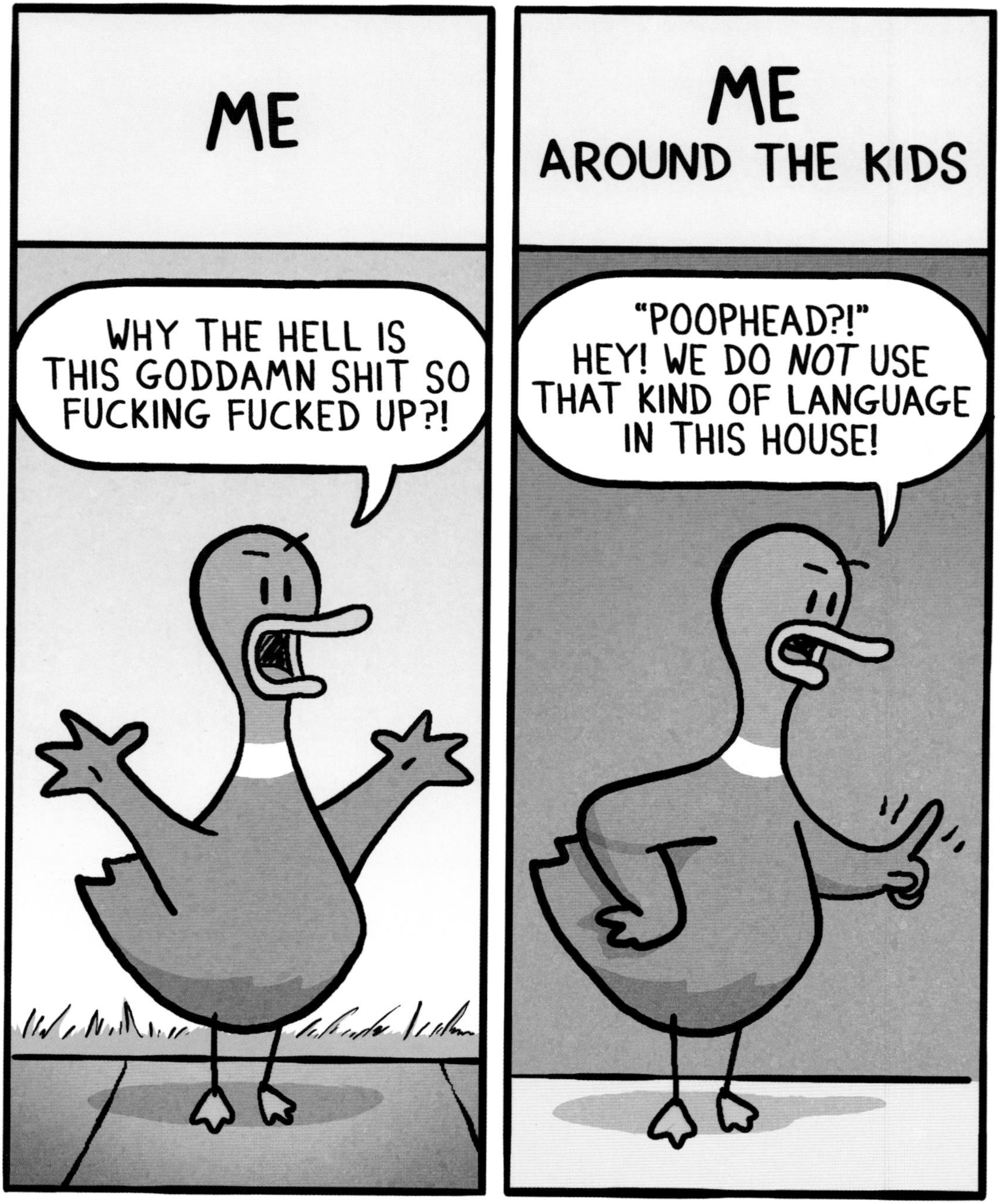
ME
WHY THE HELL IS THIS GODDAMN SHIT SO FUCKING FUCKED UP?!
ME AROUND THE KIDS
"POOPHEAD?!" HEY! WE DO *NOT* USE THAT KIND OF LANGUAGE IN THIS HOUSE!

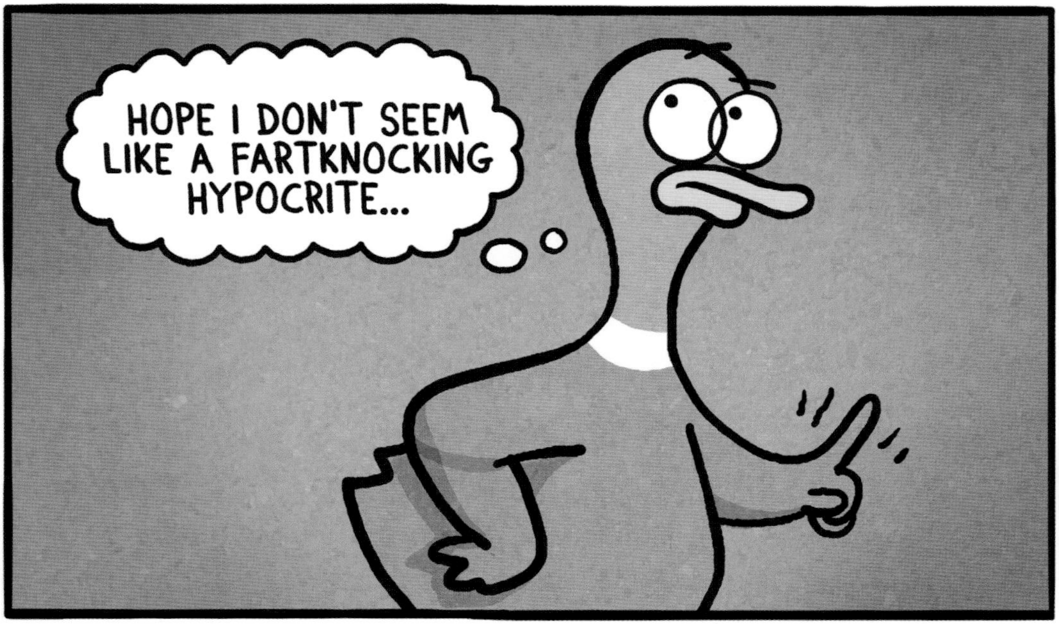
HOPE I DON'T SEEM LIKE A FARTKNOCKING HYPOCRITE...

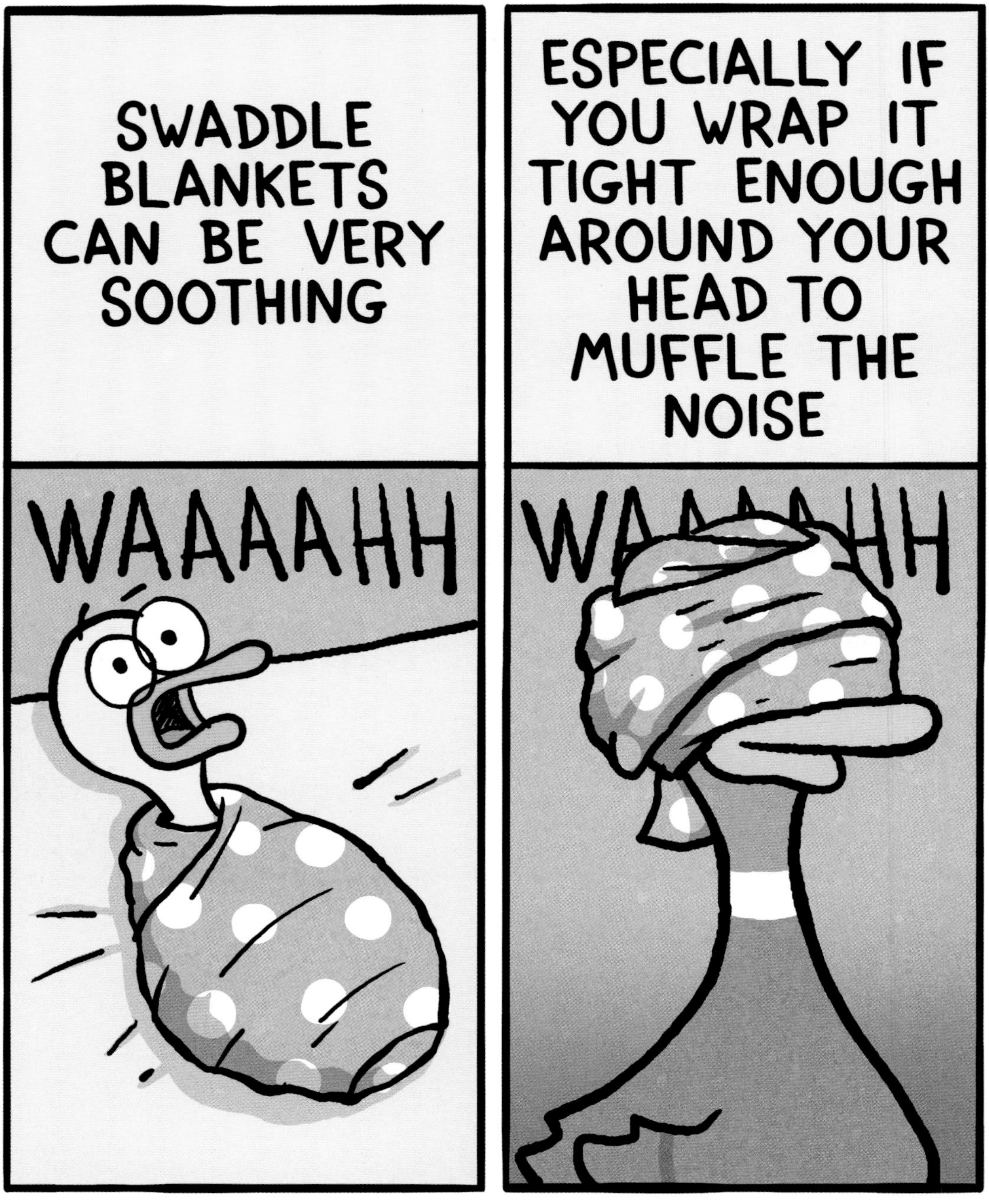
SWADDLE BLANKETS CAN BE VERY SOOTHING
WAAAAHH
ESPECIALLY IF YOU WRAP IT TIGHT ENOUGH AROUND YOUR HEAD TO MUFFLE THE NOISE

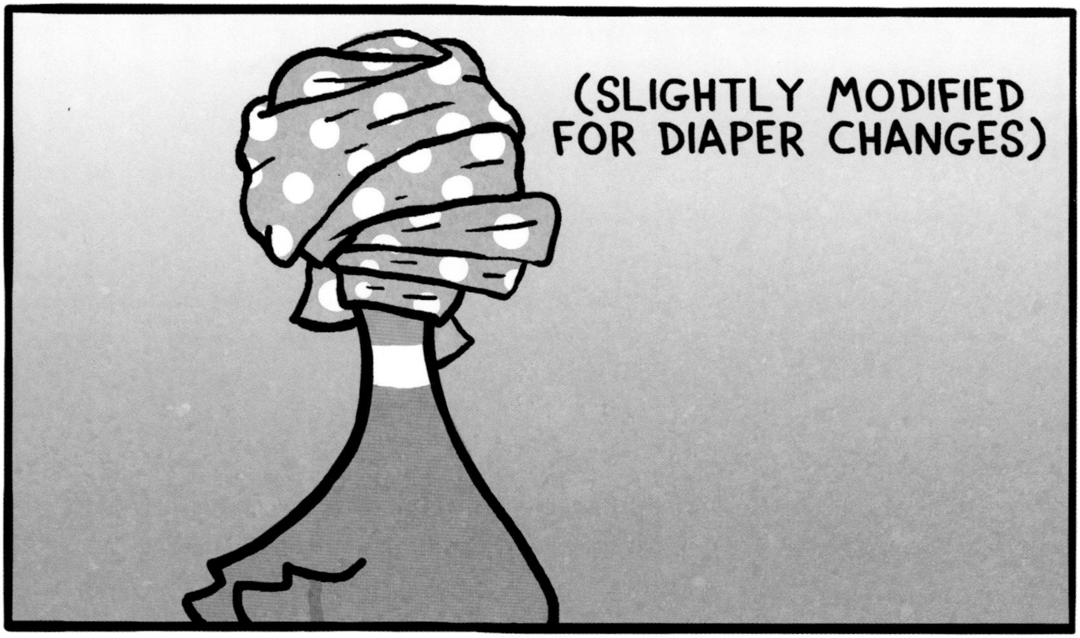
(SLIGHTLY MODIFIED FOR DIAPER CHANGES)

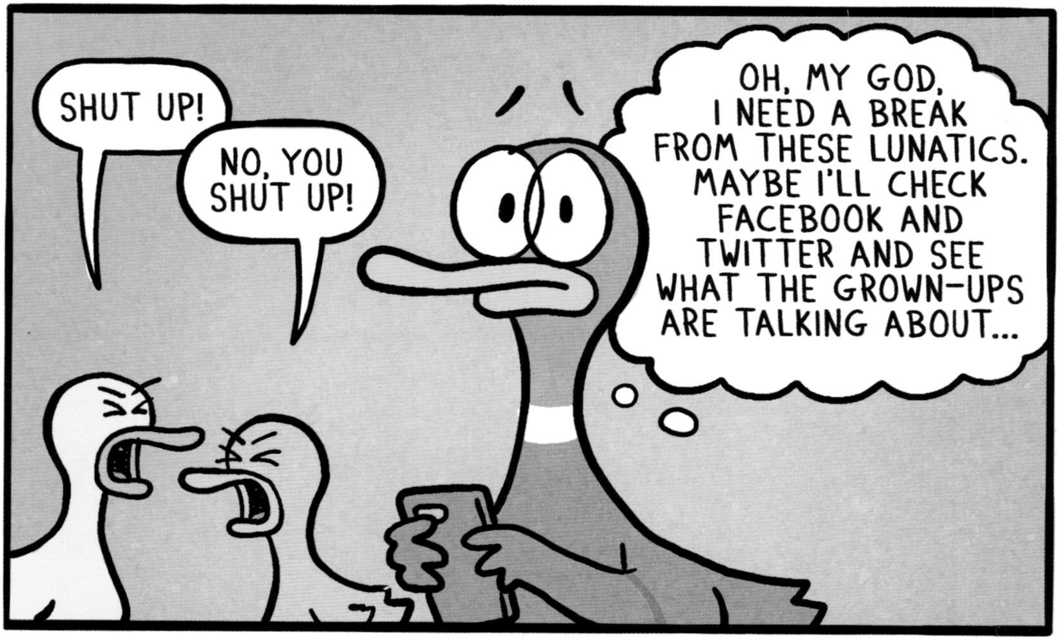
SHUT UP!
NO, YOU SHUT UP!
OH, MY GOD, I NEED A BREAK FROM THESE LUNATICS. MAYBE I'LL CHECK FACEBOOK AND TWITTER AND SEE WHAT THE GROWN-UPS ARE TALKING ABOUT...

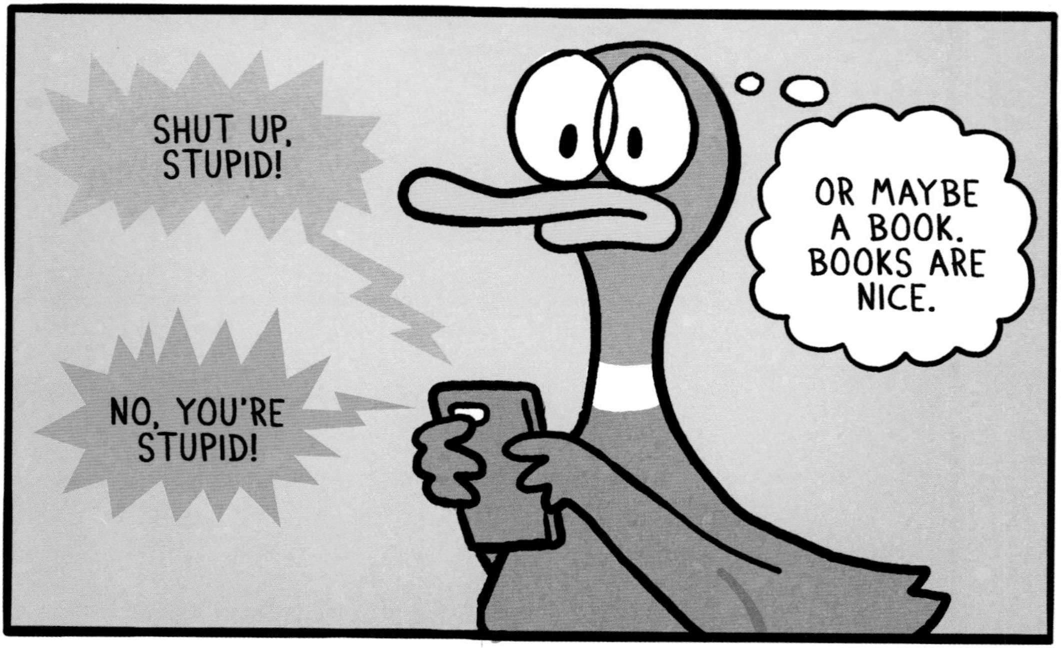
SHUT UP, STUPID!
NO, YOU'RE STUPID!
OR MAYBE A BOOK. BOOKS ARE NICE.

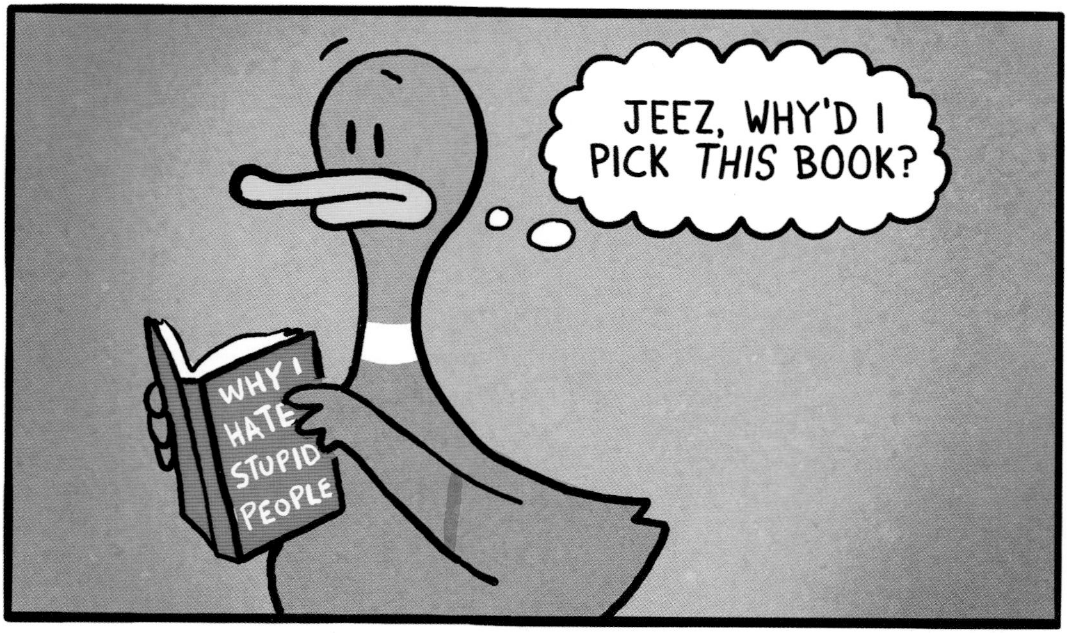
JEEZ, WHY'D I PICK *THIS* BOOK?
WHY I HATE STUPID PEOPLE

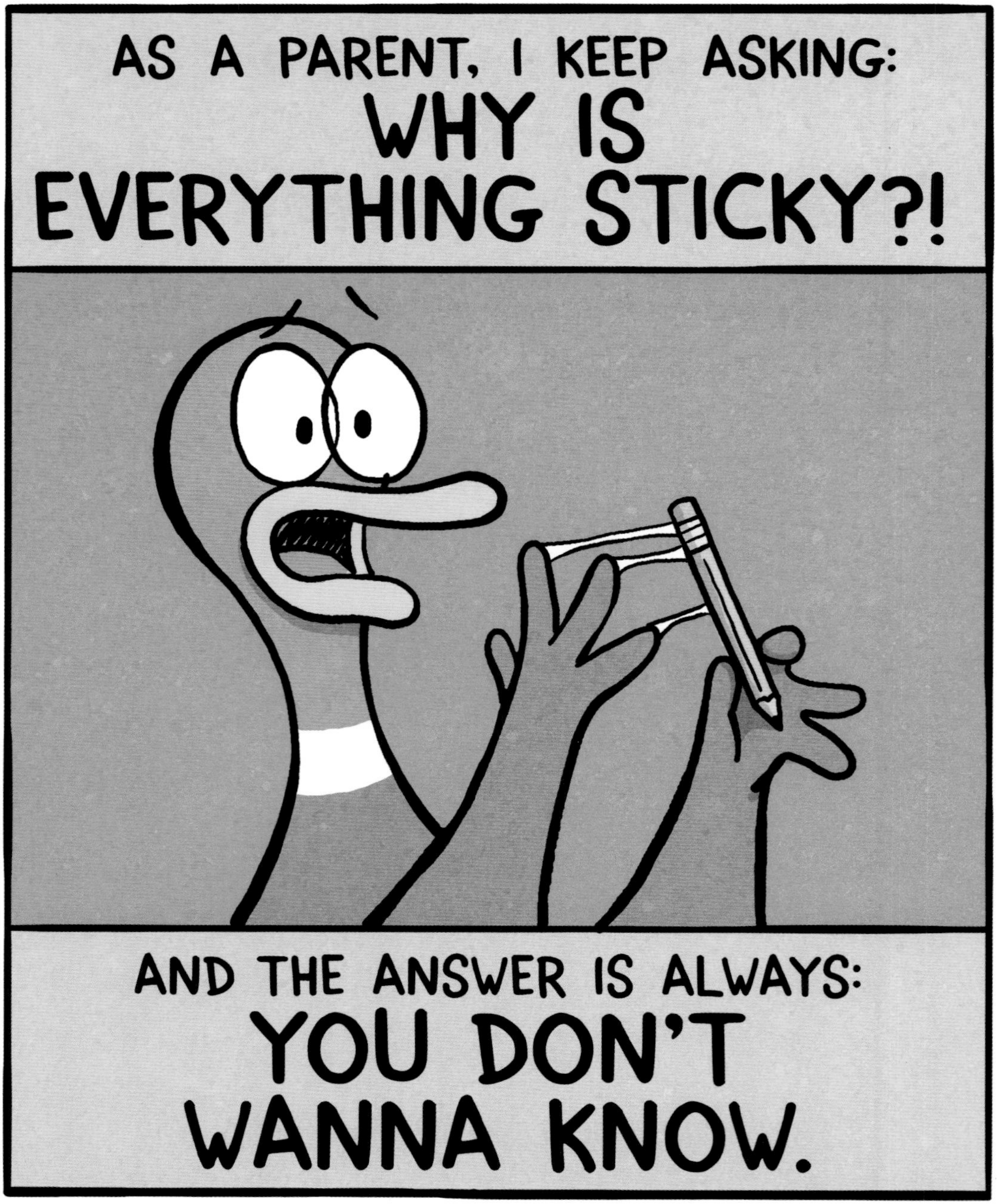
AS A PARENT, I KEEP ASKING:
WHY IS EVERYTHING STICKY?!
AND THE ANSWER IS ALWAYS:
YOU DON'T WANNA KNOW.

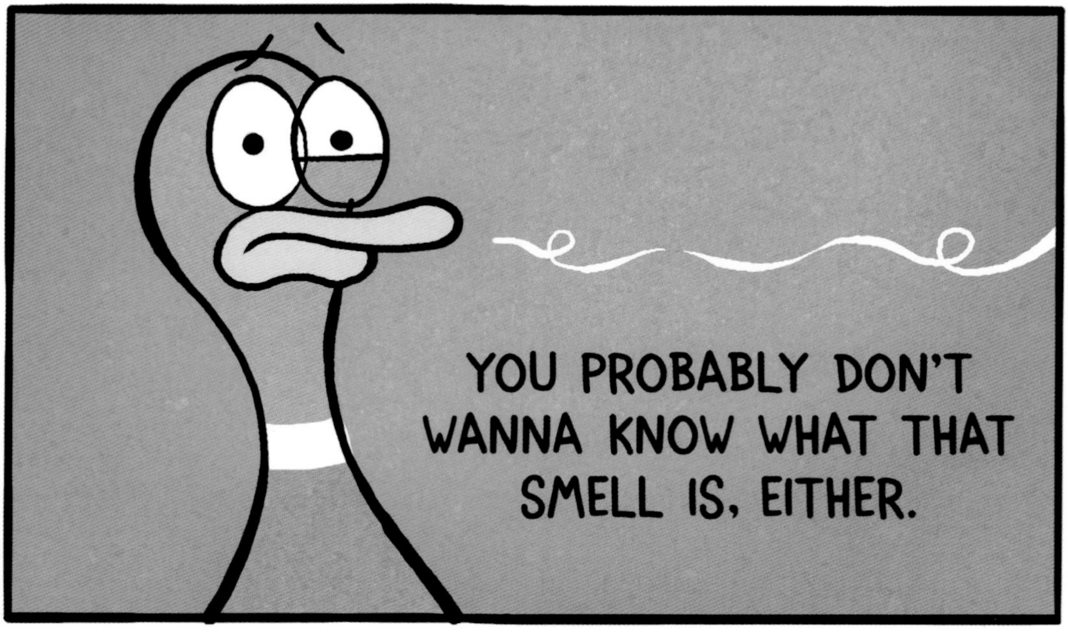
YOU PROBABLY DON'T WANNA KNOW WHAT THAT SMELL IS, EITHER.

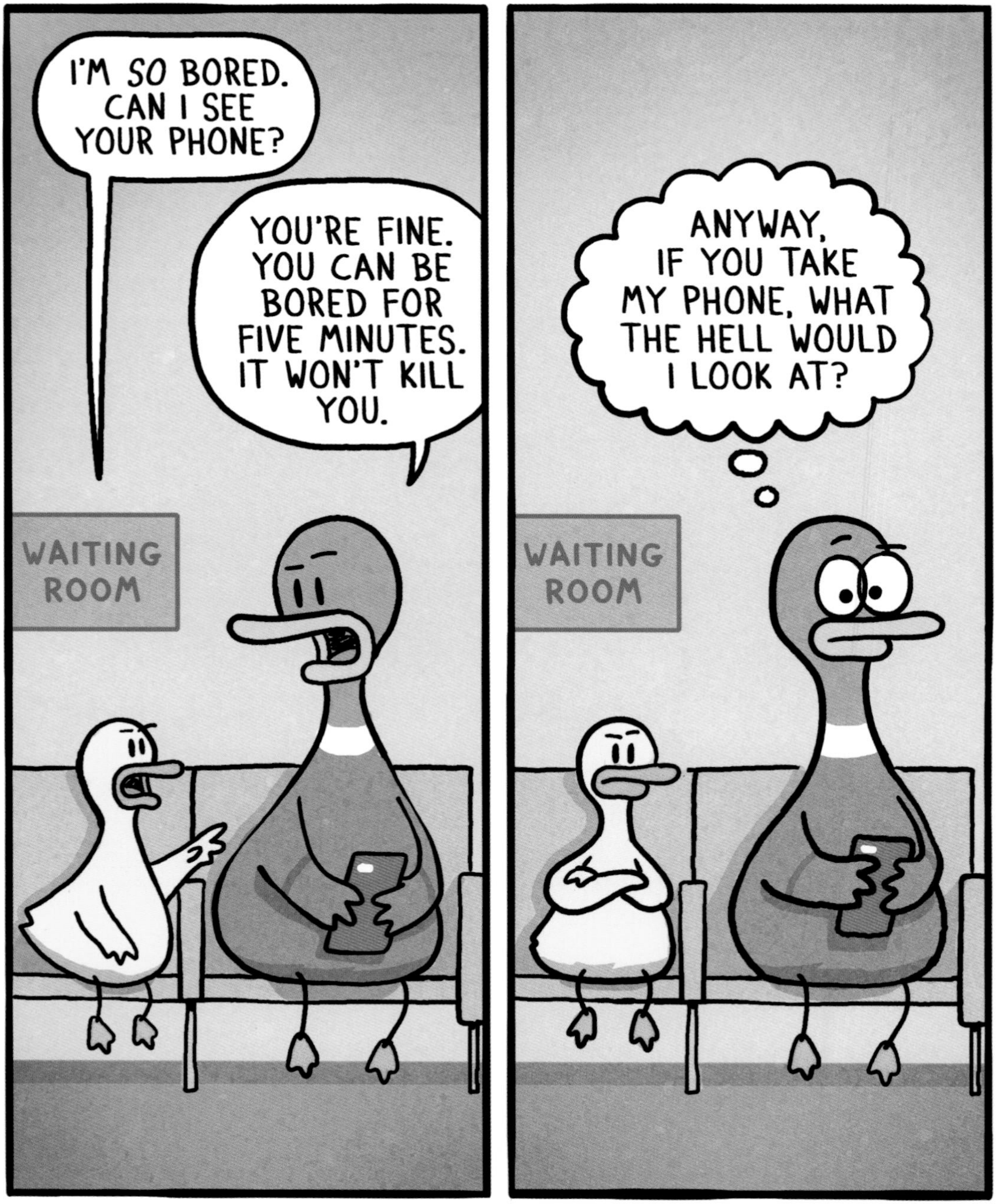
I'M SO BORED. CAN I SEE YOUR PHONE?
YOU'RE FINE. YOU CAN BE BORED FOR FIVE MINUTES. IT WON'T KILL YOU.
WAITING ROOM
WAITING ROOM
ANYWAY, IF YOU TAKE MY PHONE, WHAT THE HELL WOULD I LOOK AT?

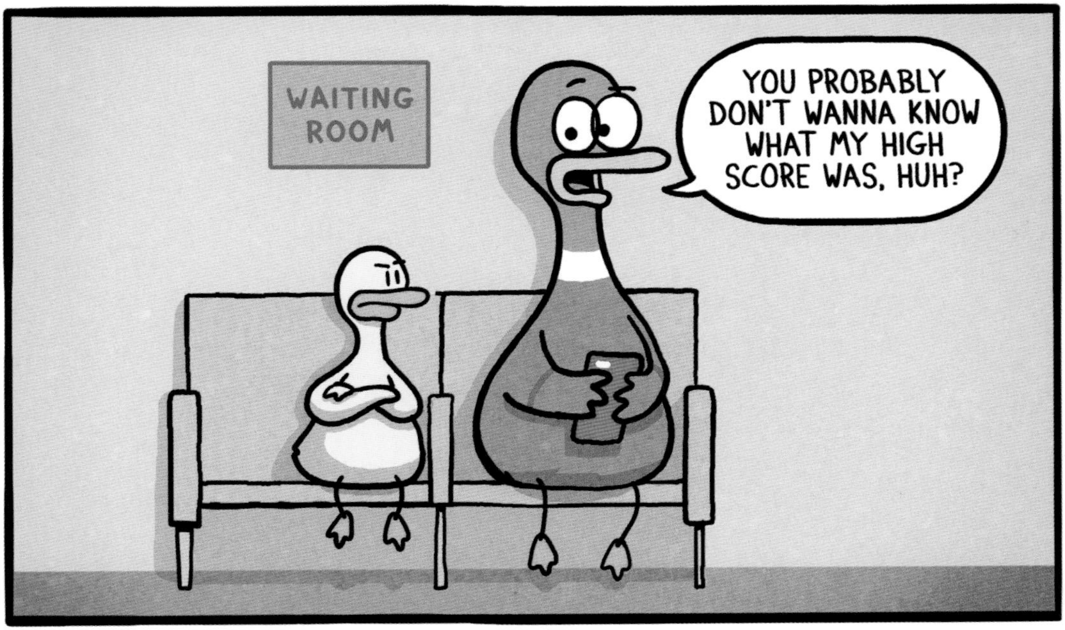
WAITING ROOM
YOU PROBABLY DON'T WANNA KNOW WHAT MY HIGH SCORE WAS, HUH?

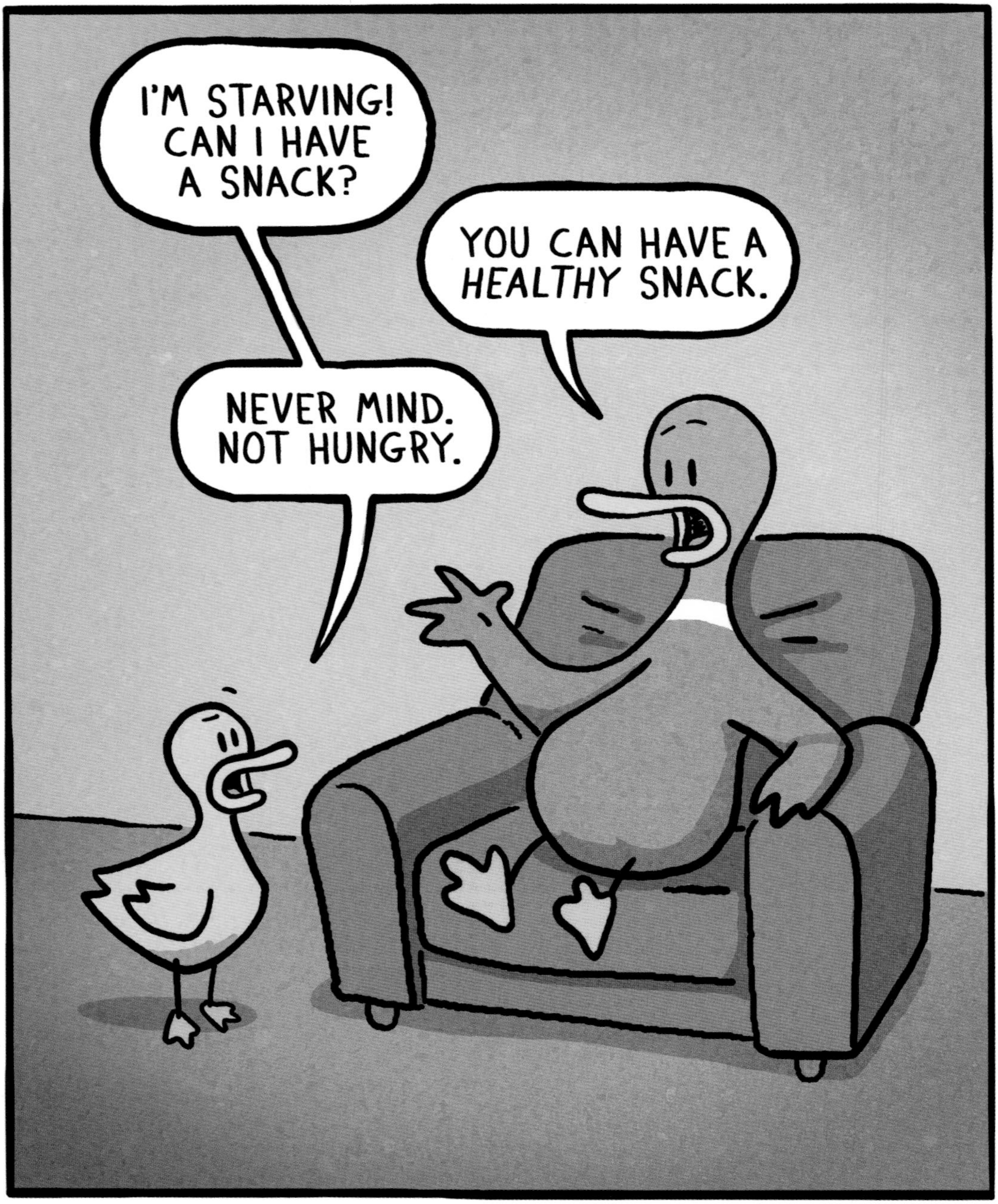
I'M STARVING! CAN I HAVE A SNACK?
YOU CAN HAVE A HEALTHY SNACK.
NEVER MIND. NOT HUNGRY.

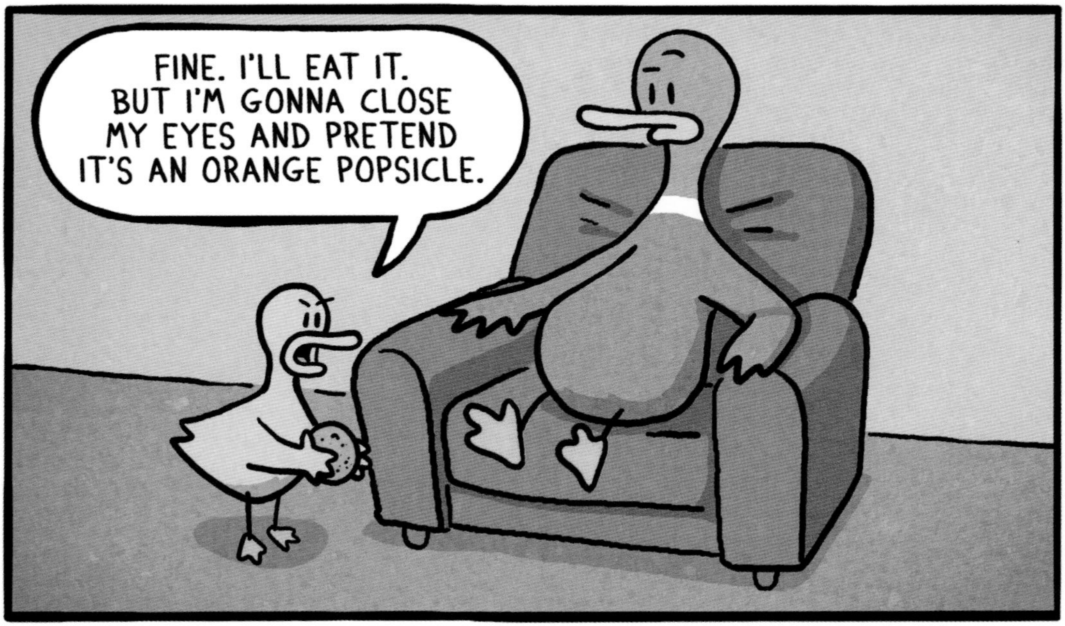
FINE. I'LL EAT IT. BUT I'M GONNA CLOSE MY EYES AND PRETEND IT'S AN ORANGE POPSICLE.

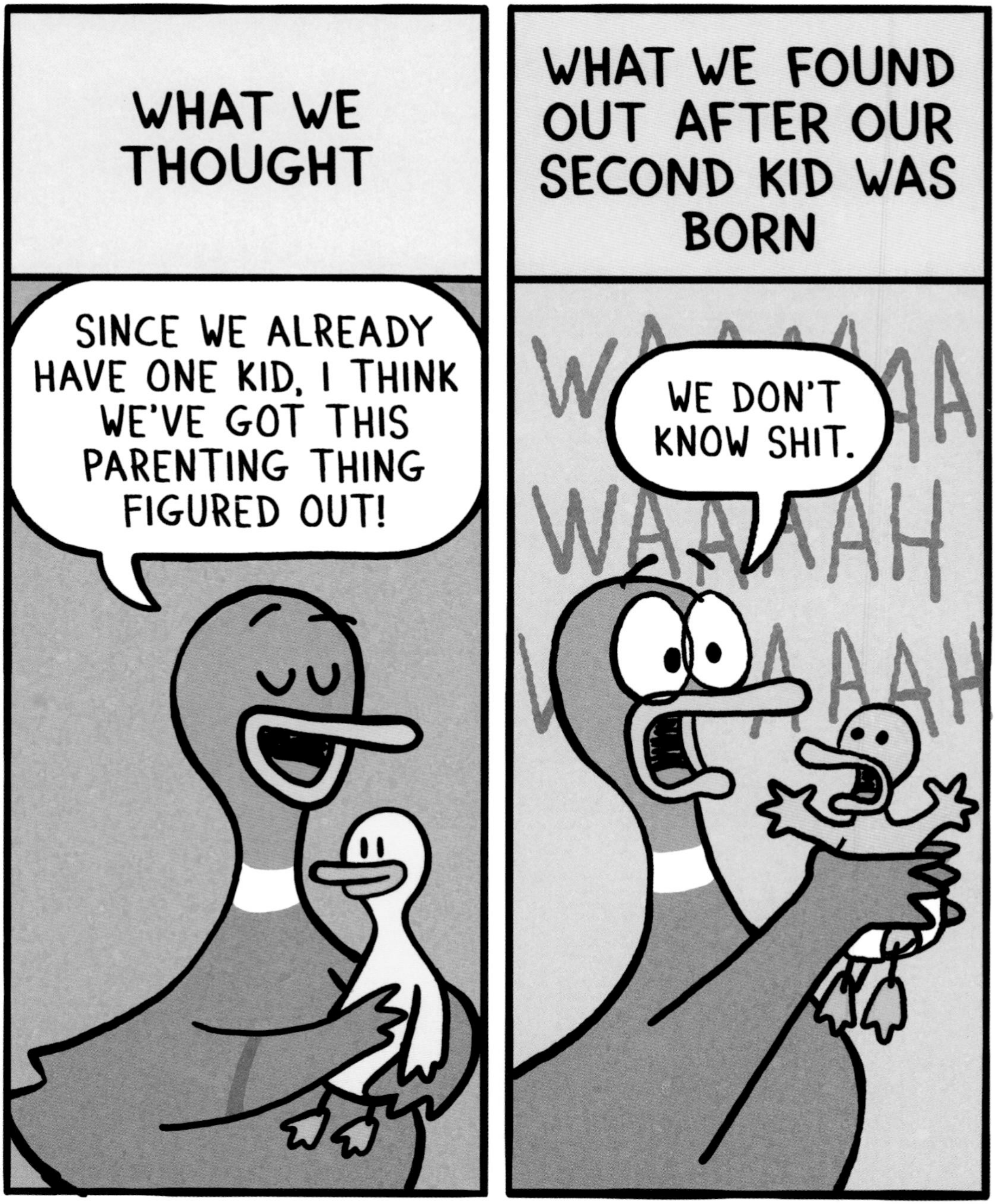
WHAT WE THOUGHT
SINCE WE ALREADY HAVE ONE KID, I THINK WE'VE GOT THIS PARENTING THING FIGURED OUT!
WHAT WE FOUND OUT AFTER OUR SECOND KID WAS BORN
WE DON'T KNOW SHIT.

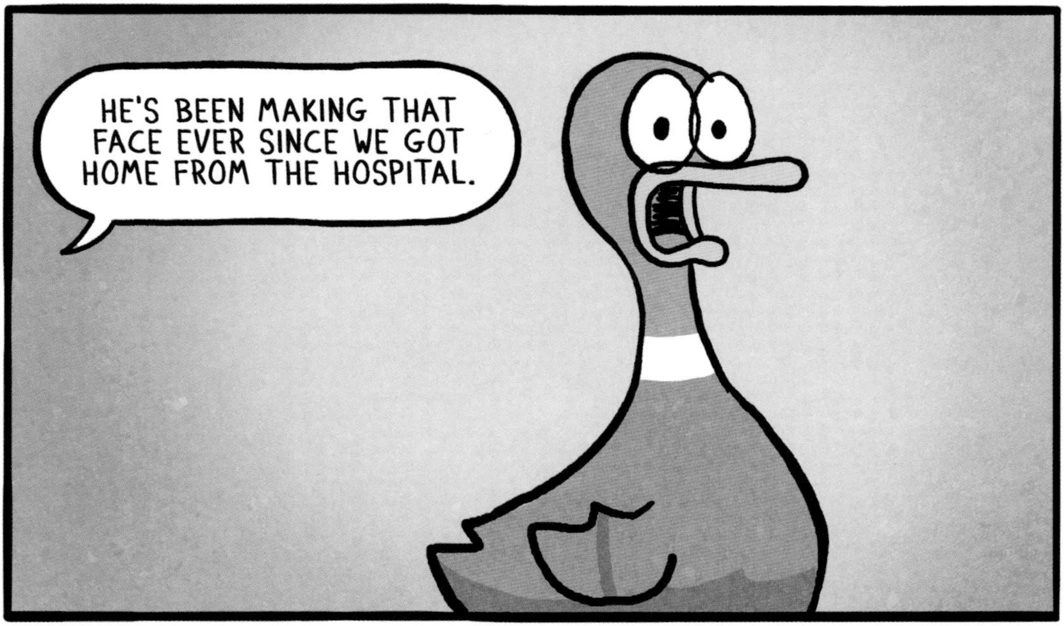
HE'S BEEN MAKING THAT FACE EVER SINCE WE GOT HOME FROM THE HOSPITAL.

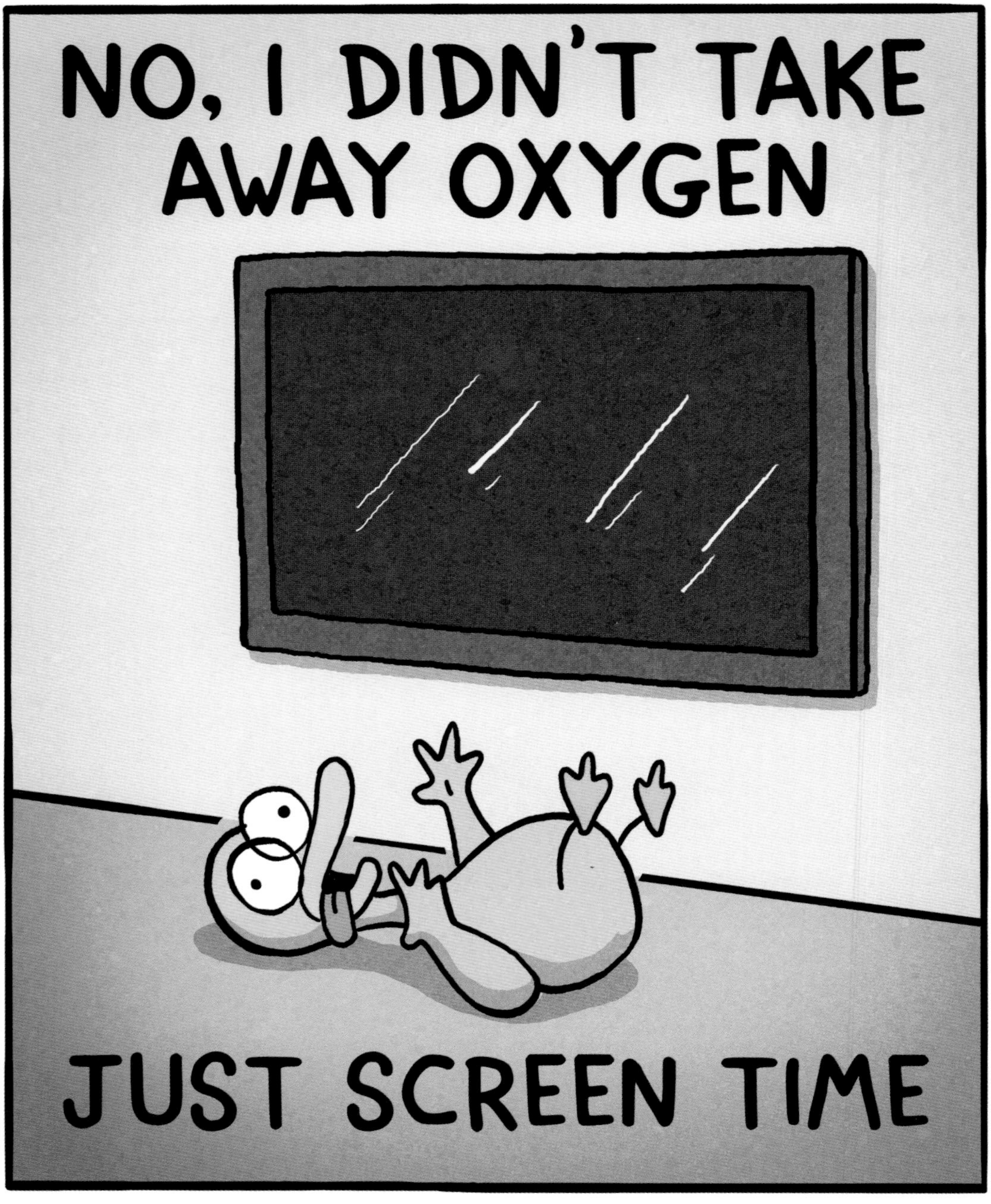
NO, I DIDN'T TAKE AWAY OXYGEN
JUST SCREEN TIME

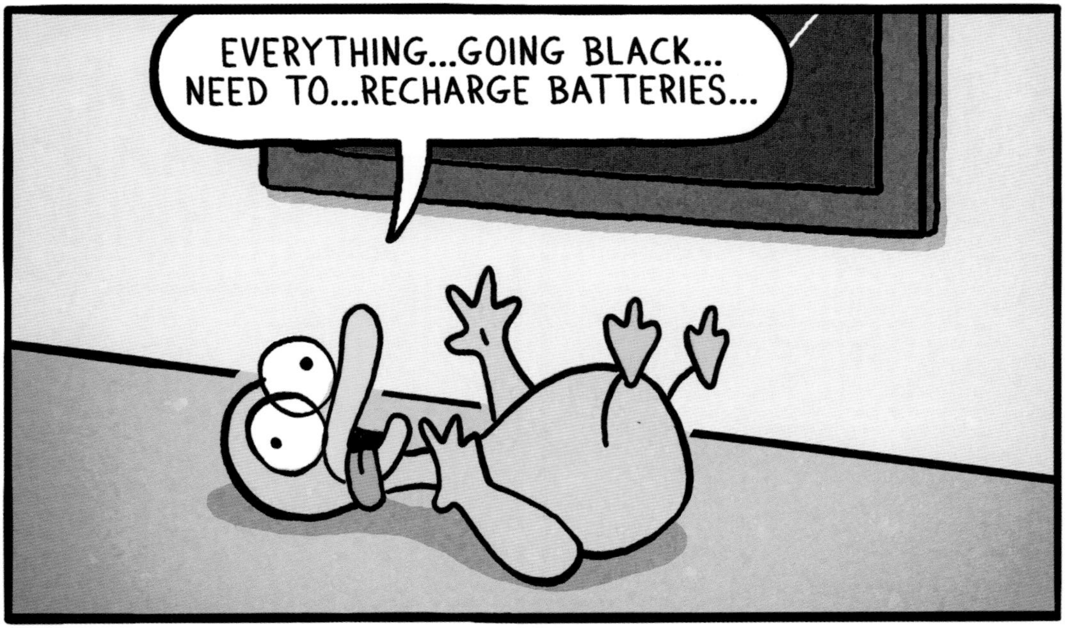
EVERYTHING...GOING BLACK...
NEED TO...RECHARGE BATTERIES...

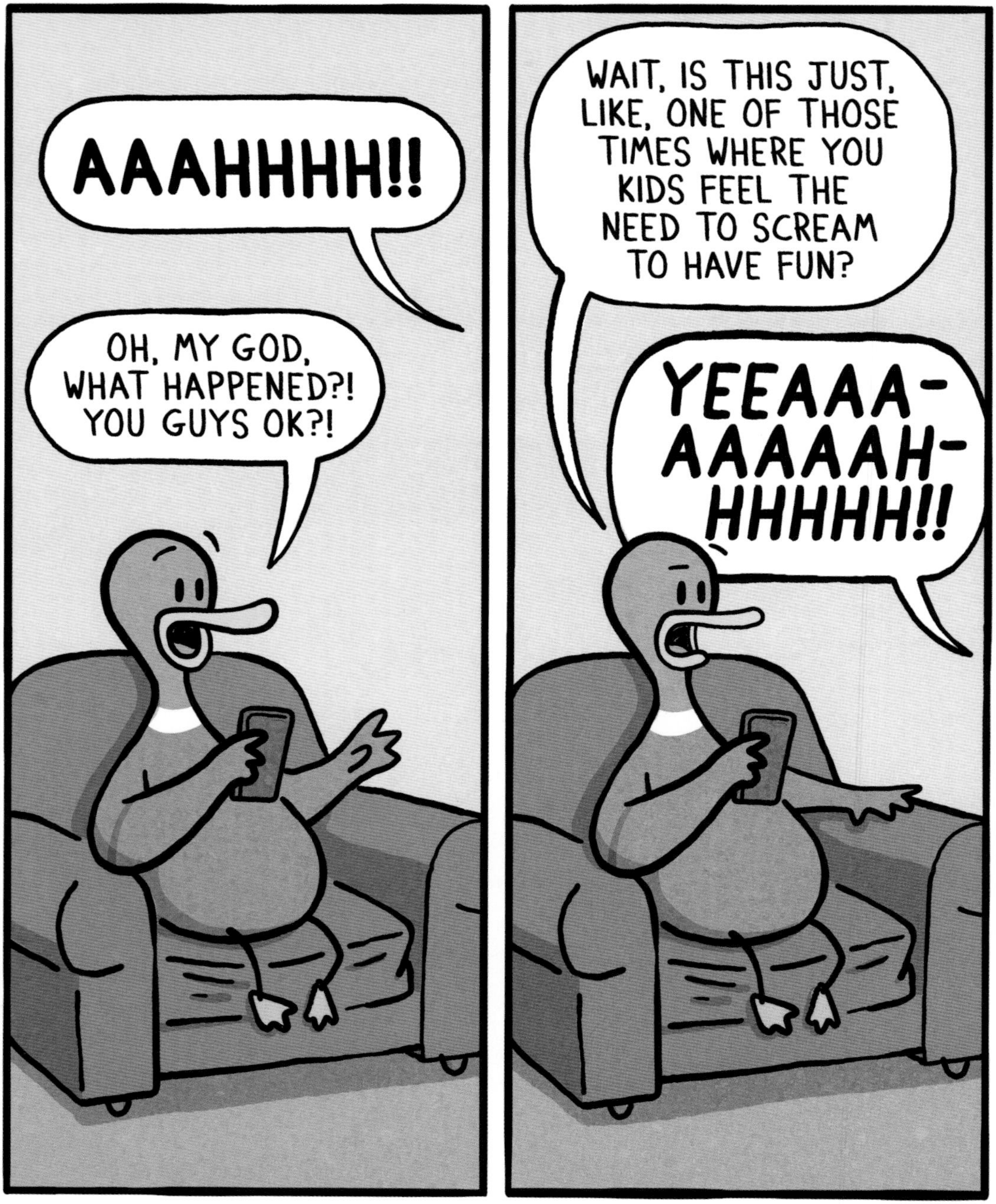
AAAHHHH!!
OH, MY GOD, WHAT HAPPENED?! YOU GUYS OK?!
WAIT, IS THIS JUST, LIKE, ONE OF THOSE TIMES WHERE YOU KIDS FEEL THE NEED TO SCREAM TO HAVE FUN?
YEEAAA-AAAAAH-HHHHH!!

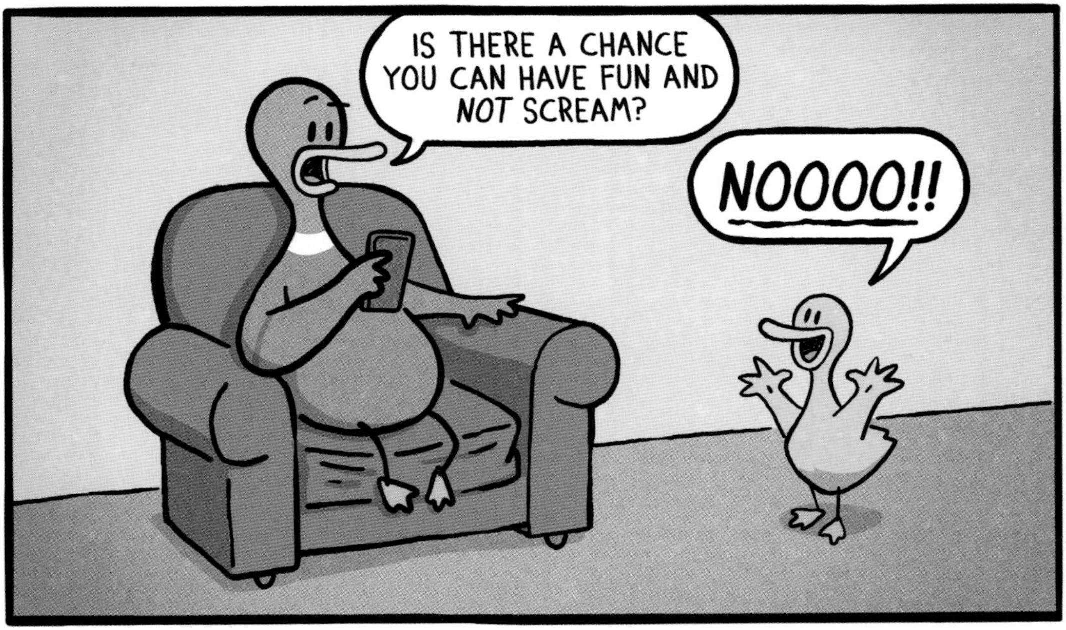
IS THERE A CHANCE YOU CAN HAVE FUN AND NOT SCREAM?
NOOOO!!

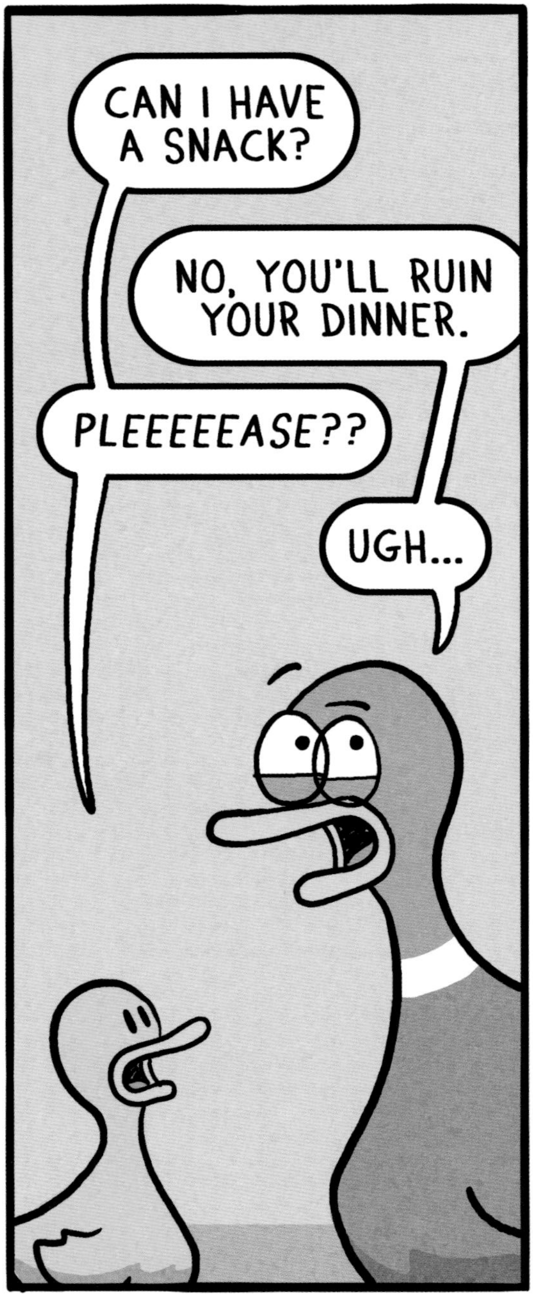
CAN I HAVE A SNACK?
NO, YOU'LL RUIN YOUR DINNER.
PLEEEEEEASE??
UGH...

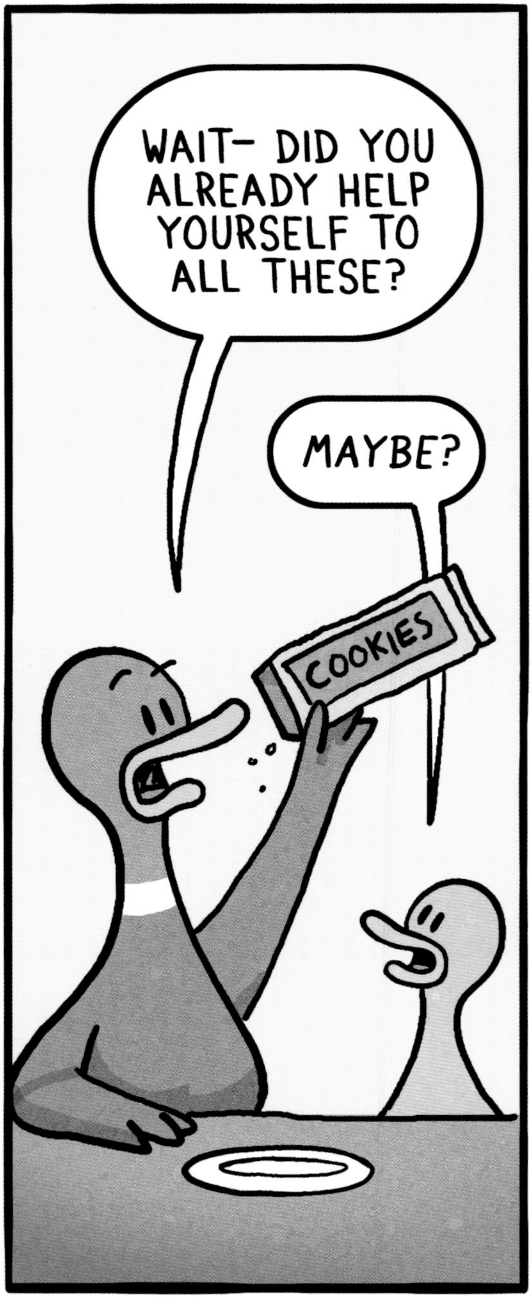
WAIT– DID YOU ALREADY HELP YOURSELF TO ALL THESE?
MAYBE?
COOKIES

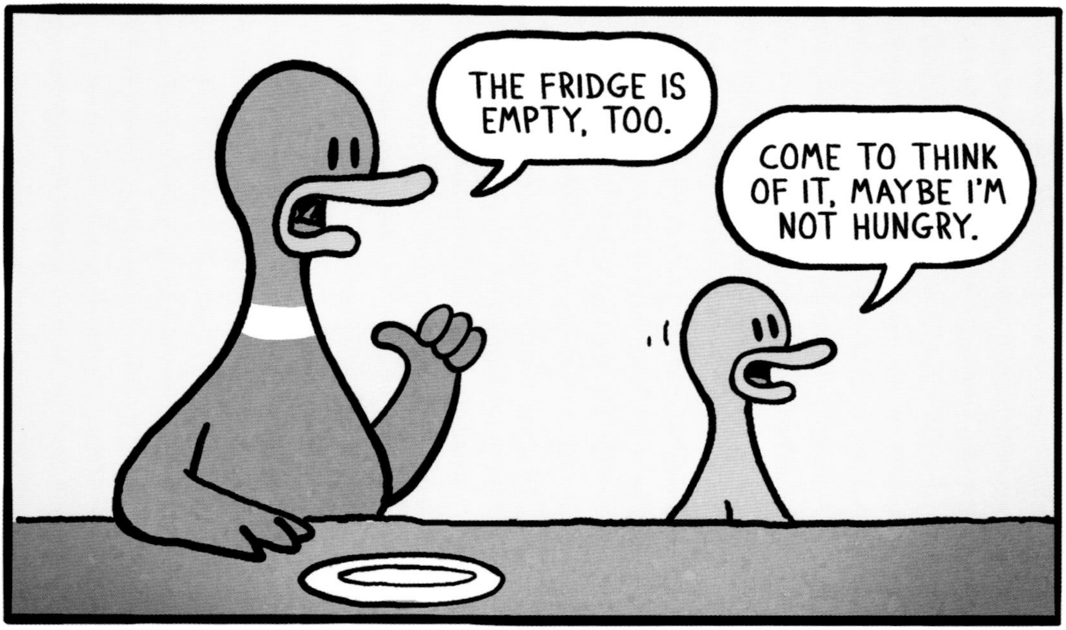
THE FRIDGE IS EMPTY, TOO.
COME TO THINK OF IT, MAYBE I'M NOT HUNGRY.

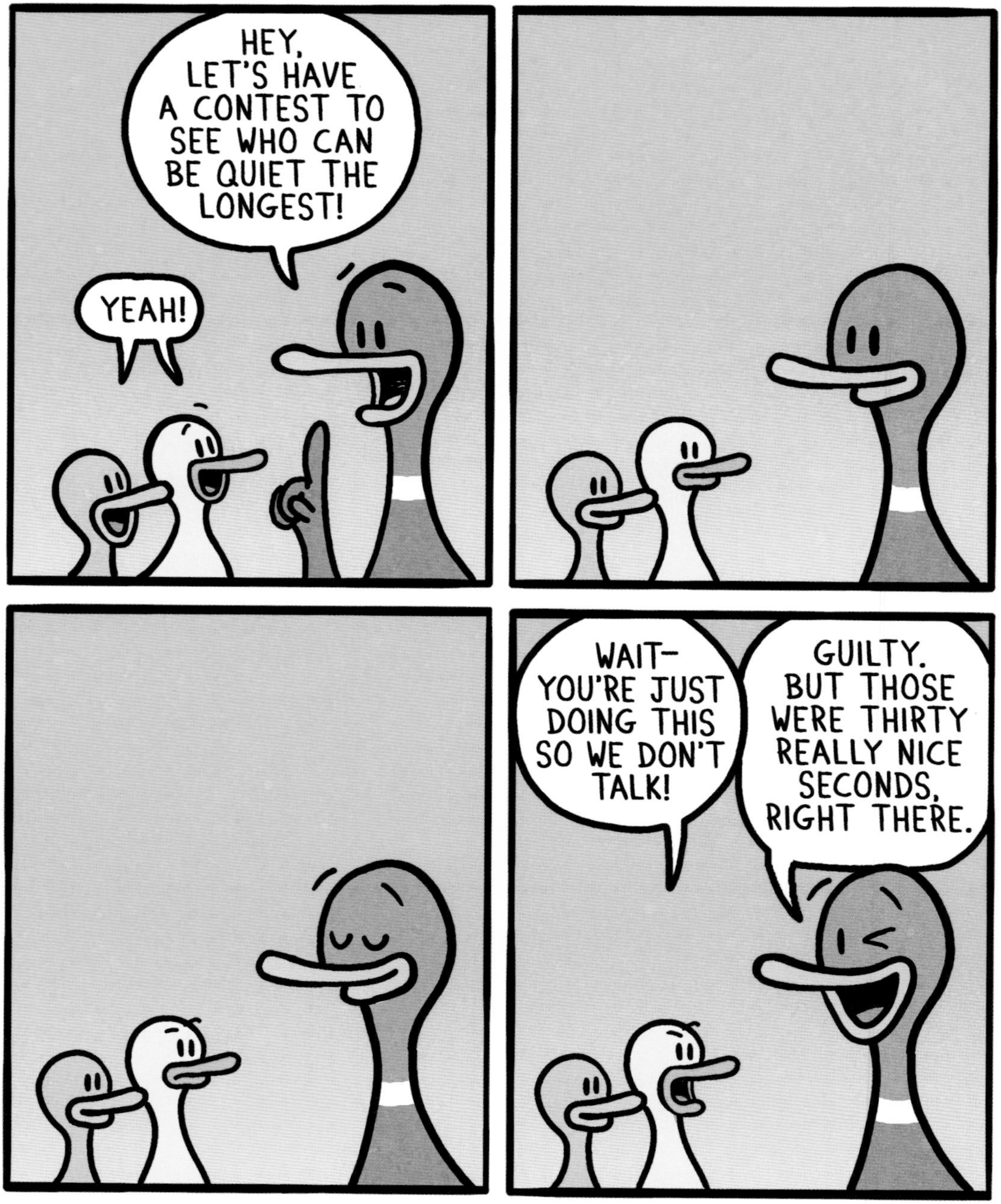
HEY, LET'S HAVE A CONTEST TO SEE WHO CAN BE QUIET THE LONGEST!
YEAH!
WAIT— YOU'RE JUST DOING THIS SO WE DON'T TALK!
GUILTY. BUT THOSE WERE THIRTY REALLY NICE SECONDS, RIGHT THERE.

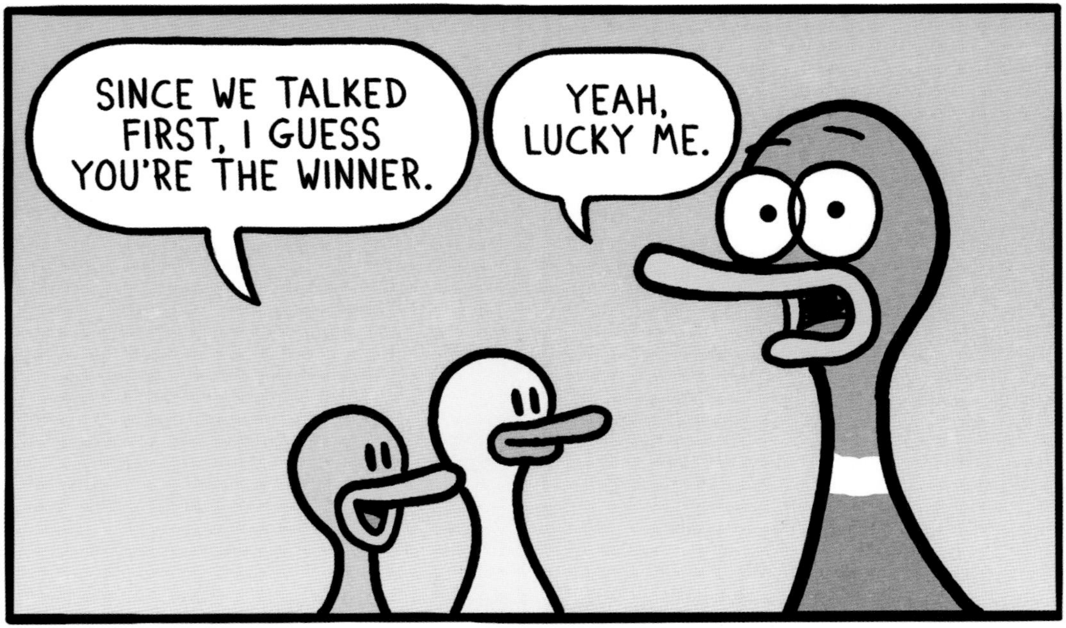
SINCE WE TALKED FIRST, I GUESS YOU'RE THE WINNER.
YEAH, LUCKY ME.

# GO PLAY OUTSIDE!

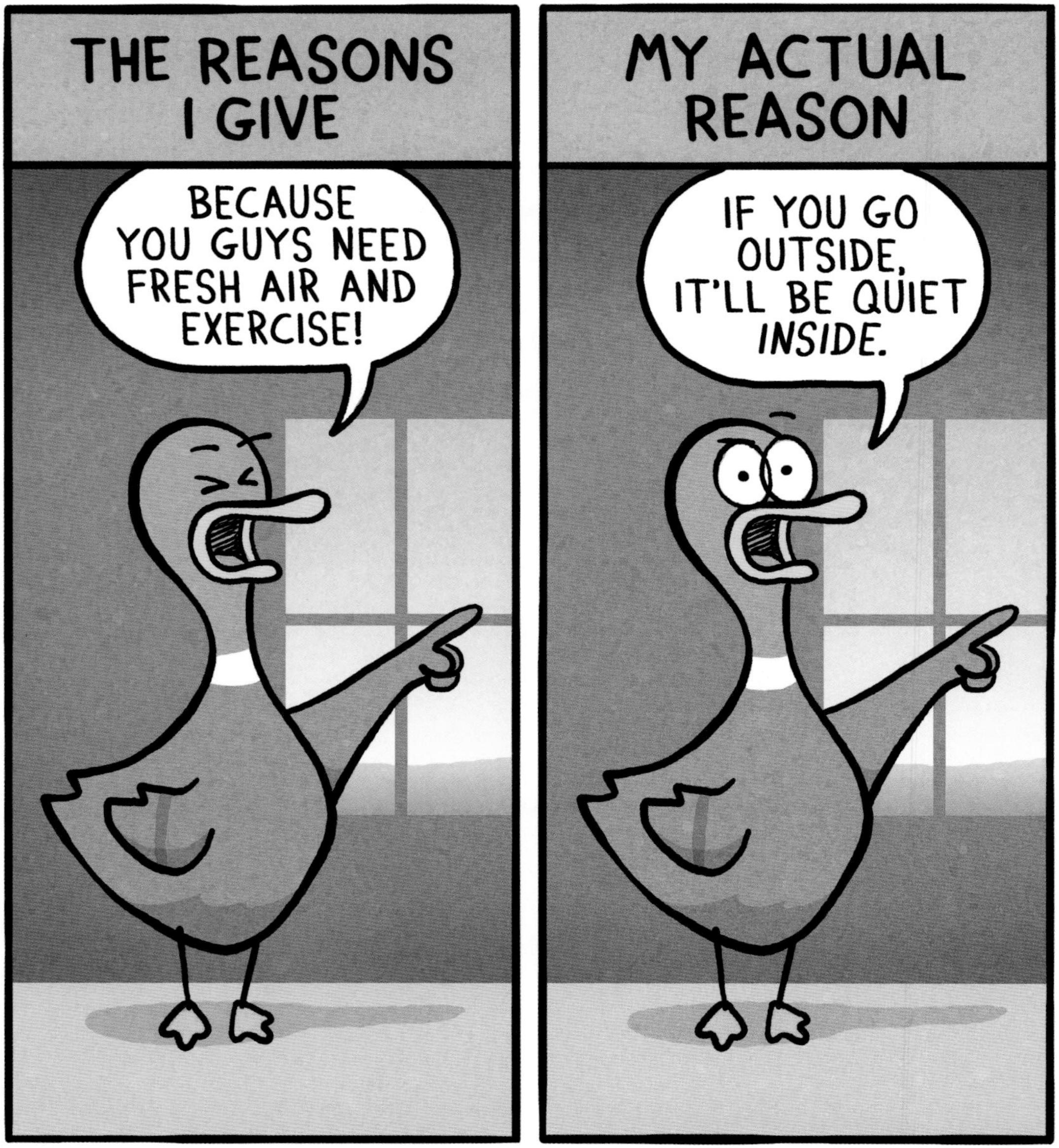
THE REASONS I GIVE
BECAUSE YOU GUYS NEED FRESH AIR AND EXERCISE!
MY ACTUAL REASON
IF YOU GO OUTSIDE, IT'LL BE QUIET *INSIDE.*

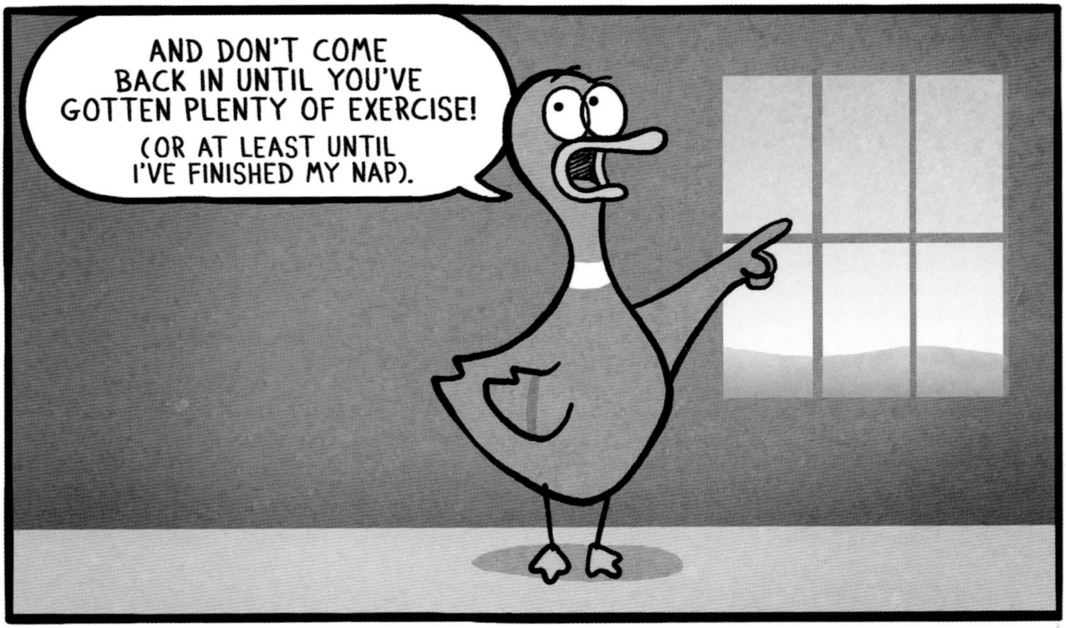
AND DON'T COME BACK IN UNTIL YOU'VE GOTTEN PLENTY OF EXERCISE! (OR AT LEAST UNTIL I'VE FINISHED MY NAP).

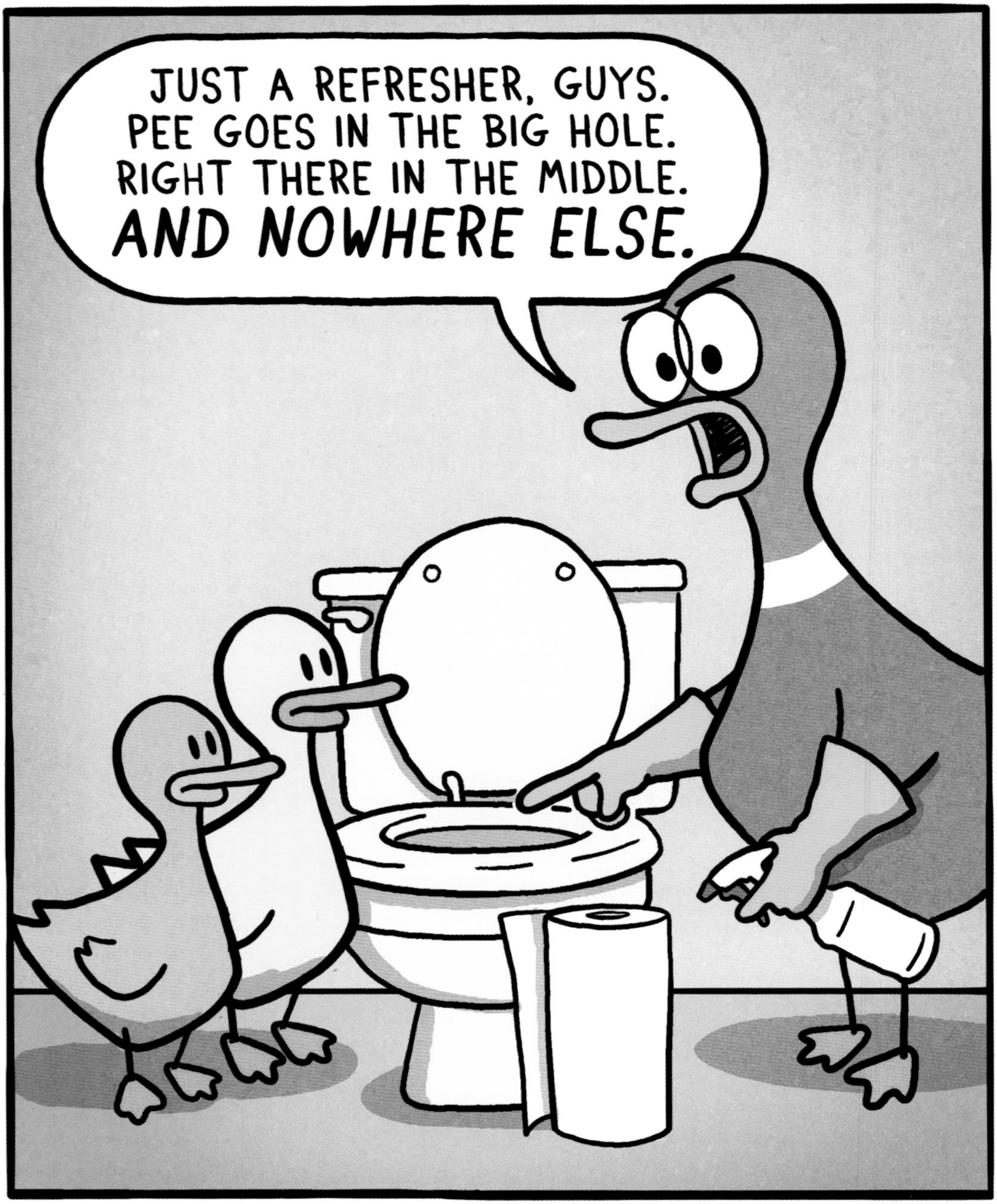
JUST A REFRESHER, GUYS. PEE GOES IN THE BIG HOLE. RIGHT THERE IN THE MIDDLE. AND NOWHERE ELSE.

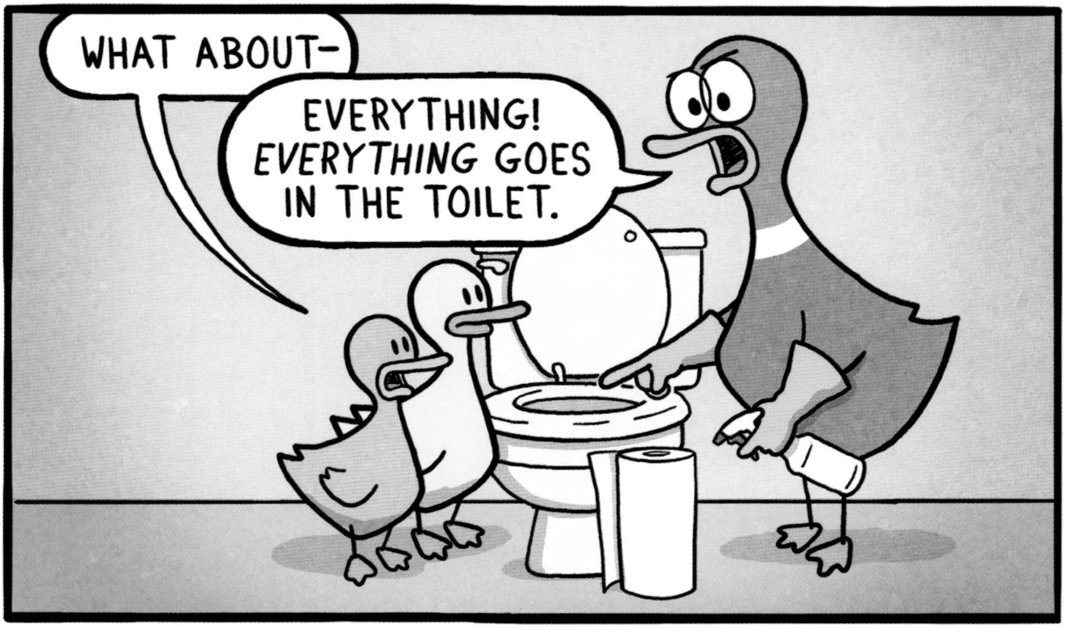
WHAT ABOUT-
EVERYTHING! *EVERYTHING* GOES IN THE TOILET.

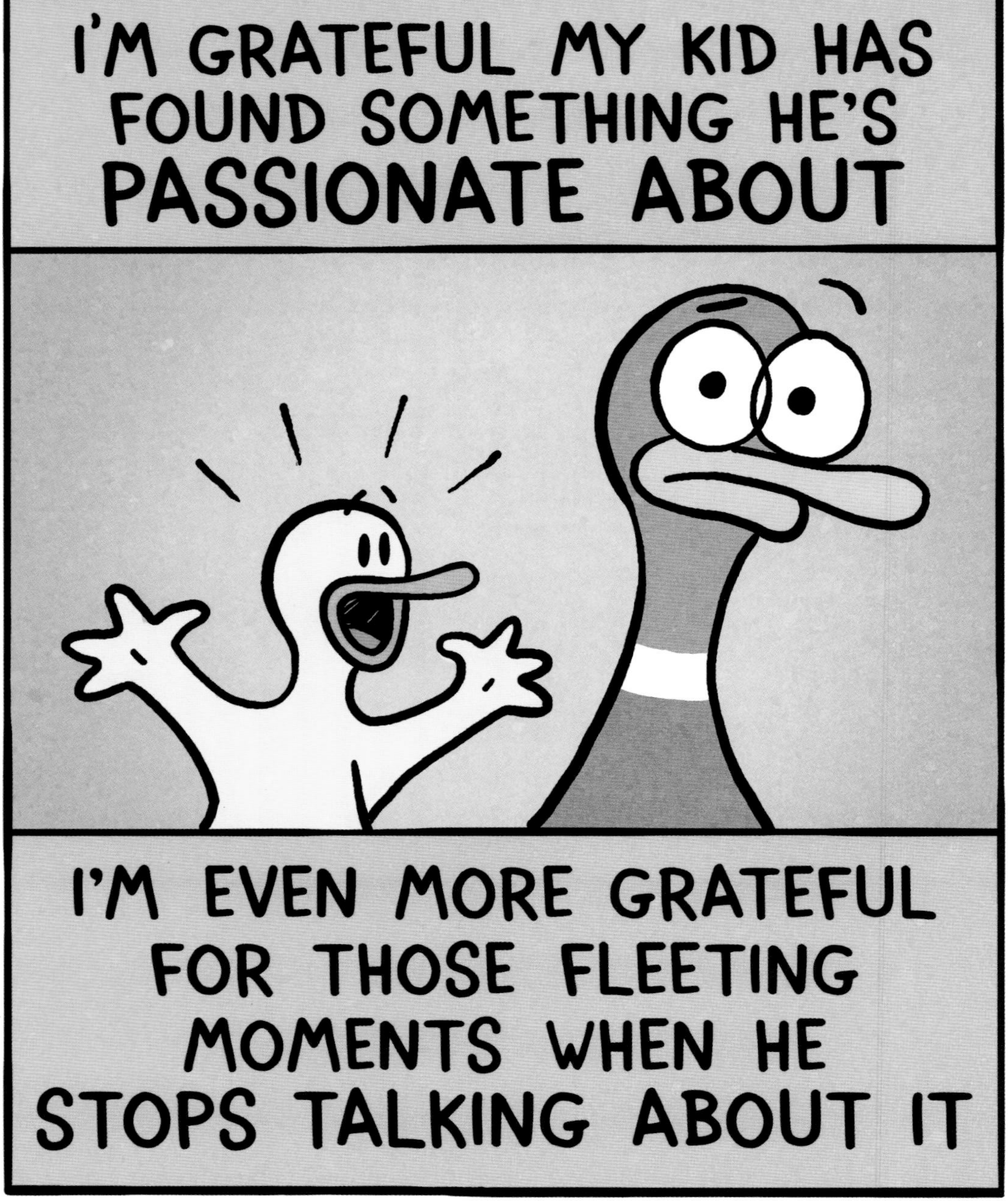
I'M GRATEFUL MY KID HAS FOUND SOMETHING HE'S PASSIONATE ABOUT
I'M EVEN MORE GRATEFUL FOR THOSE FLEETING MOMENTS WHEN HE STOPS TALKING ABOUT IT

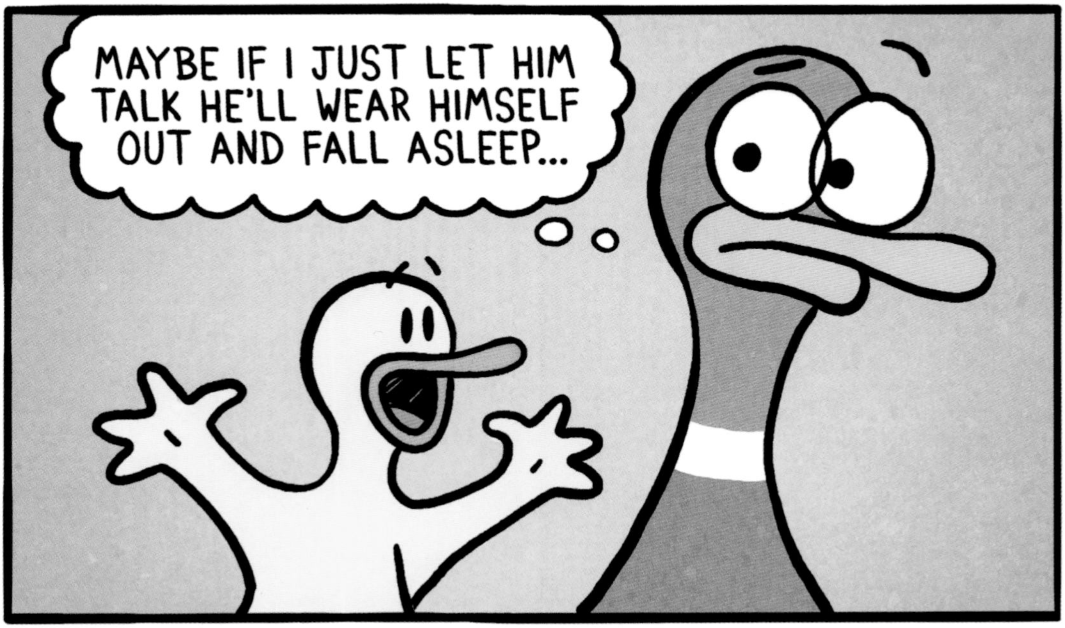
MAYBE IF I JUST LET HIM TALK HE'LL WEAR HIMSELF OUT AND FALL ASLEEP...

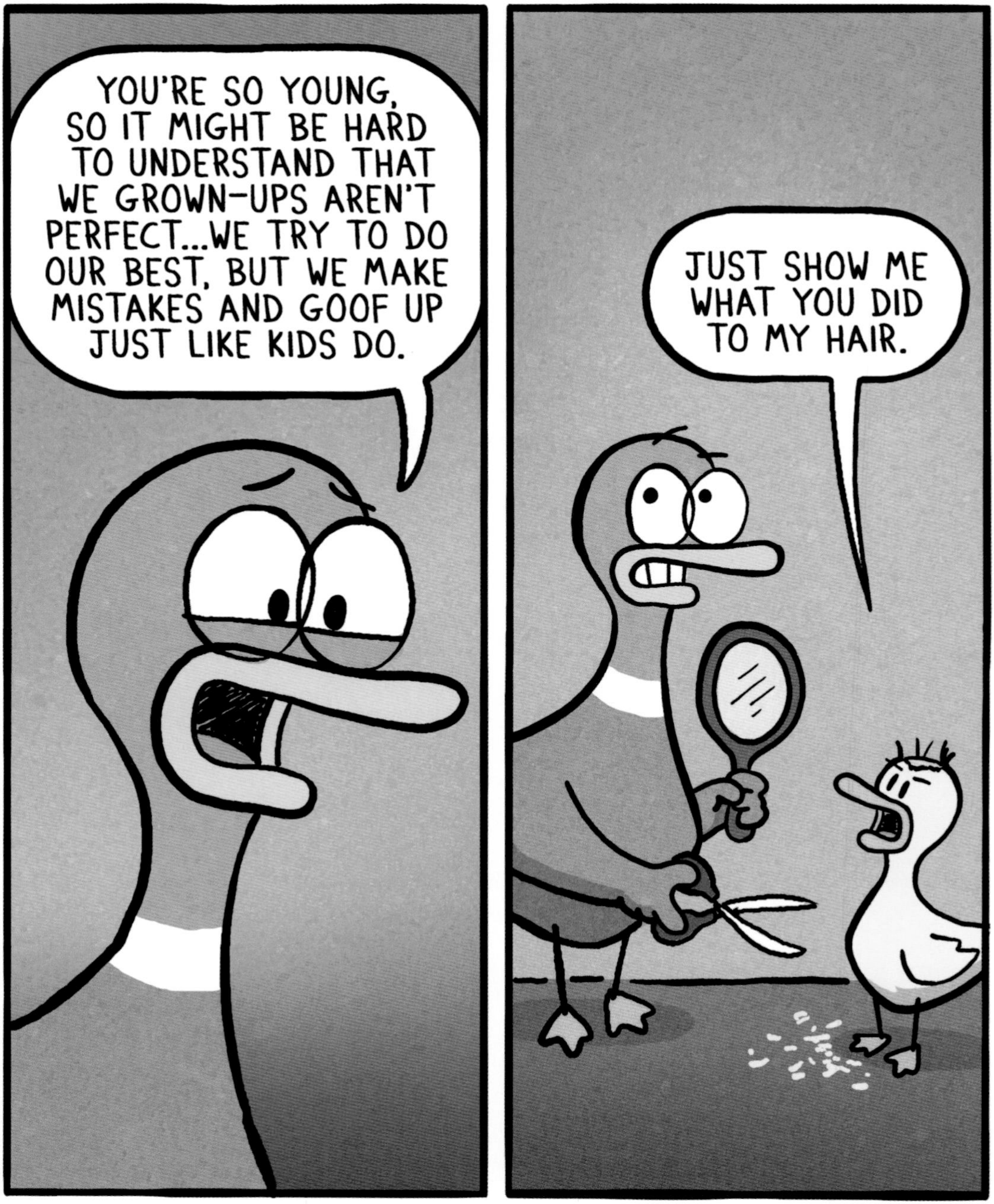
YOU'RE SO YOUNG, SO IT MIGHT BE HARD TO UNDERSTAND THAT WE GROWN-UPS AREN'T PERFECT...WE TRY TO DO OUR BEST, BUT WE MAKE MISTAKES AND GOOF UP JUST LIKE KIDS DO.
JUST SHOW ME WHAT YOU DID TO MY HAIR.

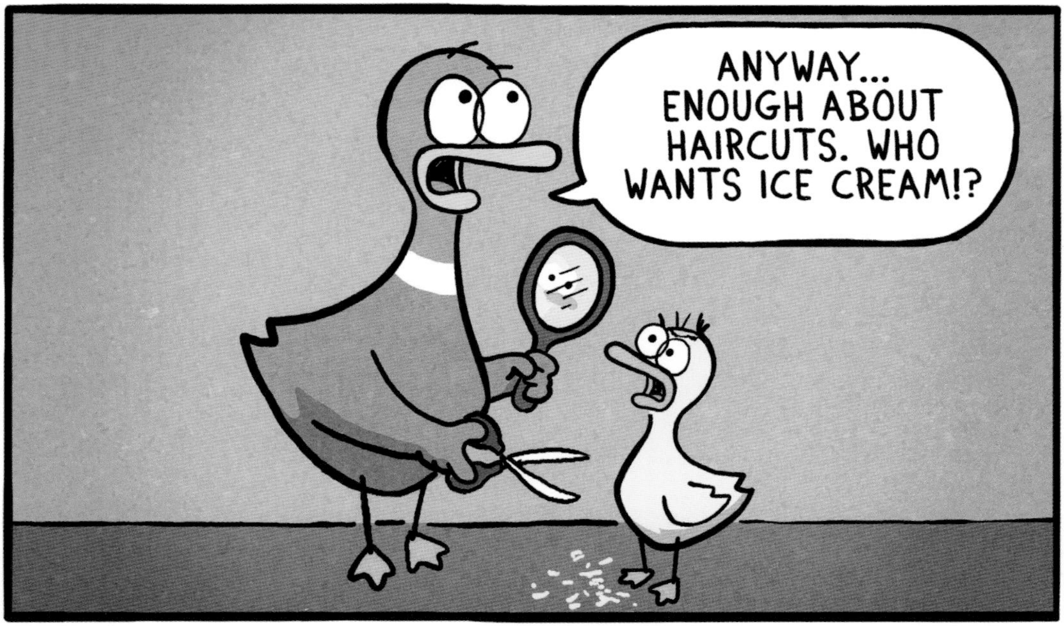
ANYWAY... ENOUGH ABOUT HAIRCUTS. WHO WANTS ICE CREAM!?

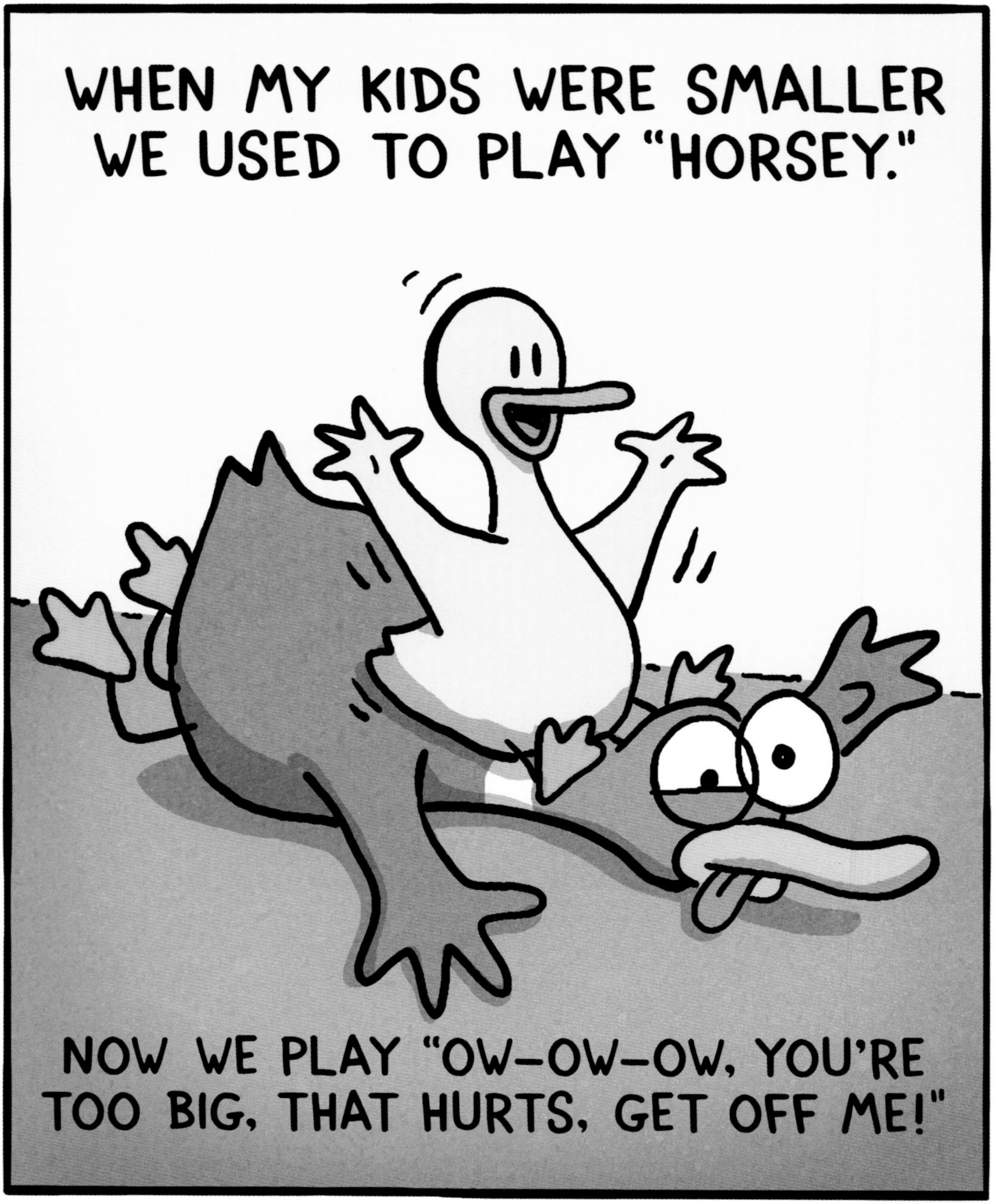
WHEN MY KIDS WERE SMALLER WE USED TO PLAY "HORSEY."
NOW WE PLAY "OW-OW-OW, YOU'RE TOO BIG, THAT HURTS, GET OFF ME!"

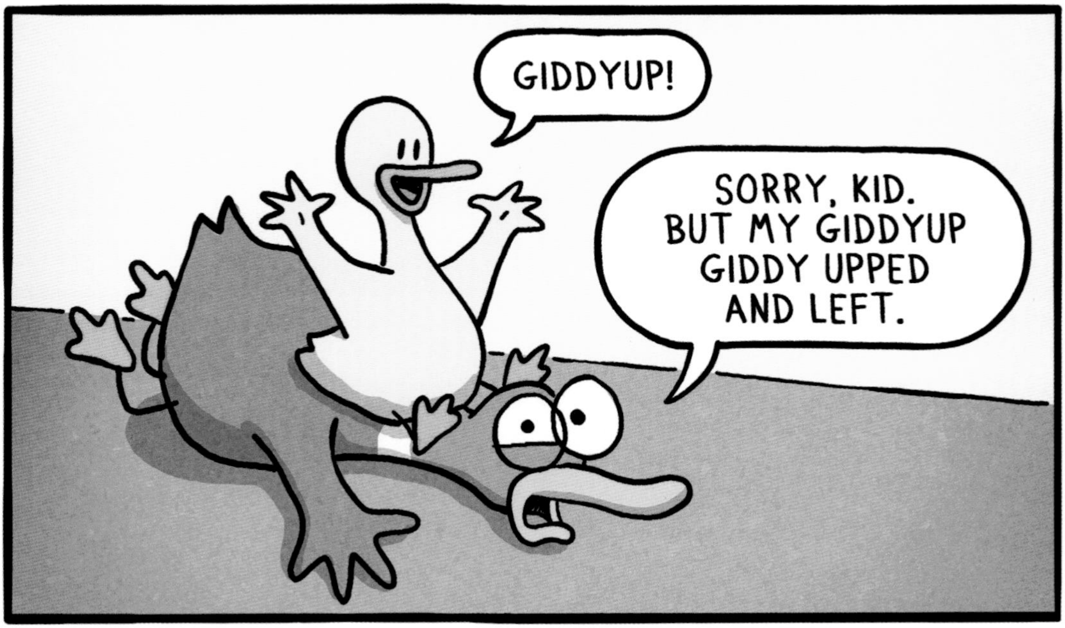
GIDDYUP!
SORRY, KID. BUT MY GIDDYUP GIDDY UPPED AND LEFT.

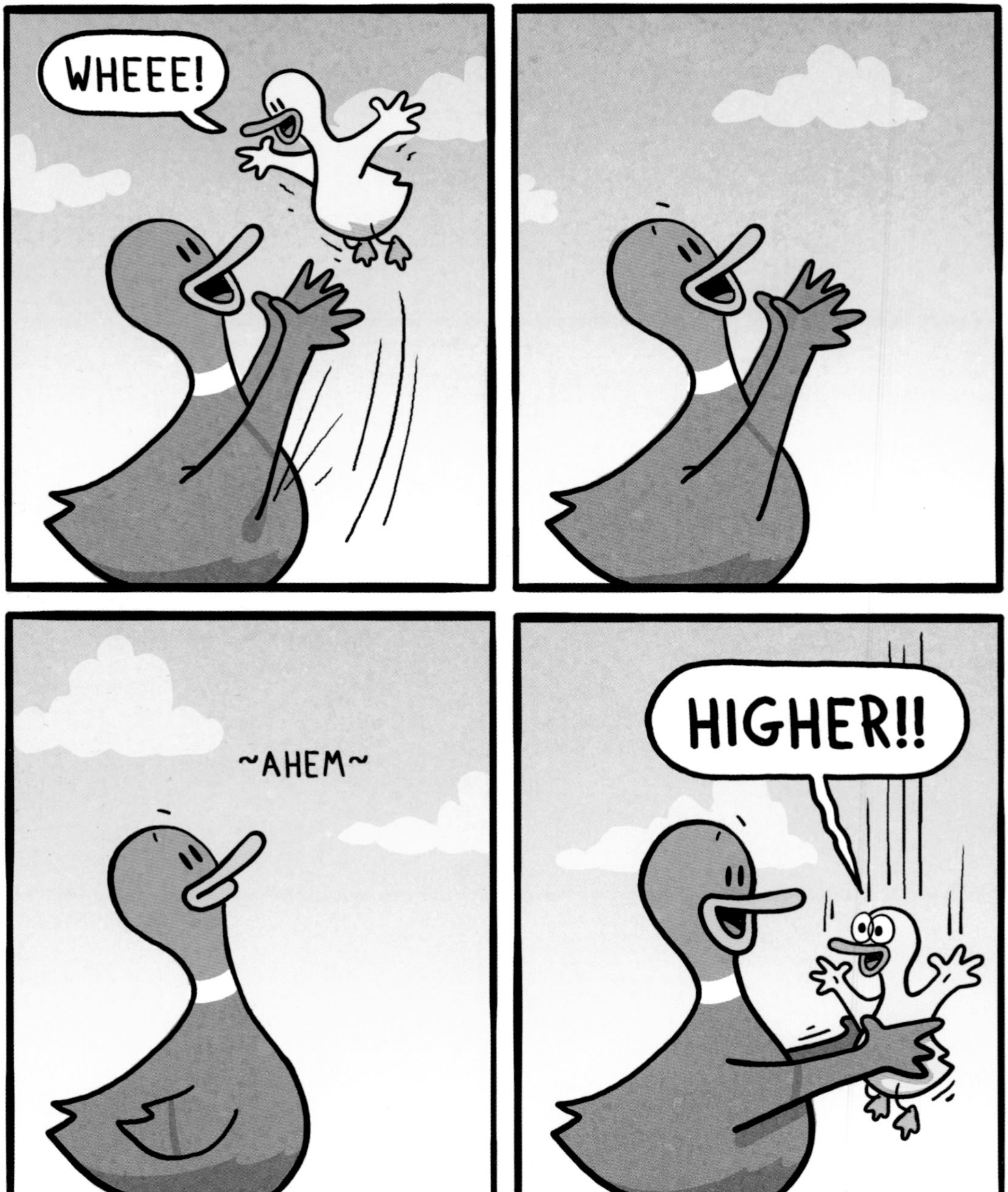
WHEEE!
~AHEM~
HIGHER!!

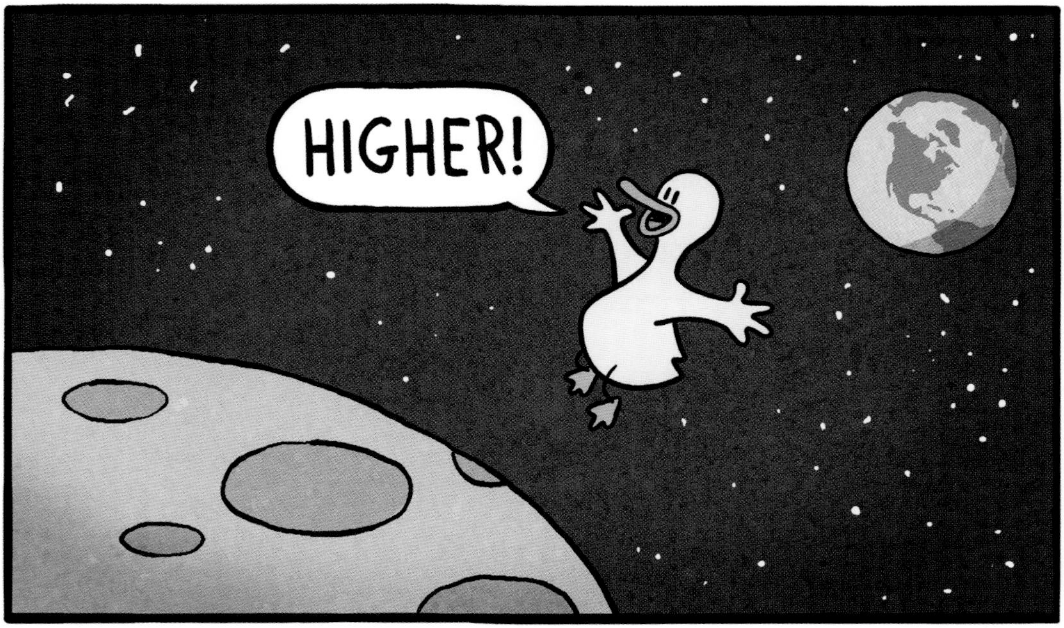
HIGHER!

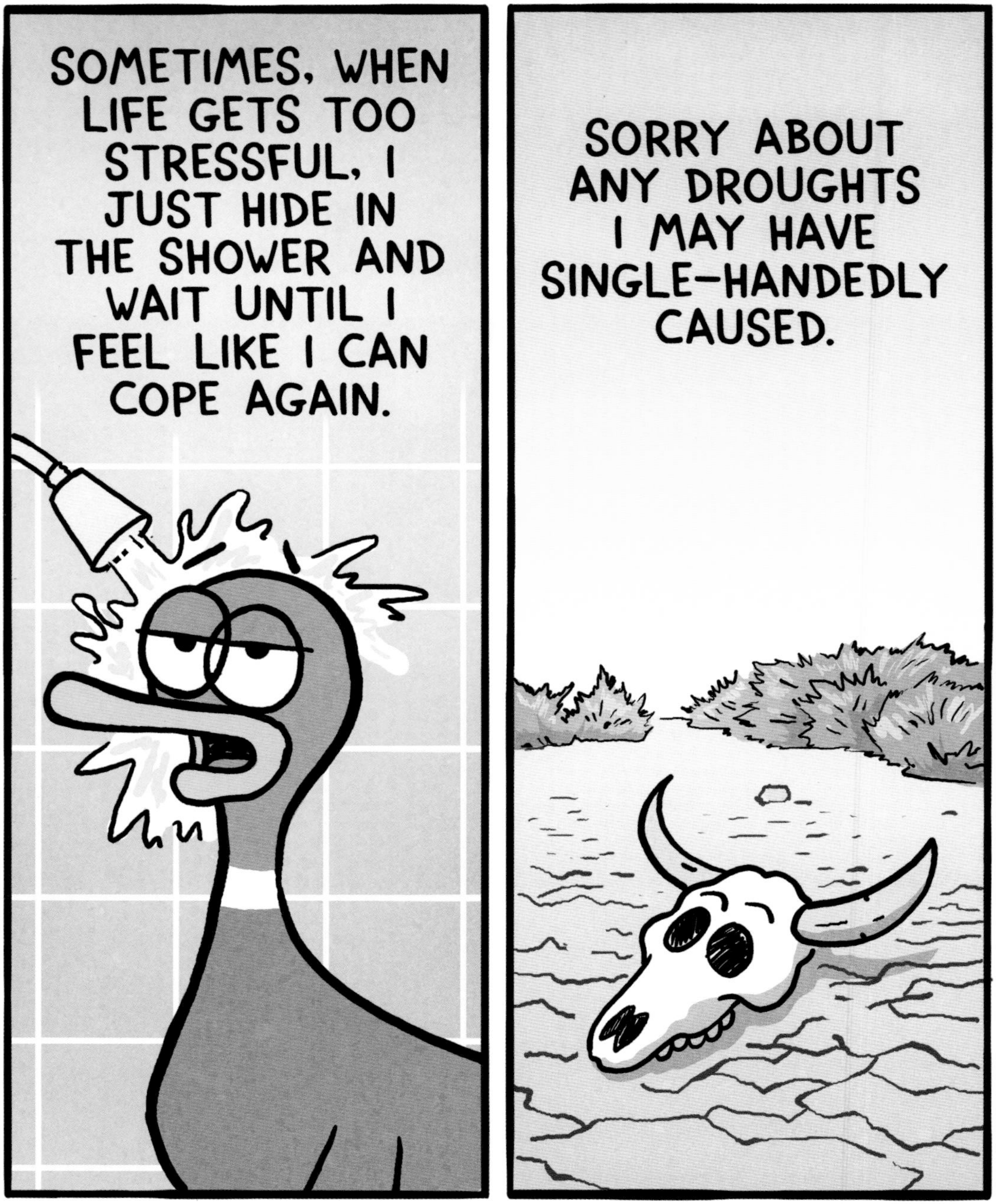
SOMETIMES, WHEN LIFE GETS TOO STRESSFUL, I JUST HIDE IN THE SHOWER AND WAIT UNTIL I FEEL LIKE I CAN COPE AGAIN.
SORRY ABOUT ANY DROUGHTS I MAY HAVE SINGLE-HANDEDLY CAUSED.

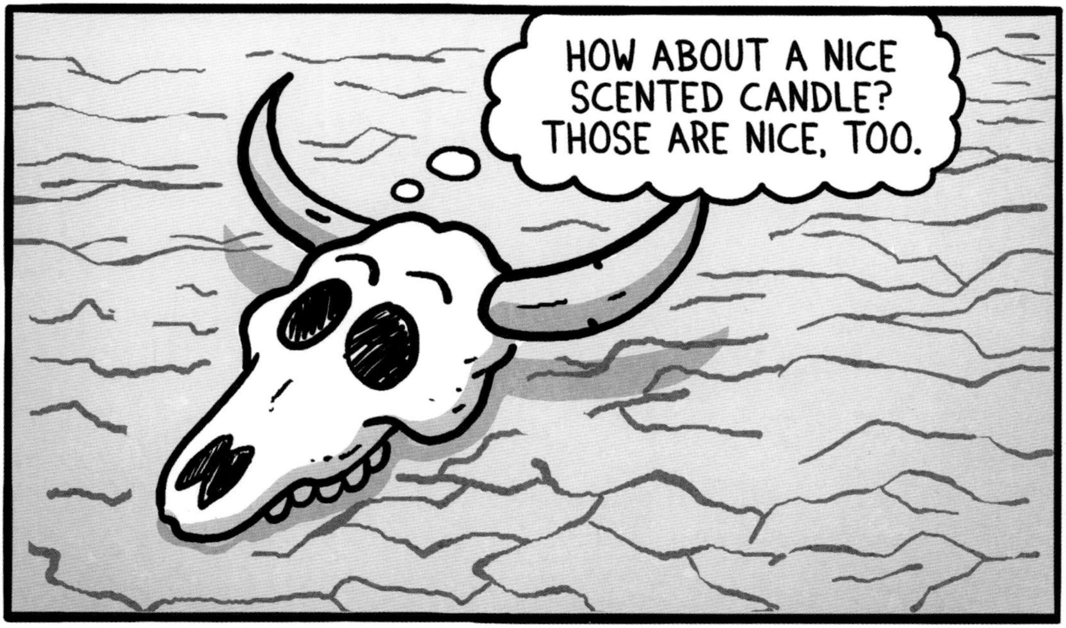
HOW ABOUT A NICE SCENTED CANDLE? THOSE ARE NICE, TOO.

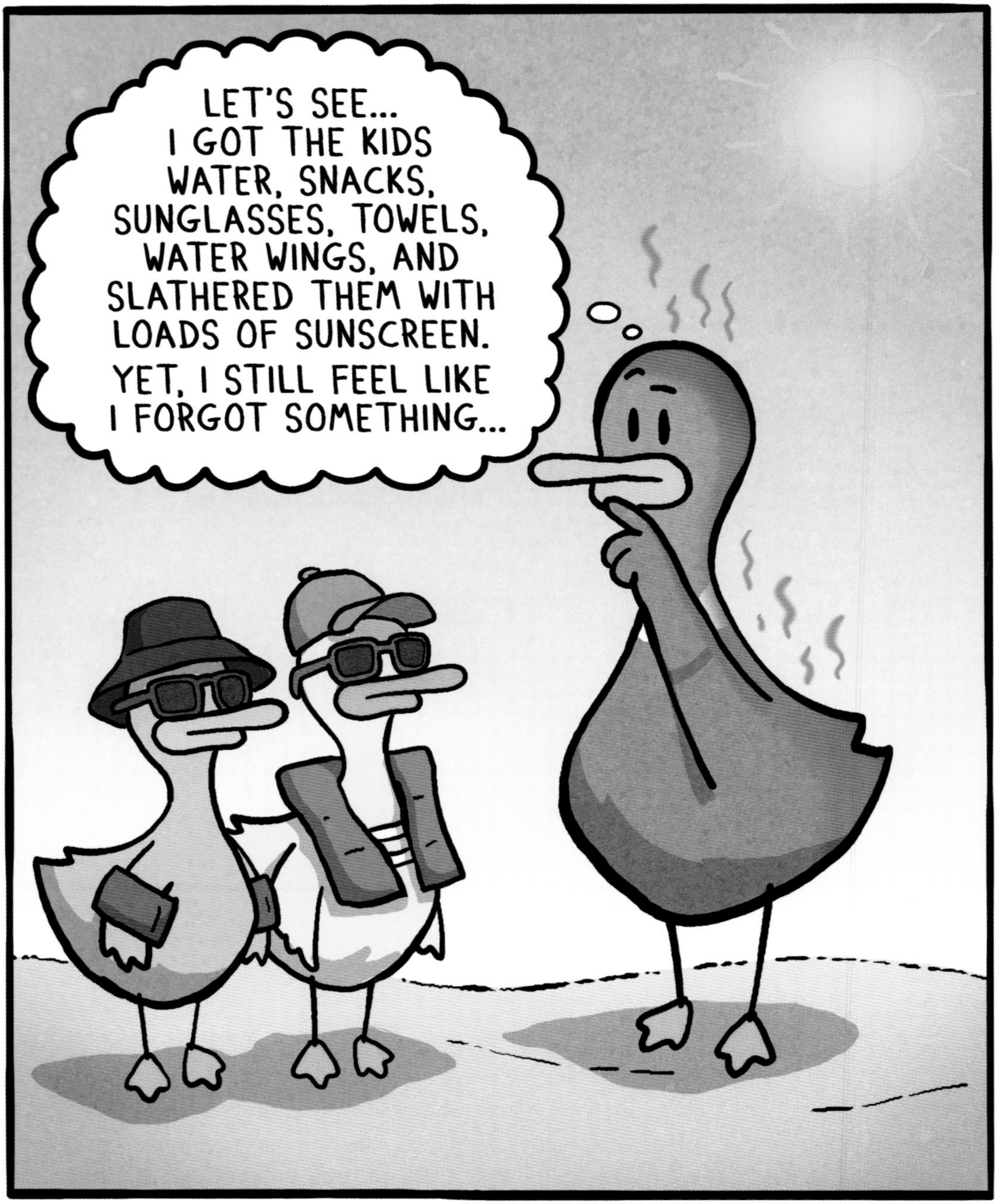
LET'S SEE... I GOT THE KIDS WATER, SNACKS, SUNGLASSES, TOWELS, WATER WINGS, AND SLATHERED THEM WITH LOADS OF SUNSCREEN. YET, I STILL FEEL LIKE I FORGOT SOMETHING...

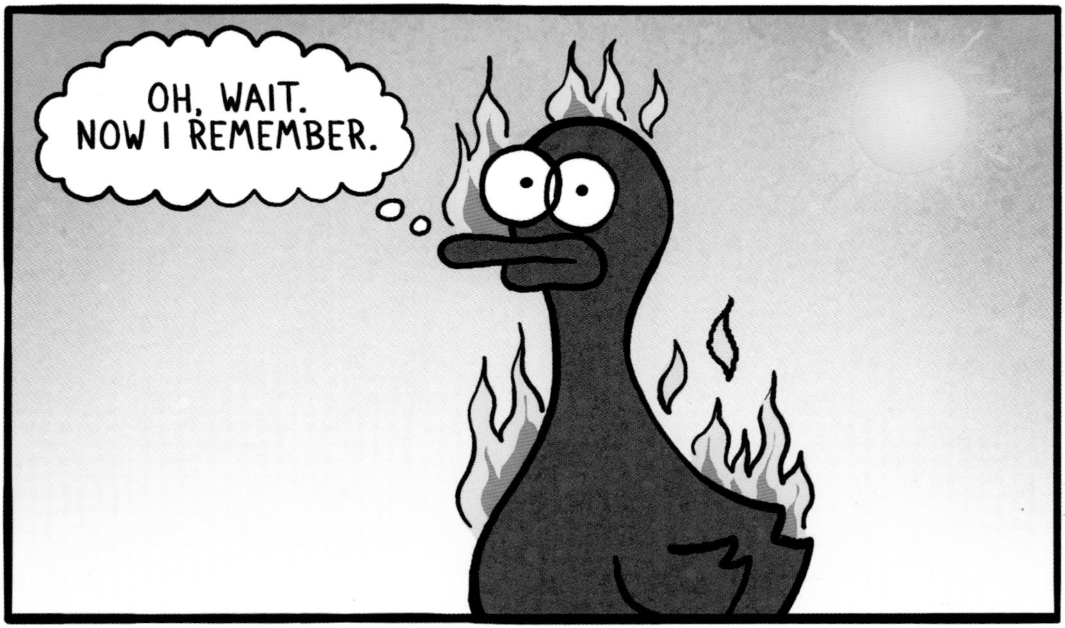
OH, WAIT.
NOW I REMEMBER.

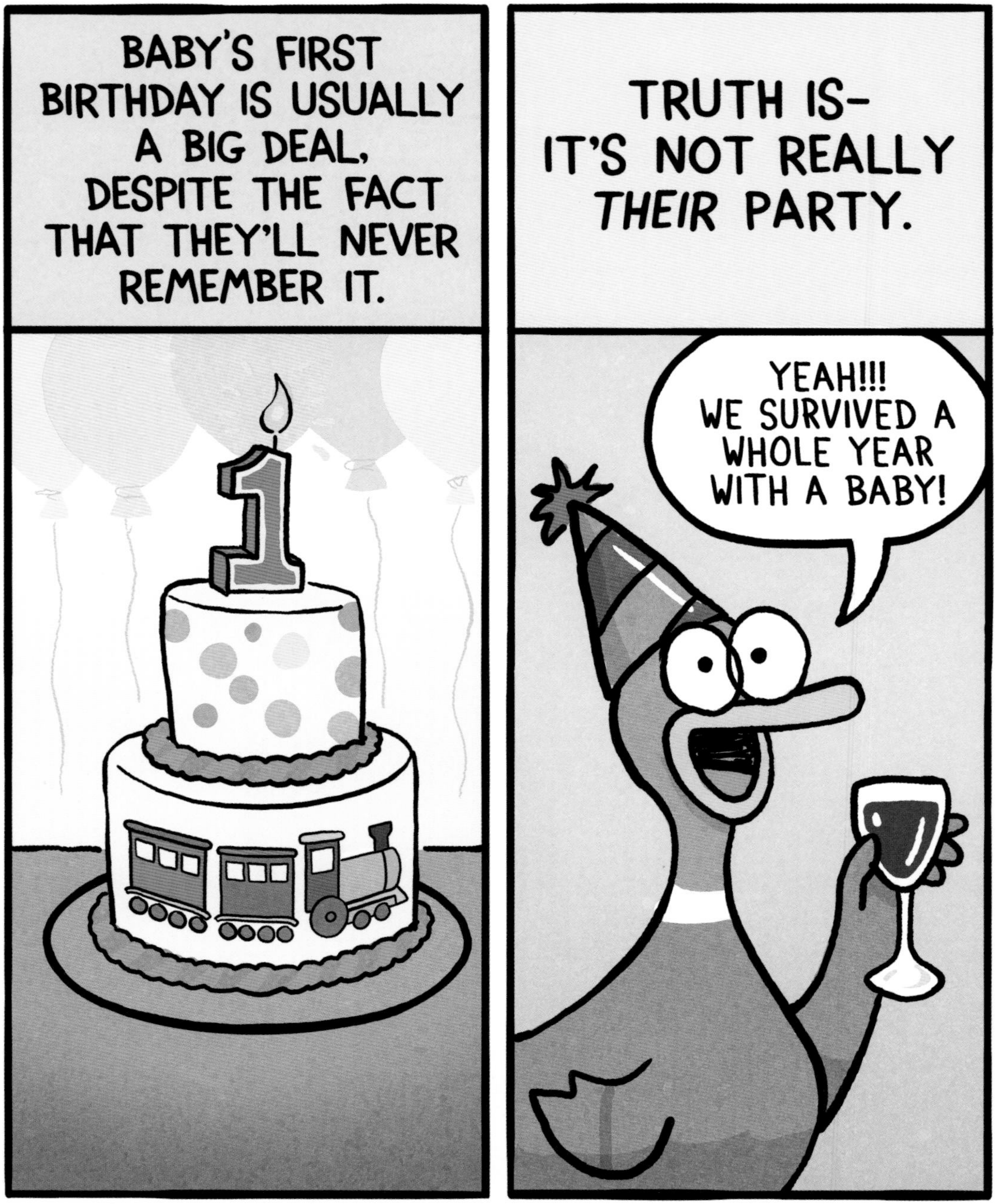
BABY'S FIRST BIRTHDAY IS USUALLY A BIG DEAL, DESPITE THE FACT THAT THEY'LL NEVER REMEMBER IT.
TRUTH IS- IT'S NOT REALLY *THEIR* PARTY.
YEAH!!! WE SURVIVED A WHOLE YEAR WITH A BABY!

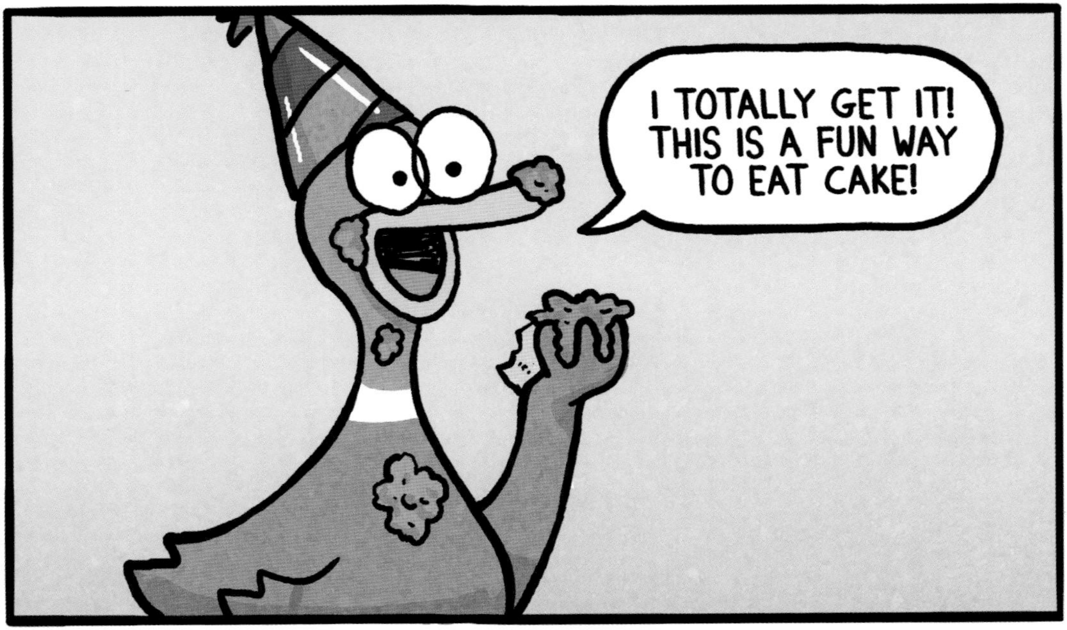
I TOTALLY GET IT! THIS IS A FUN WAY TO EAT CAKE!

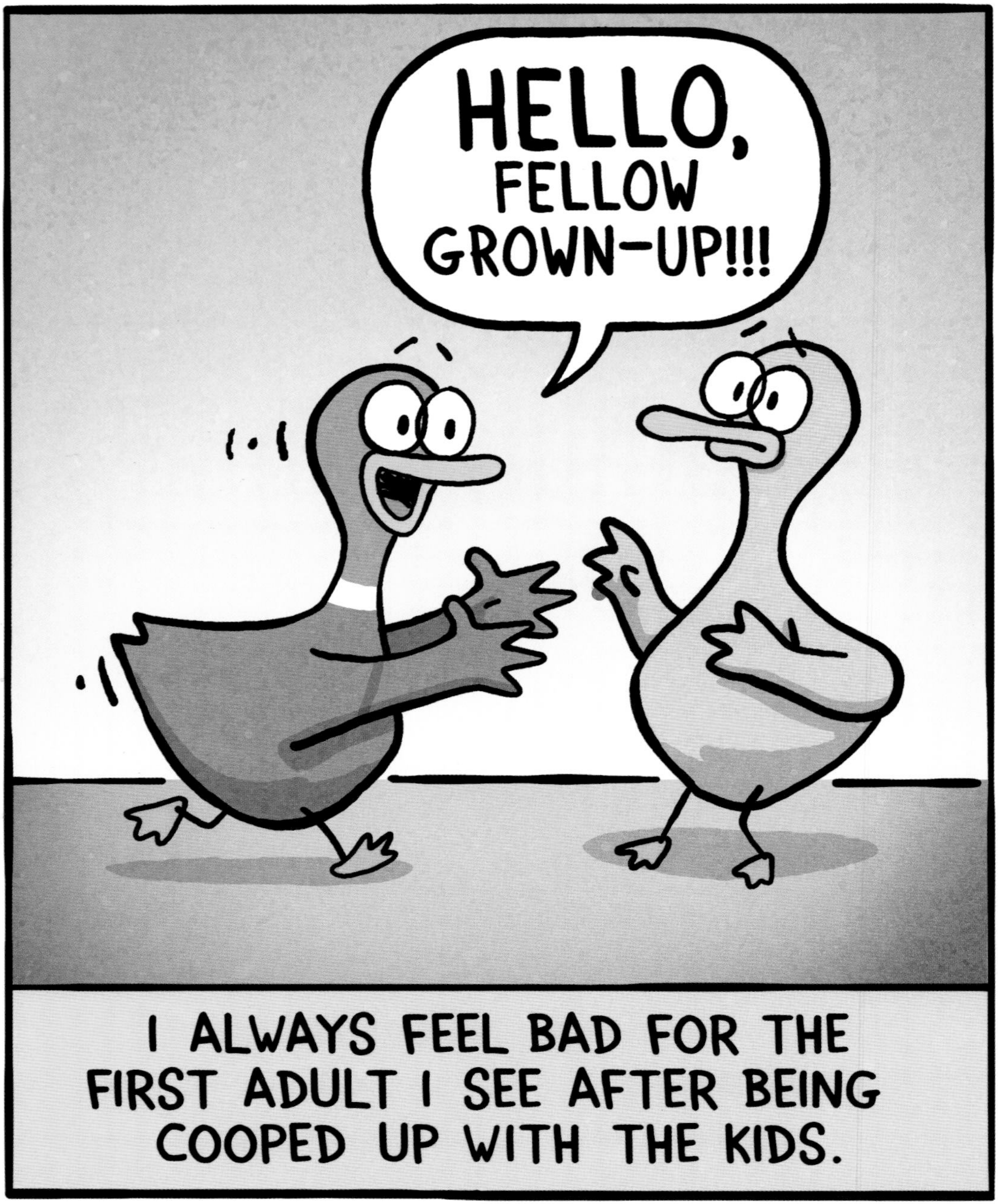
HELLO, FELLOW GROWN-UP!!!
I ALWAYS FEEL BAD FOR THE FIRST ADULT I SEE AFTER BEING COOPED UP WITH THE KIDS.

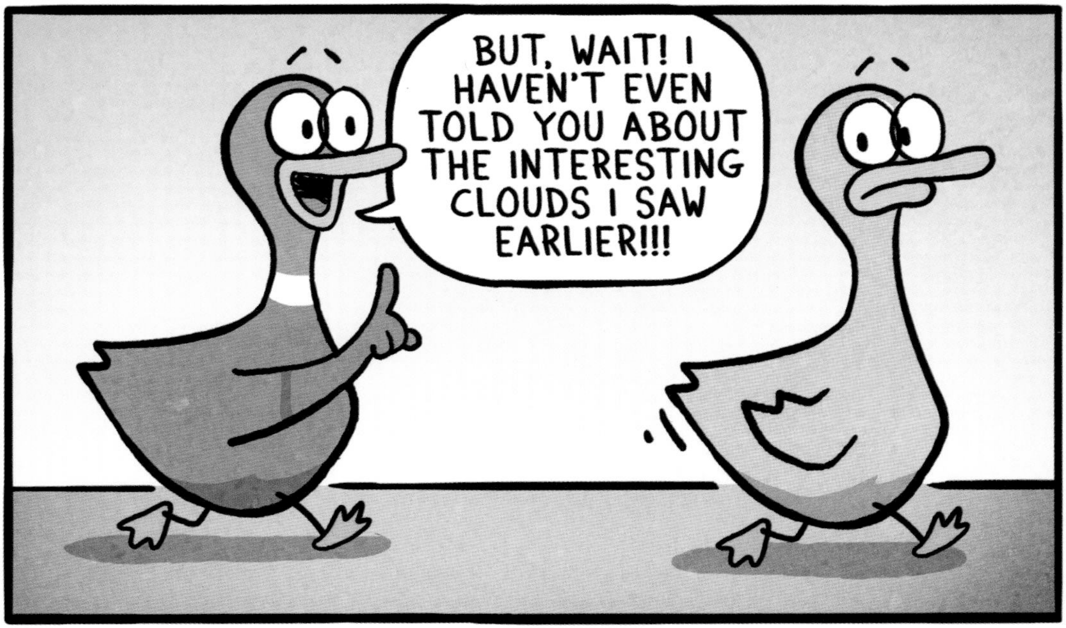
BUT, WAIT! I HAVEN'T EVEN TOLD YOU ABOUT THE INTERESTING CLOUDS I SAW EARLIER!!!

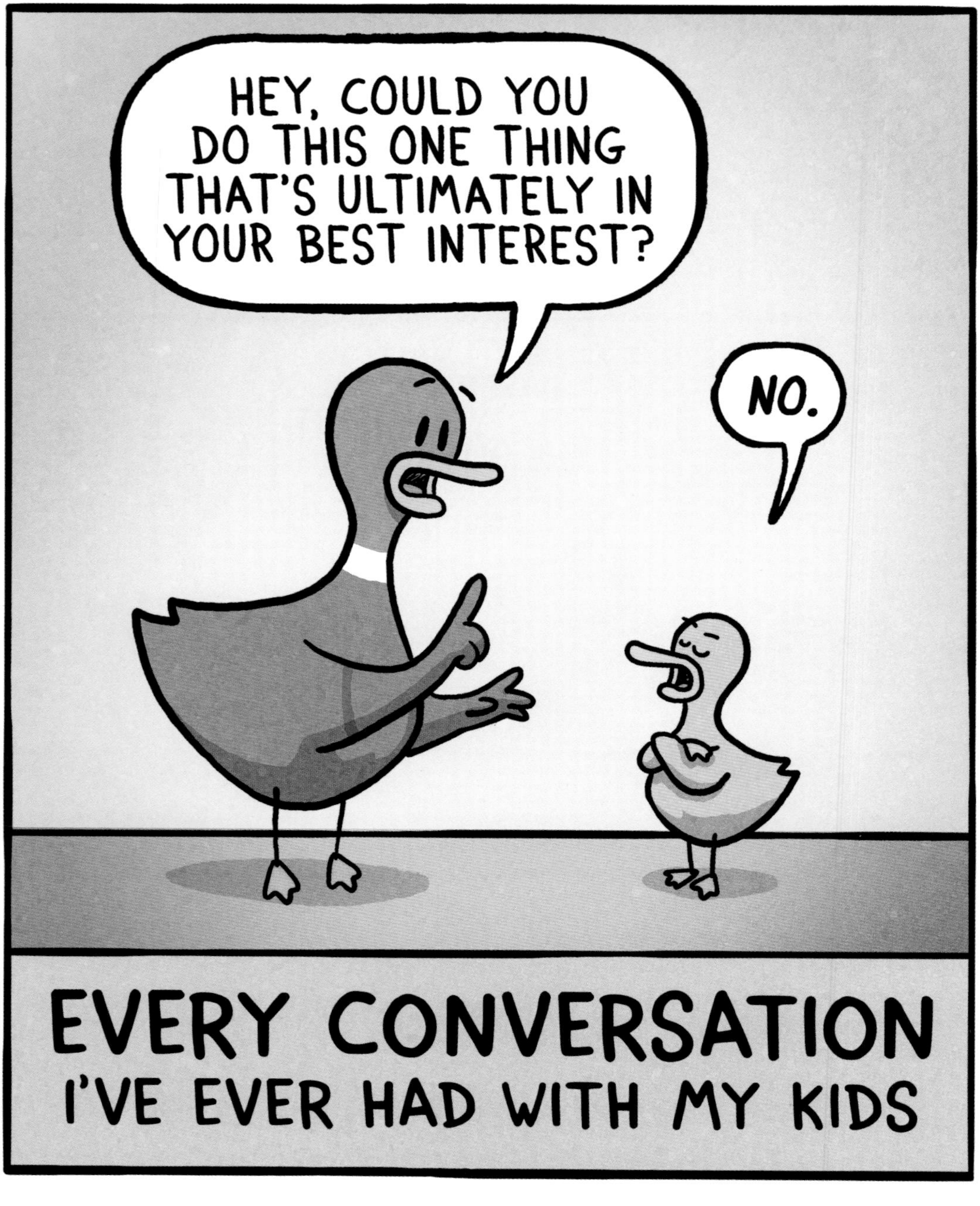
HEY, COULD YOU DO THIS ONE THING THAT'S ULTIMATELY IN YOUR BEST INTEREST?
NO.
EVERY CONVERSATION I'VE EVER HAD WITH MY KIDS

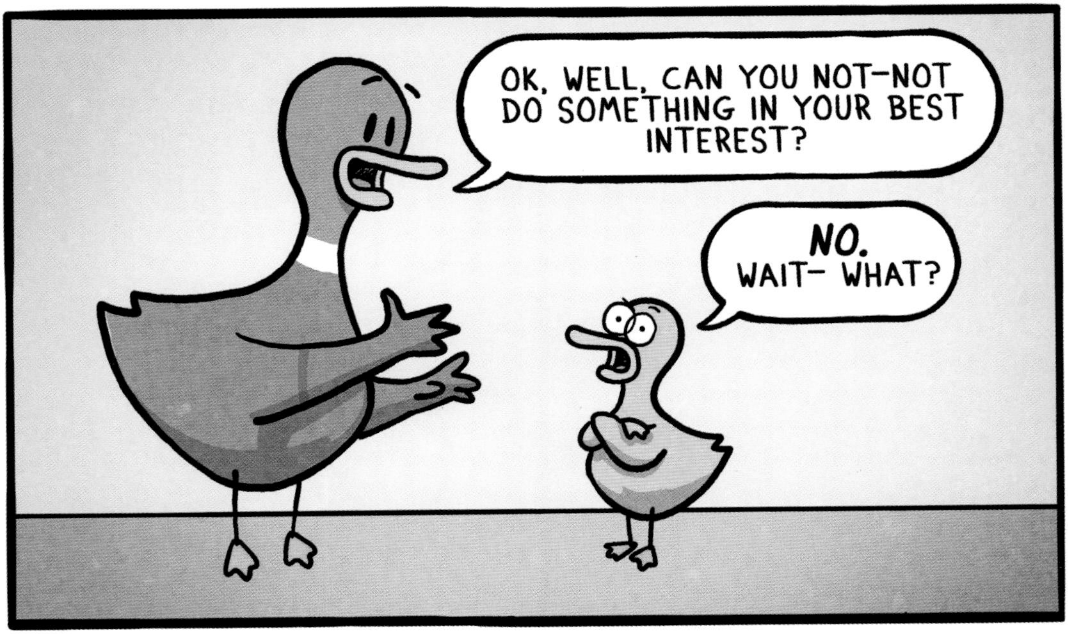
OK, WELL, CAN YOU NOT-NOT DO SOMETHING IN YOUR BEST INTEREST?
NO.
WAIT- WHAT?

# NAPS

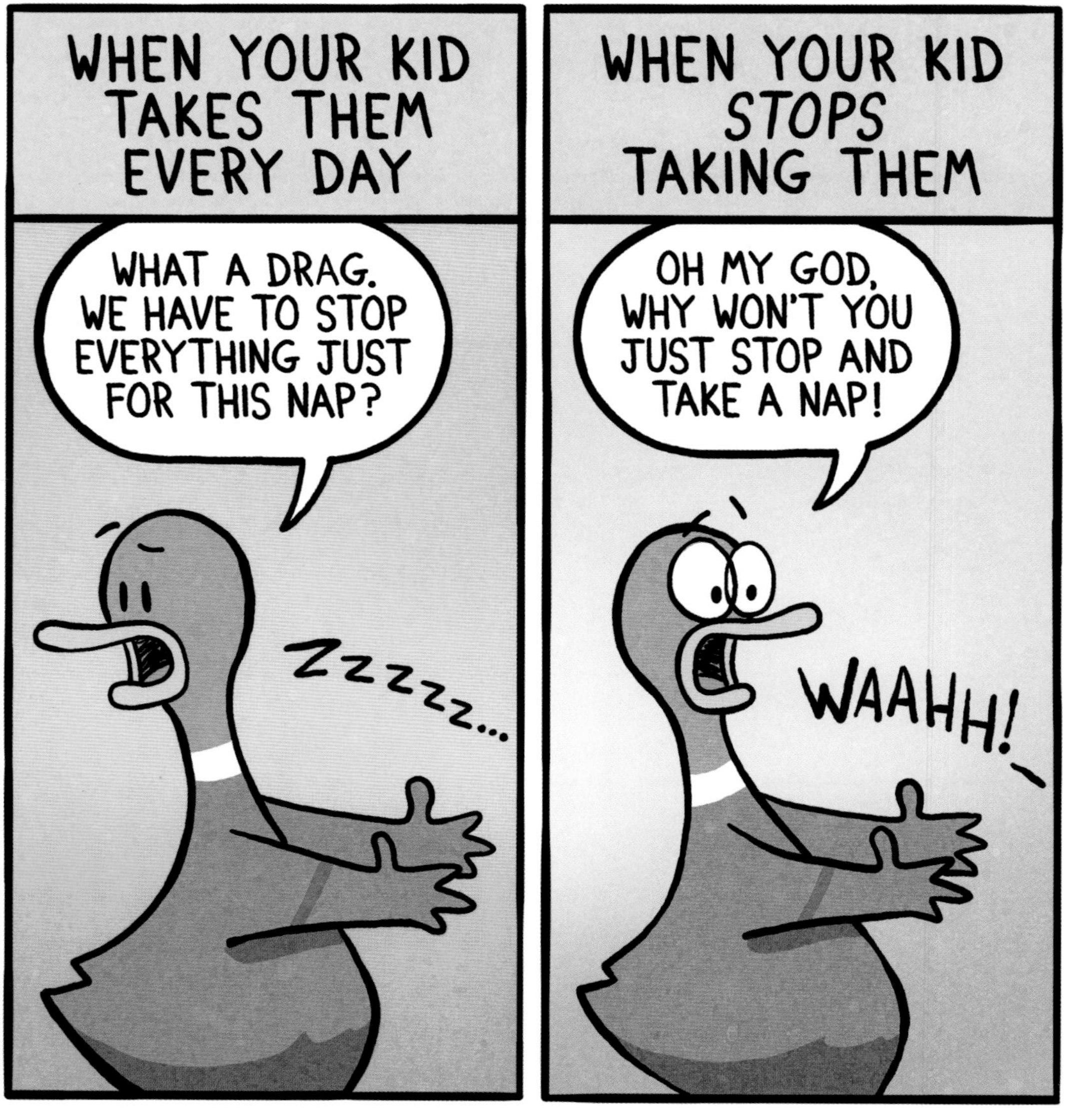
WHEN YOUR KID TAKES THEM EVERY DAY
WHAT A DRAG. WE HAVE TO STOP EVERYTHING JUST FOR THIS NAP?
ZZZZZZ...
WHEN YOUR KID *STOPS* TAKING THEM
OH MY GOD, WHY WON'T YOU JUST STOP AND TAKE A NAP!
WAAHH!

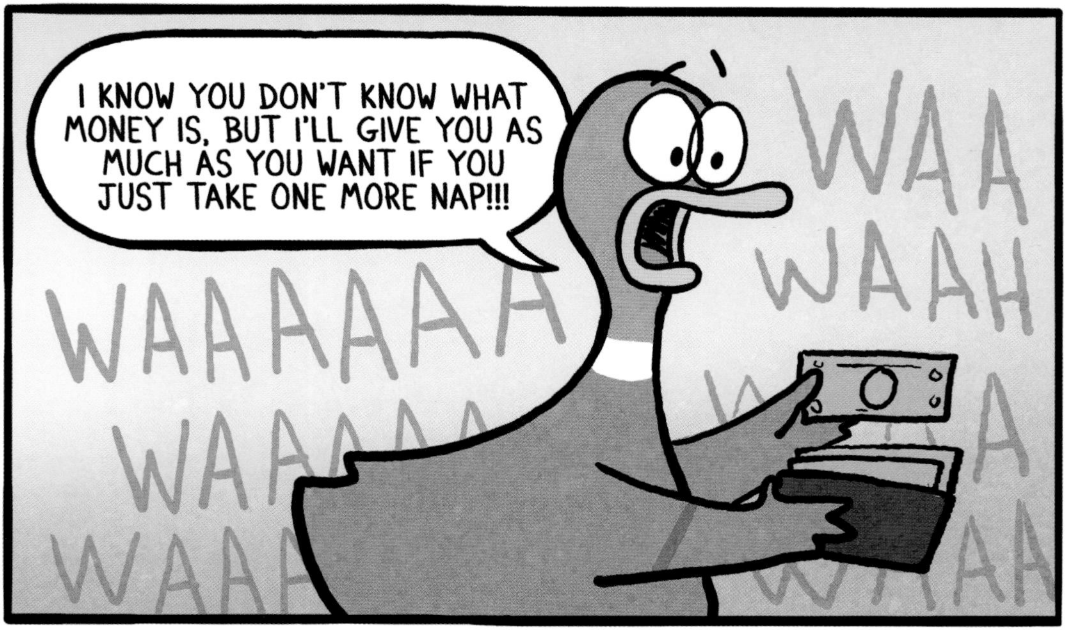
I KNOW YOU DON'T KNOW WHAT MONEY IS, BUT I'LL GIVE YOU AS MUCH AS YOU WANT IF YOU JUST TAKE ONE MORE NAP!!!
WAAAAAA
WAA
WAAH

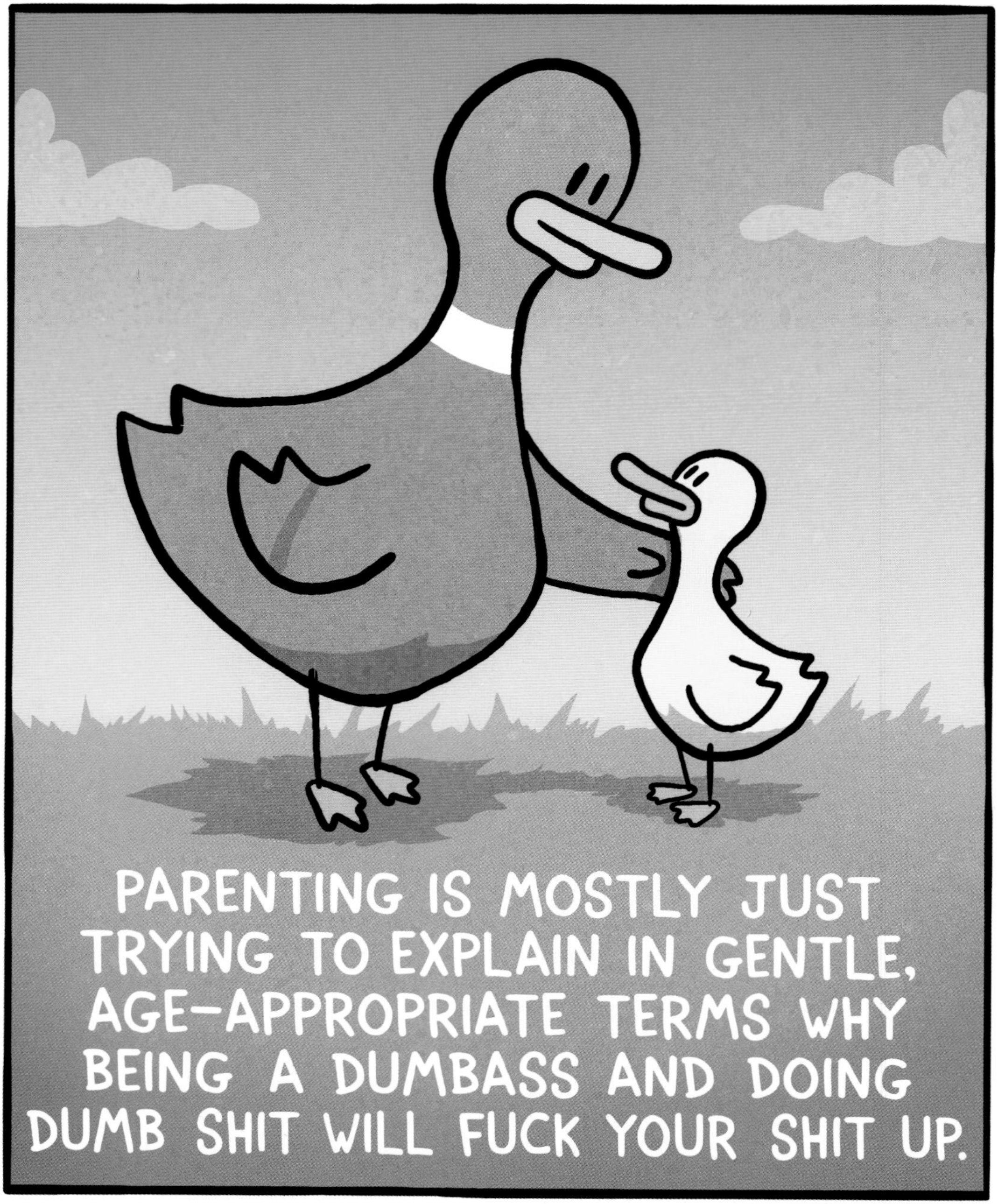
PARENTING IS MOSTLY JUST TRYING TO EXPLAIN IN GENTLE, AGE-APPROPRIATE TERMS WHY BEING A DUMBASS AND DOING DUMB SHIT WILL FUCK YOUR SHIT UP.

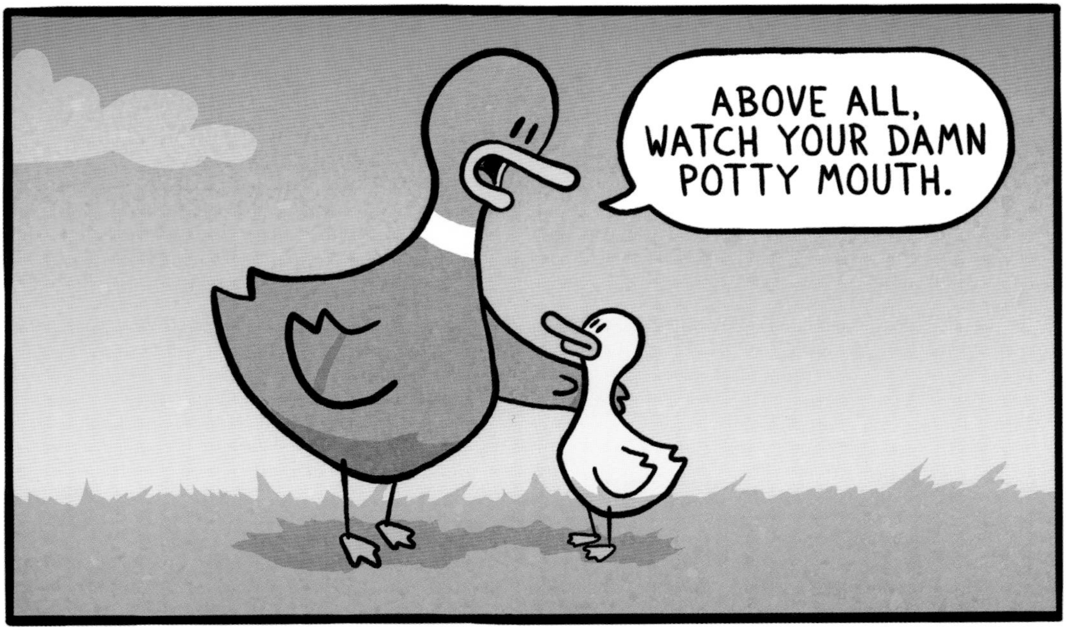
ABOVE ALL, WATCH YOUR DAMN POTTY MOUTH.

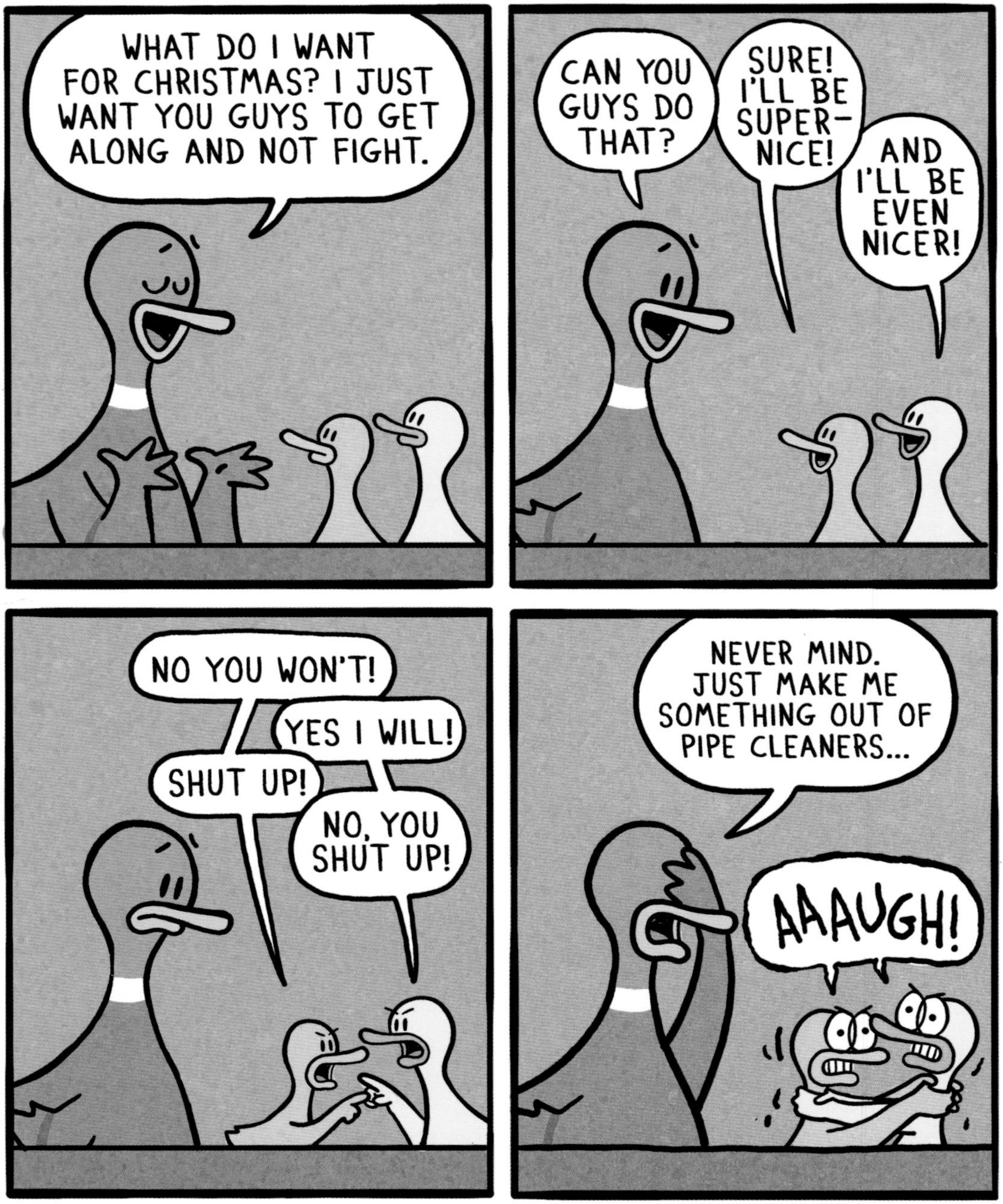
WHAT DO I WANT FOR CHRISTMAS? I JUST WANT YOU GUYS TO GET ALONG AND NOT FIGHT.
CAN YOU GUYS DO THAT?
SURE! I'LL BE SUPER-NICE!
AND I'LL BE EVEN NICER!
NO YOU WON'T!
YES I WILL!
SHUT UP!
NO, YOU SHUT UP!
NEVER MIND. JUST MAKE ME SOMETHING OUT OF PIPE CLEANERS...
AAAUGH!

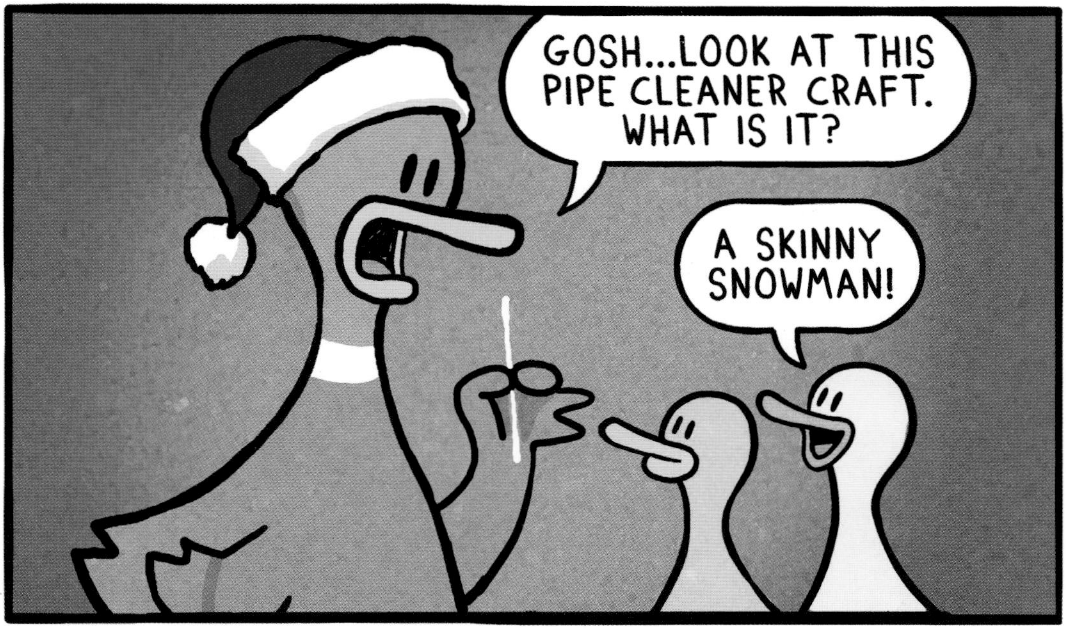
GOSH...LOOK AT THIS PIPE CLEANER CRAFT. WHAT IS IT?
A SKINNY SNOWMAN!

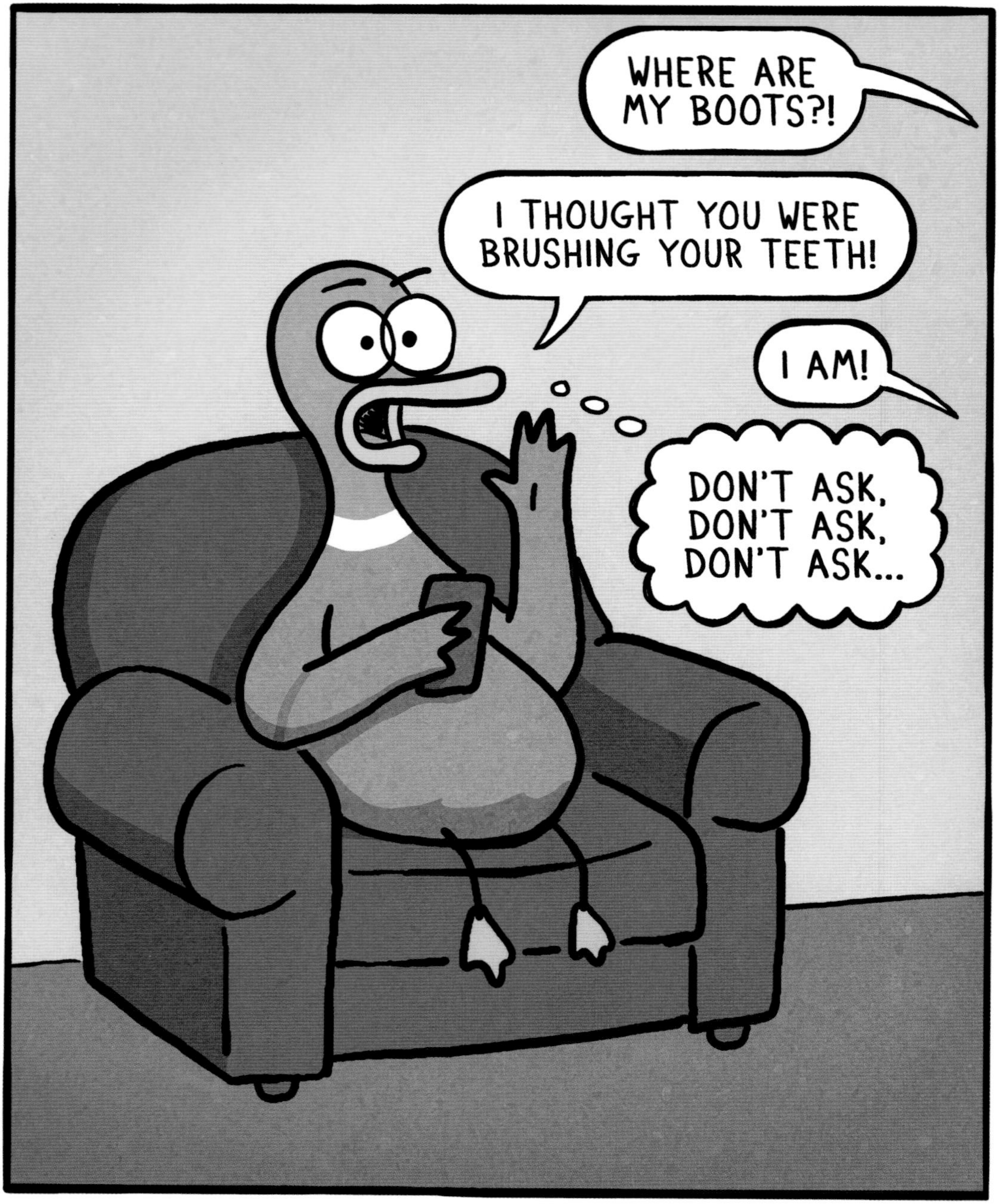
WHERE ARE MY BOOTS?!
I THOUGHT YOU WERE BRUSHING YOUR TEETH!
I AM!
DON'T ASK, DON'T ASK, DON'T ASK...

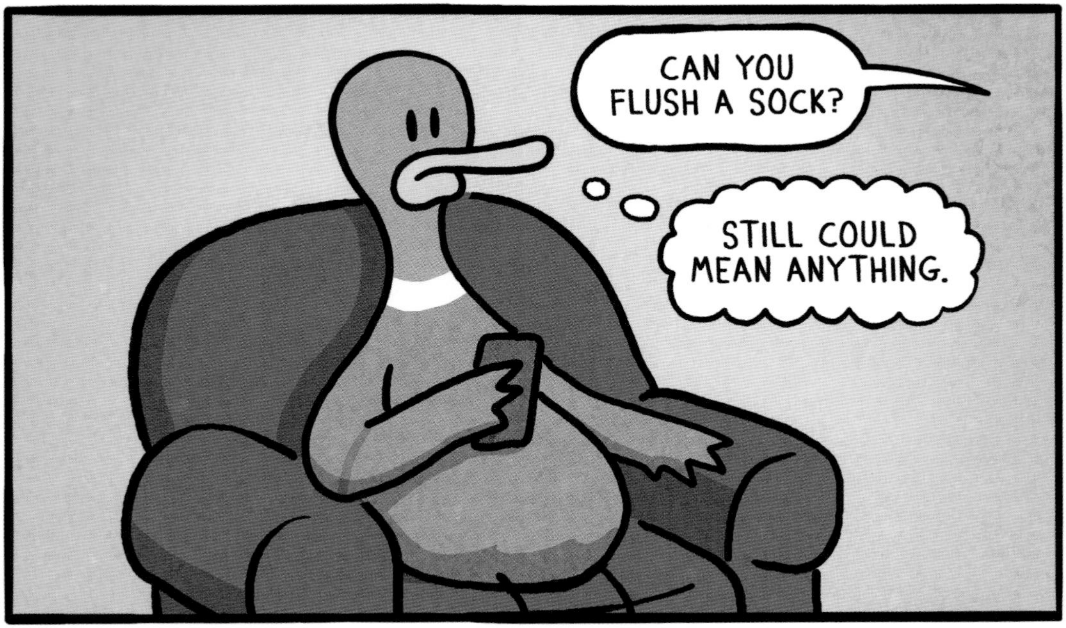
CAN YOU FLUSH A SOCK?
STILL COULD MEAN ANYTHING.

# HOW TO GET A CHILD'S ATTENTION

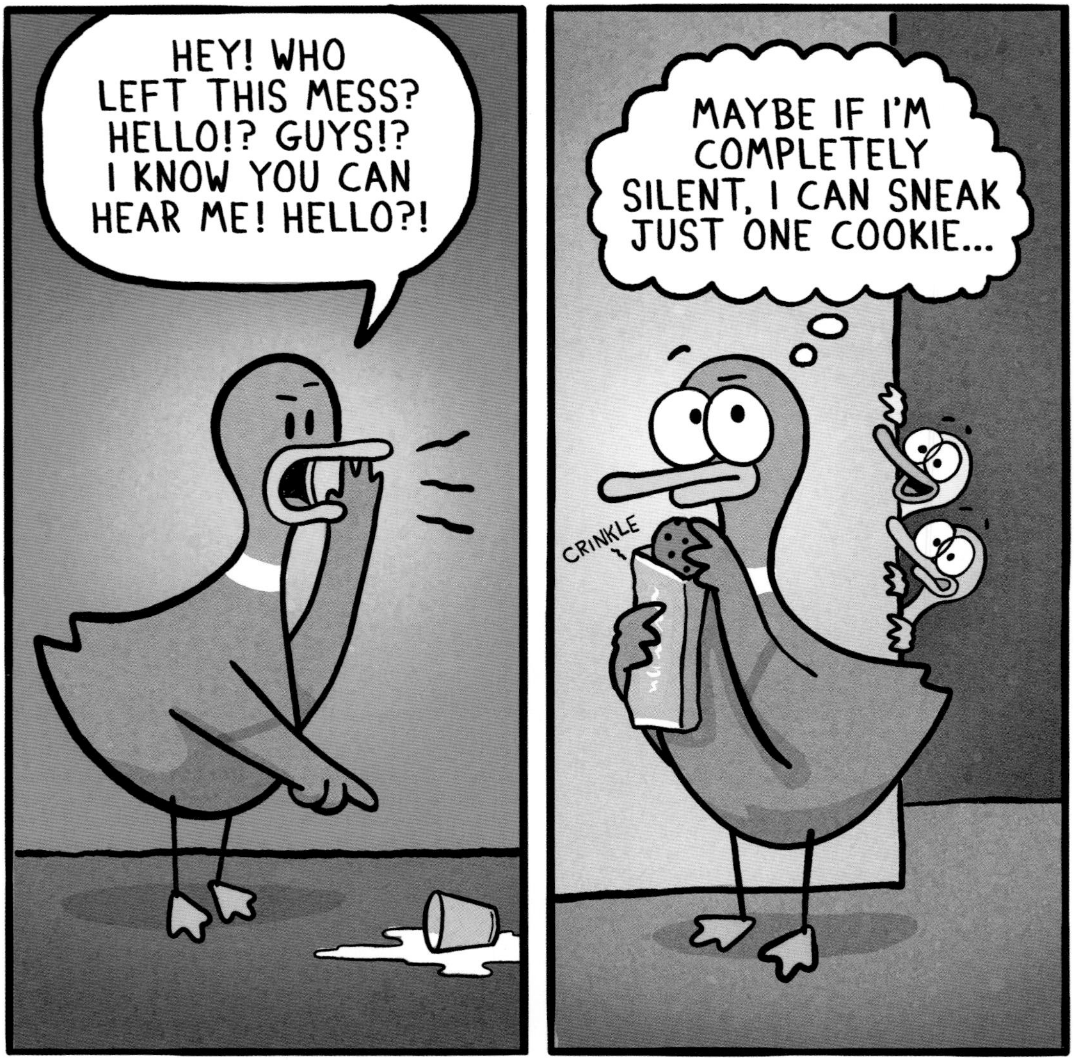
HEY! WHO LEFT THIS MESS? HELLO!? GUYS!? I KNOW YOU CAN HEAR ME! HELLO?!
MAYBE IF I'M COMPLETELY SILENT, I CAN SNEAK JUST ONE COOKIE...
CRINKLE

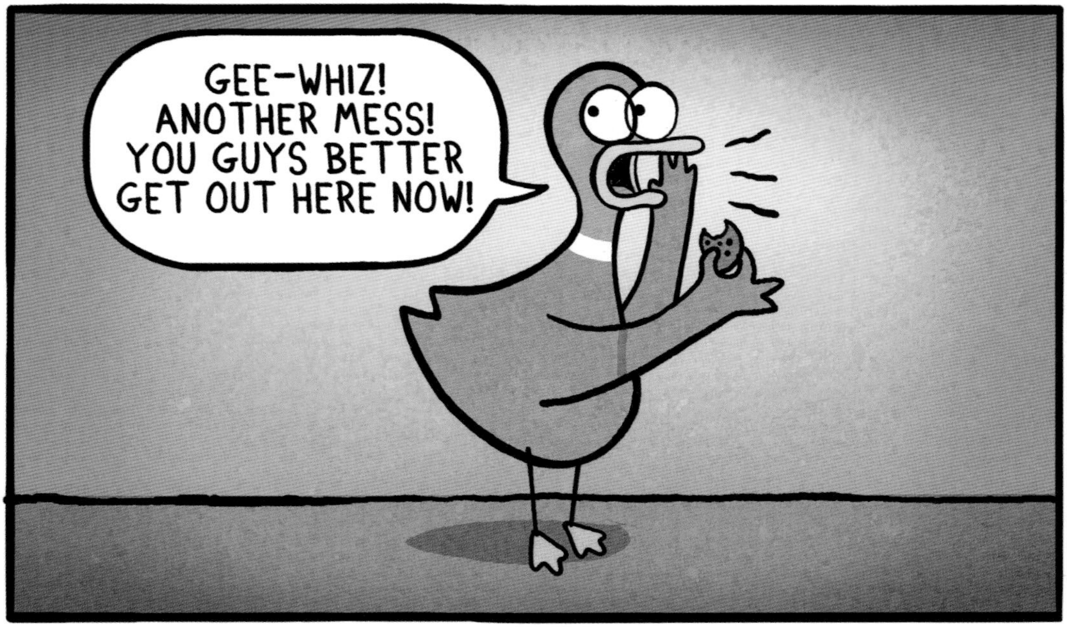
GEE-WHIZ! ANOTHER MESS! YOU GUYS BETTER GET OUT HERE NOW!

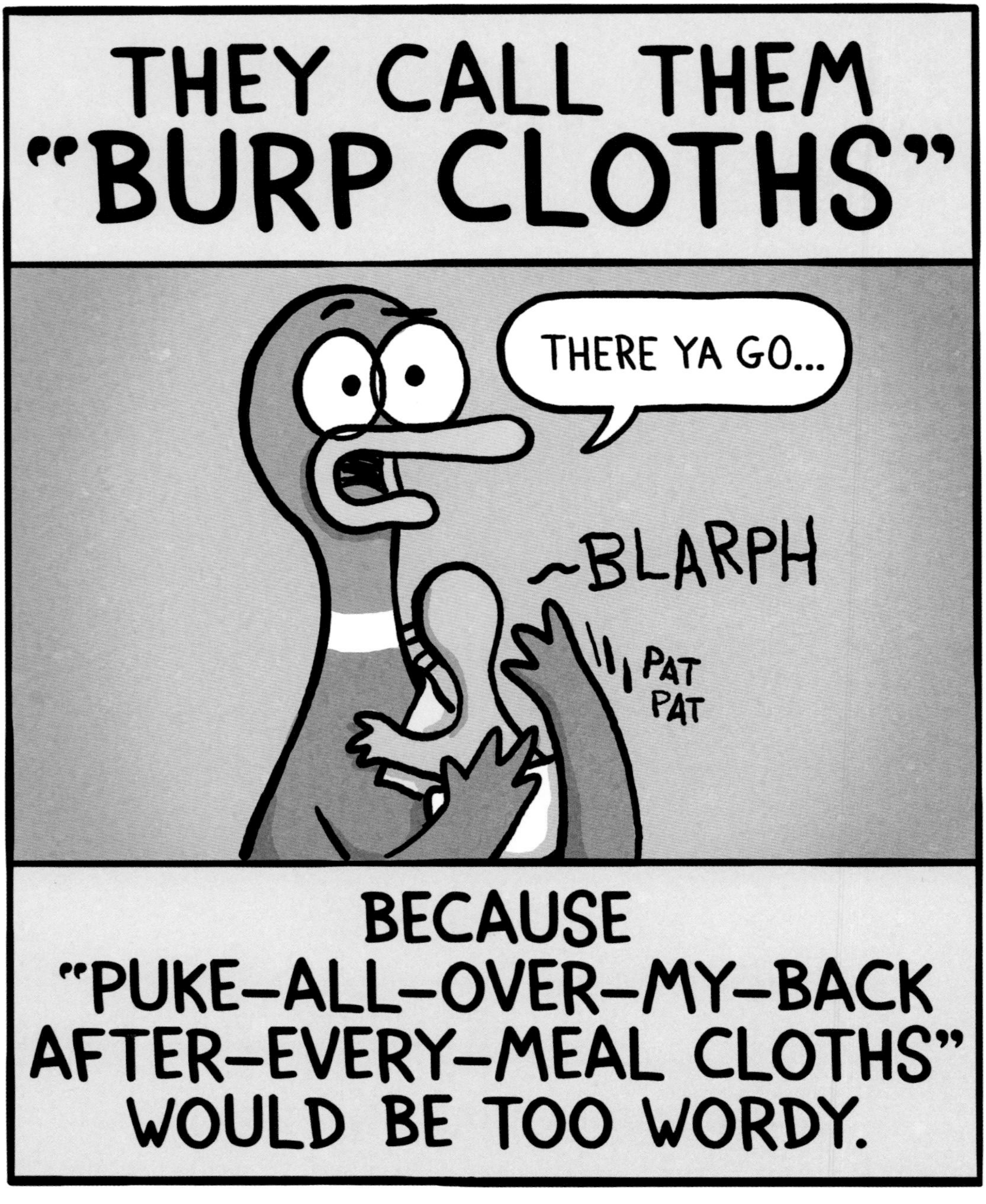
THEY CALL THEM "BURP CLOTHS"
THERE YA GO...
~BLARPH
PAT PAT
BECAUSE "PUKE-ALL-OVER-MY-BACK AFTER-EVERY-MEAL CLOTHS" WOULD BE TOO WORDY.

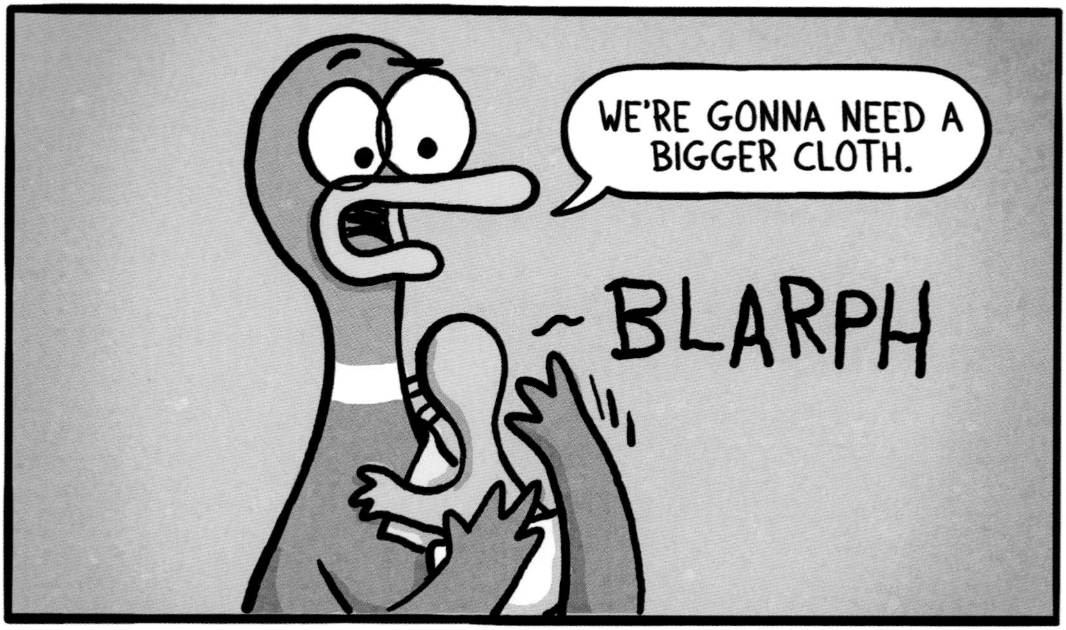
WE'RE GONNA NEED A BIGGER CLOTH.
~BLARPH

# BATHROOM RULES

1. PEE GOES IN THE TOILET. *ONLY* IN THE TOILET.

2. ONE WORD, FOUR LETTERS. WIPE.

3. WASH YOUR HANDS.

4. DID YOU *REALLY...?* LET ME SEE THEM.

5. YEAH, THAT'S WHAT I THOUGHT.

6. WASH! YOUR! HANDS!

7. OH, FOR THE LOVE OF GOD—
   YOU LEFT THE WATER ON!

8. THANK YOU.

9. WHAT DO YOU MEAN,
   *YOU HAVE TO GO AGAIN?!*

# THE PROBLEM WITH BABY SHOWER GIFTS

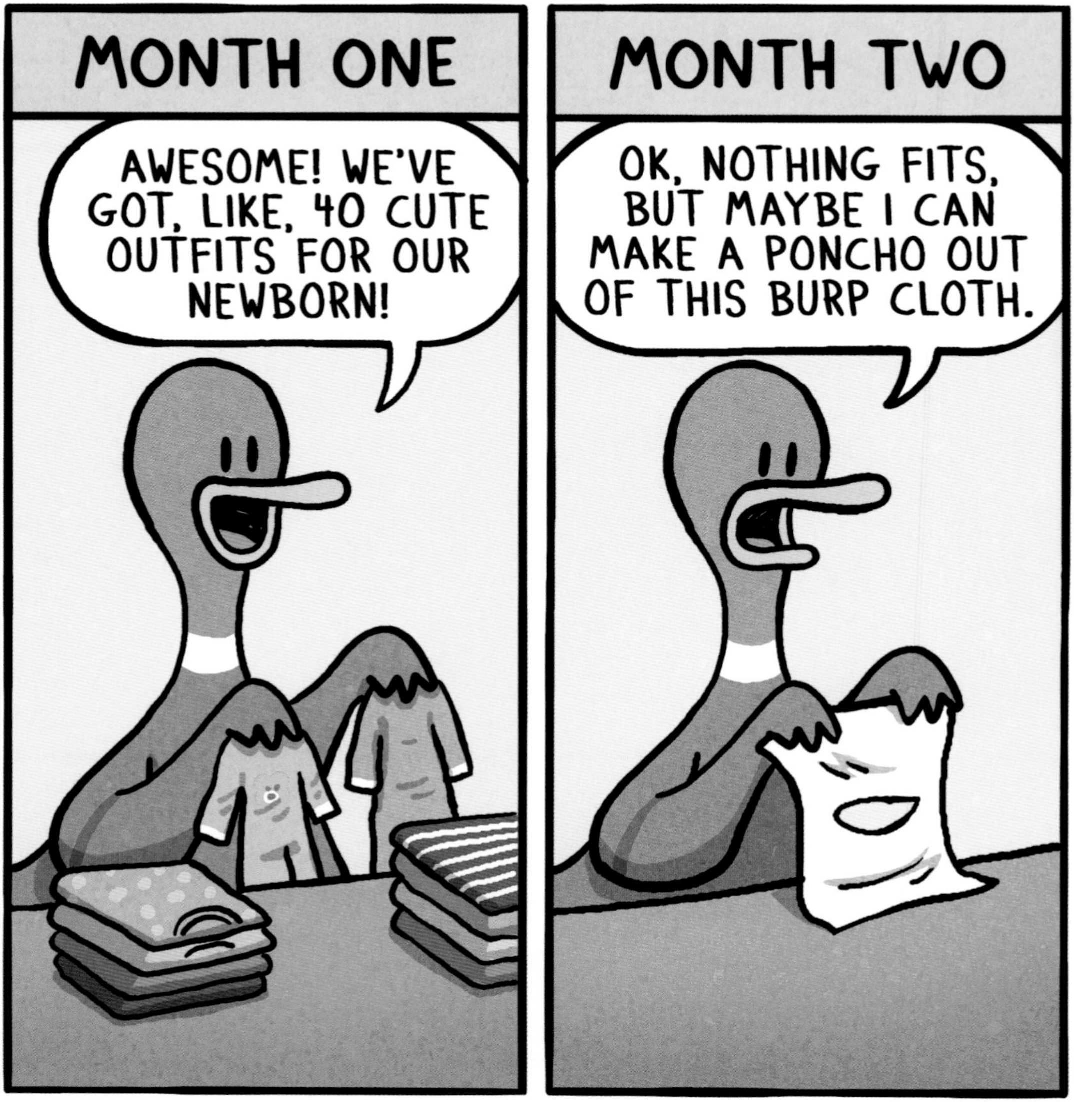
MONTH ONE
AWESOME! WE'VE GOT, LIKE, 40 CUTE OUTFITS FOR OUR NEWBORN!
MONTH TWO
OK, NOTHING FITS, BUT MAYBE I CAN MAKE A PONCHO OUT OF THIS BURP CLOTH.

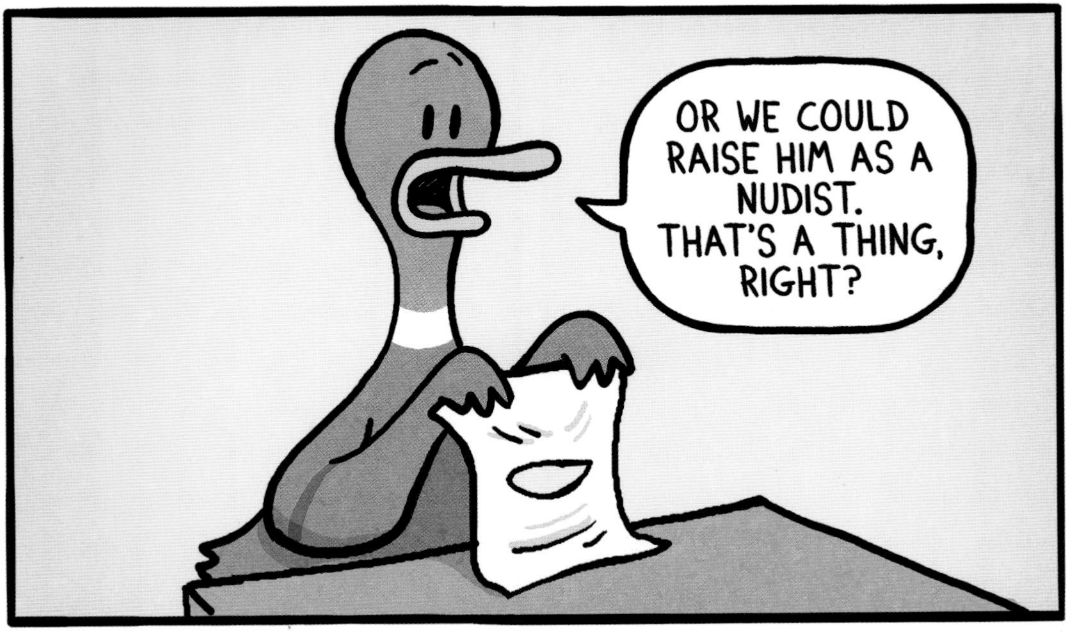
OR WE COULD RAISE HIM AS A NUDIST. THAT'S A THING, RIGHT?

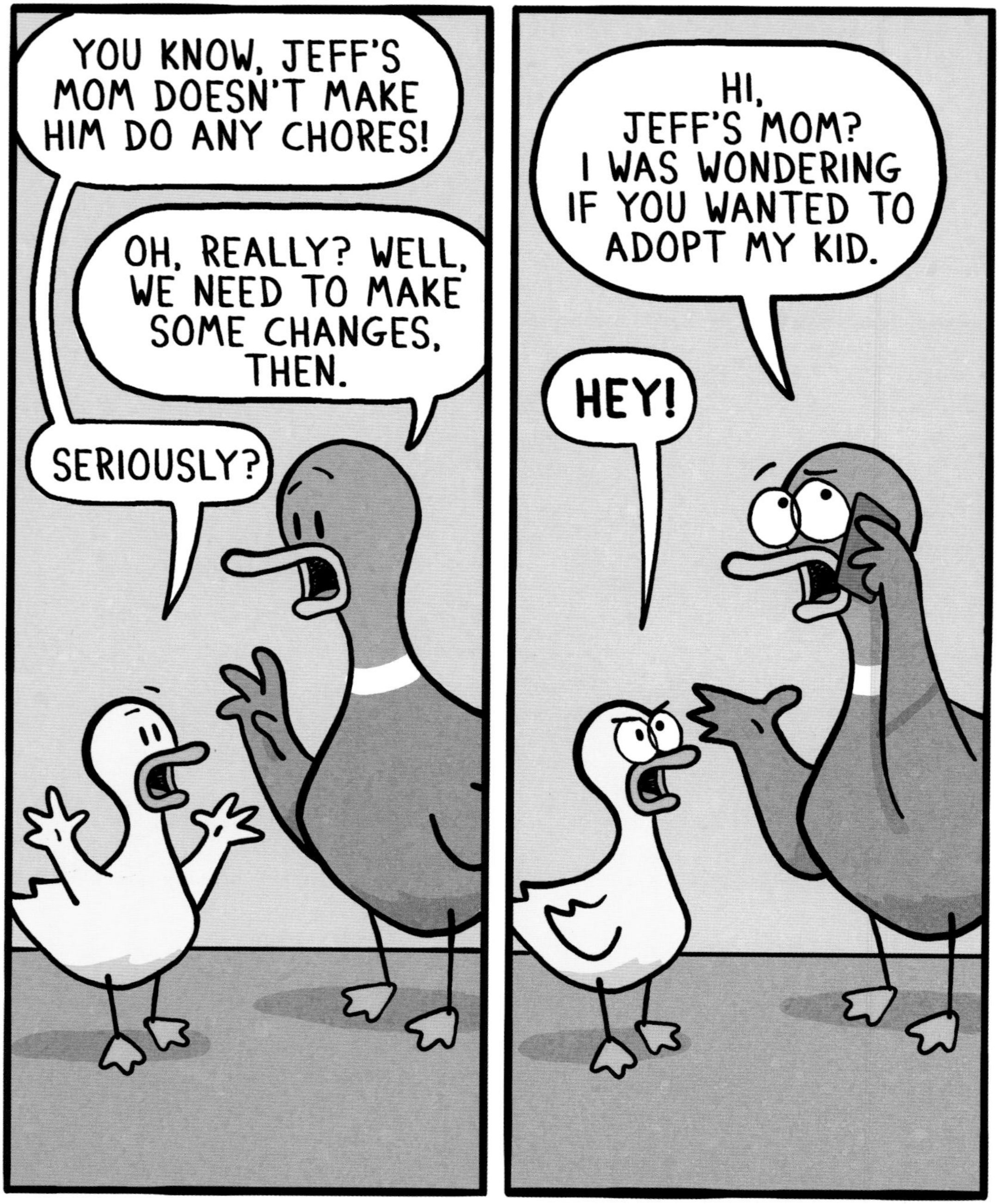
YOU KNOW, JEFF'S MOM DOESN'T MAKE HIM DO ANY CHORES!
OH, REALLY? WELL, WE NEED TO MAKE SOME CHANGES, THEN.
SERIOUSLY?
HI, JEFF'S MOM? I WAS WONDERING IF YOU WANTED TO ADOPT MY KID.
HEY!

EVIDENTLY JEFF TRIED TO PULL THE SAME SCAM ON HIS MOM, TOO.

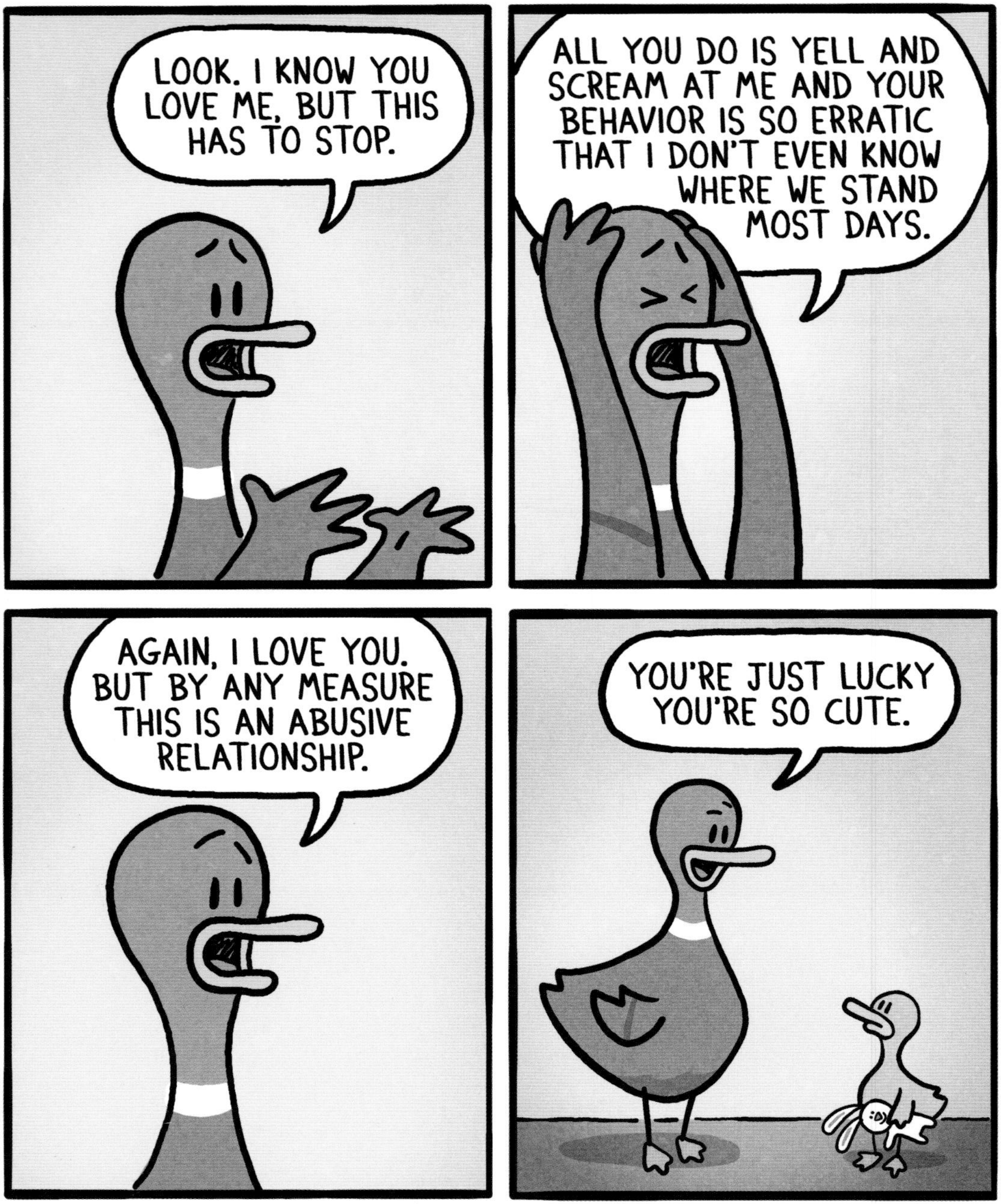
LOOK. I KNOW YOU LOVE ME, BUT THIS HAS TO STOP.
ALL YOU DO IS YELL AND SCREAM AT ME AND YOUR BEHAVIOR IS SO ERRATIC THAT I DON'T EVEN KNOW WHERE WE STAND MOST DAYS.
AGAIN, I LOVE YOU. BUT BY ANY MEASURE THIS IS AN ABUSIVE RELATIONSHIP.
YOU'RE JUST LUCKY YOU'RE SO CUTE.

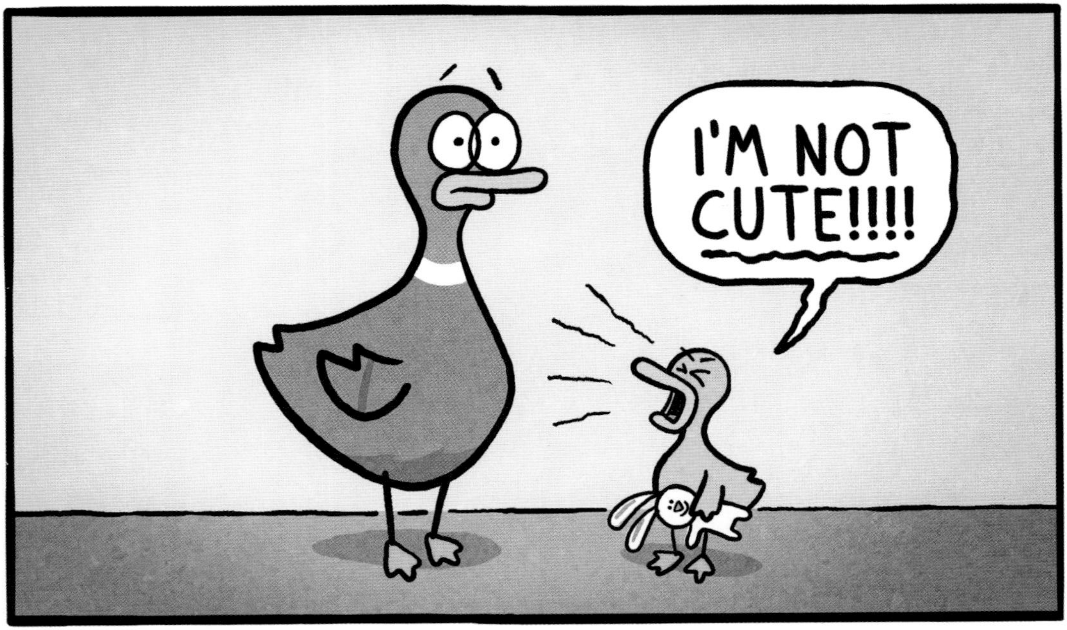
I'M NOT CUTE!!!!

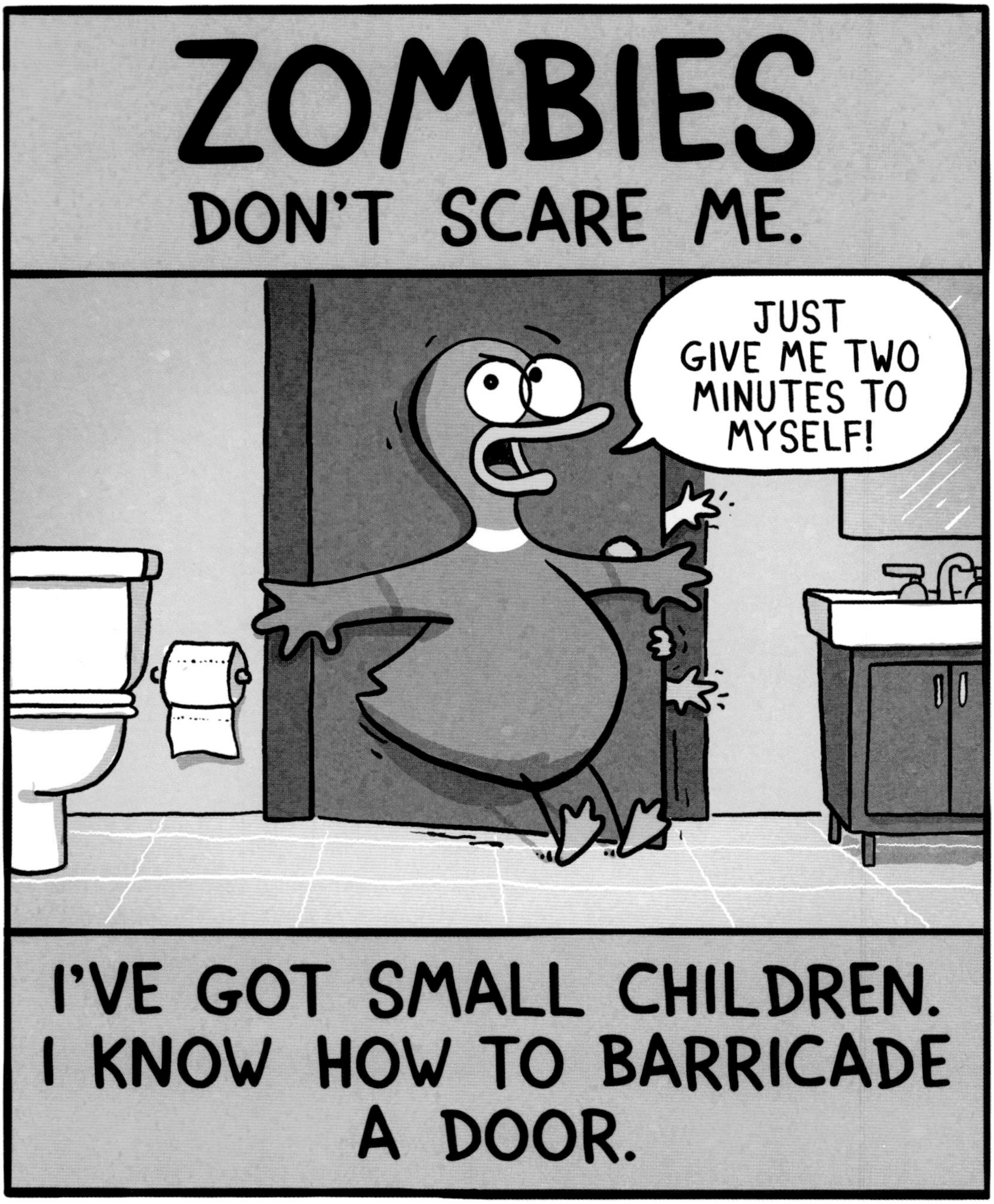
ZOMBIES
DON'T SCARE ME.
JUST GIVE ME TWO MINUTES TO MYSELF!
I'VE GOT SMALL CHILDREN. I KNOW HOW TO BARRICADE A DOOR.

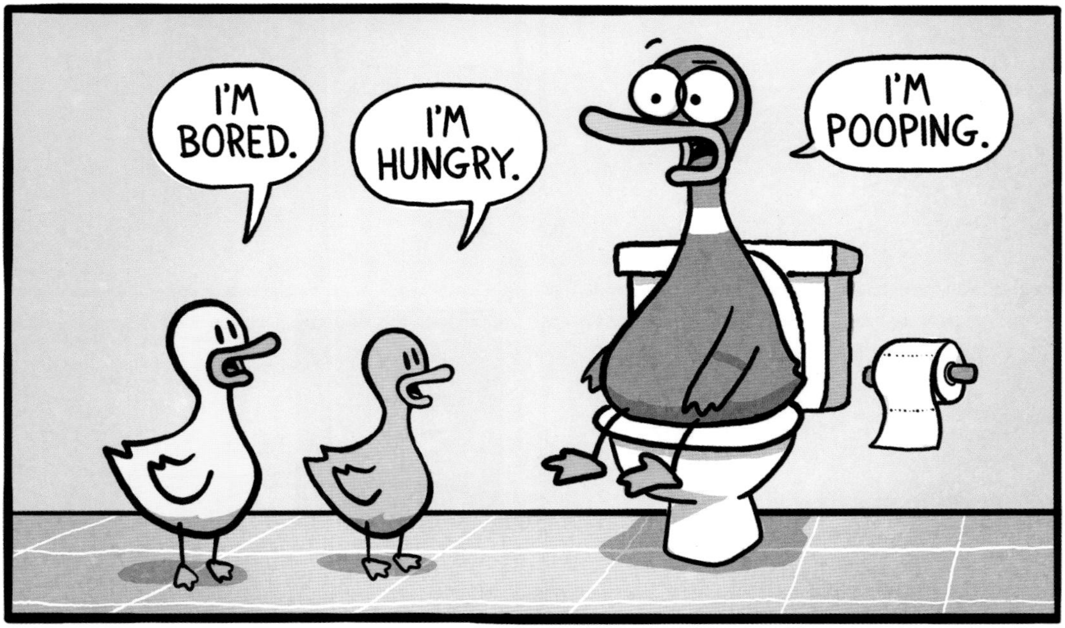
I'M BORED.
I'M HUNGRY.
I'M POOPING.

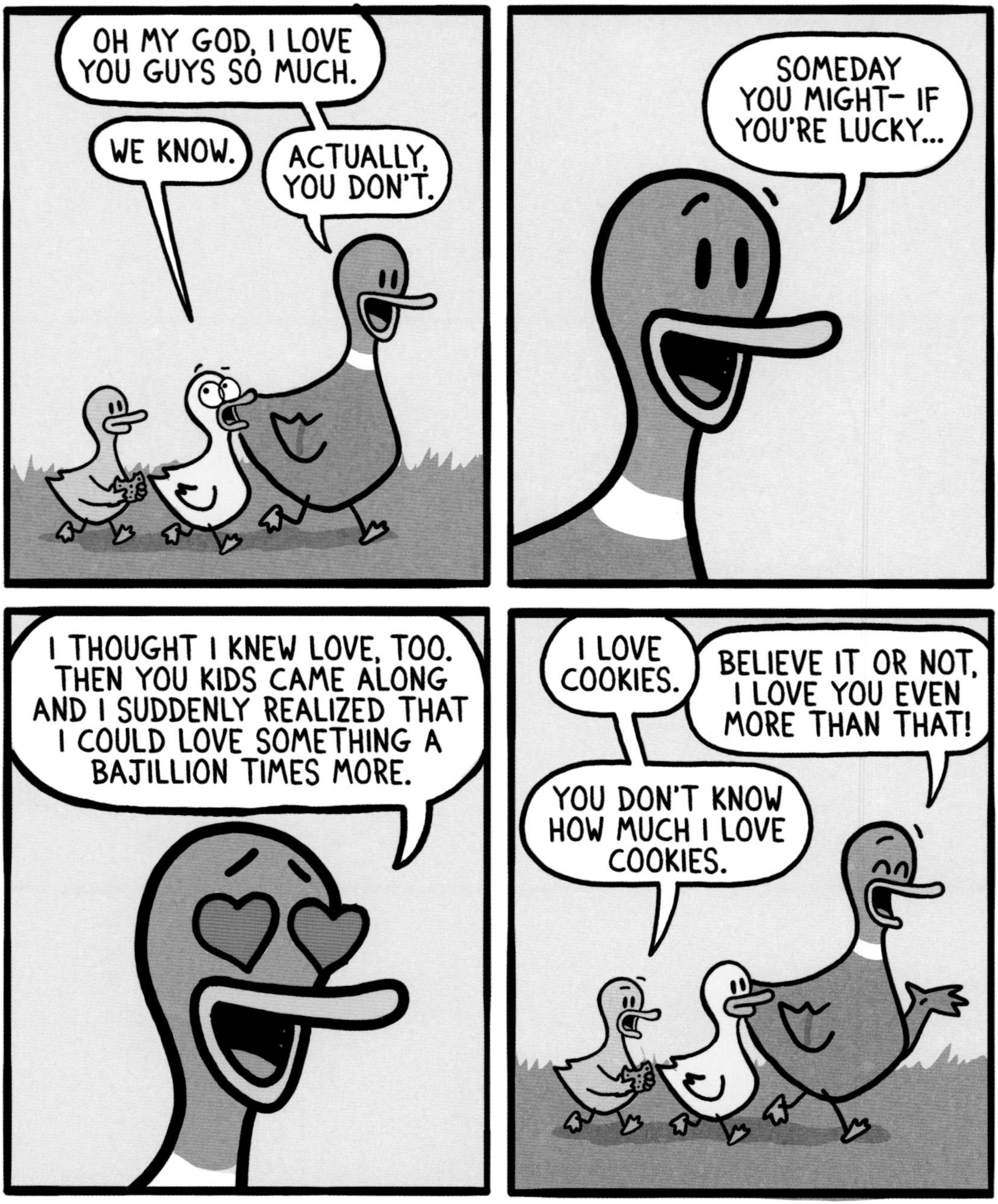
OH MY GOD, I LOVE YOU GUYS SO MUCH.
WE KNOW.
ACTUALLY, YOU DON'T.
SOMEDAY YOU MIGHT– IF YOU'RE LUCKY...
I THOUGHT I KNEW LOVE, TOO. THEN YOU KIDS CAME ALONG AND I SUDDENLY REALIZED THAT I COULD LOVE SOMETHING A BAJILLION TIMES MORE.
I LOVE COOKIES.
BELIEVE IT OR NOT, I LOVE YOU EVEN MORE THAN THAT!
YOU DON'T KNOW HOW MUCH I LOVE COOKIES.

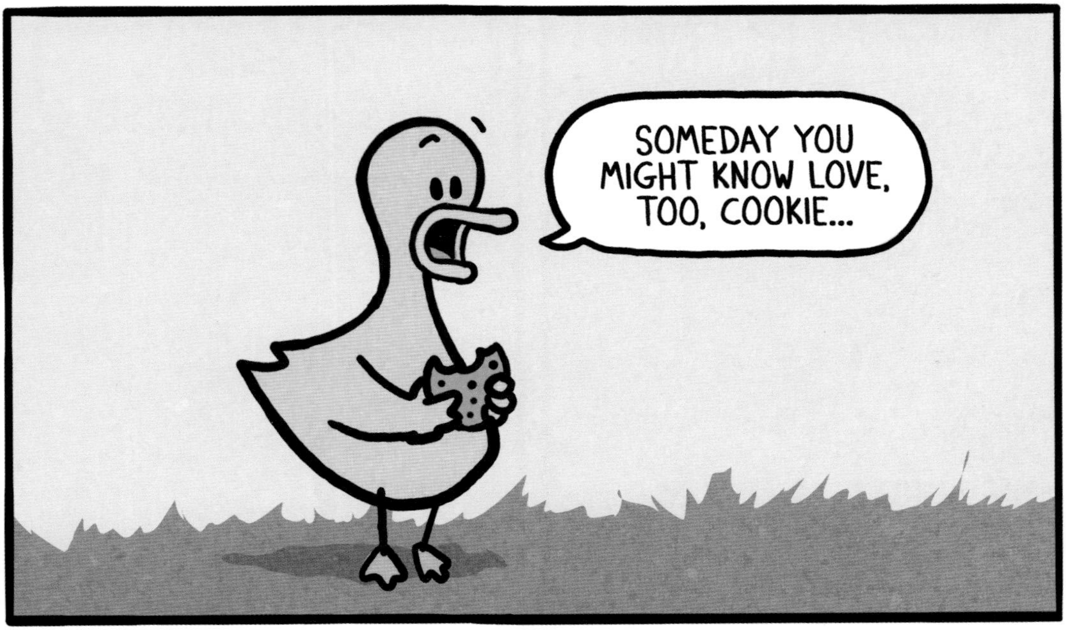
SOMEDAY YOU MIGHT KNOW LOVE, TOO, COOKIE...

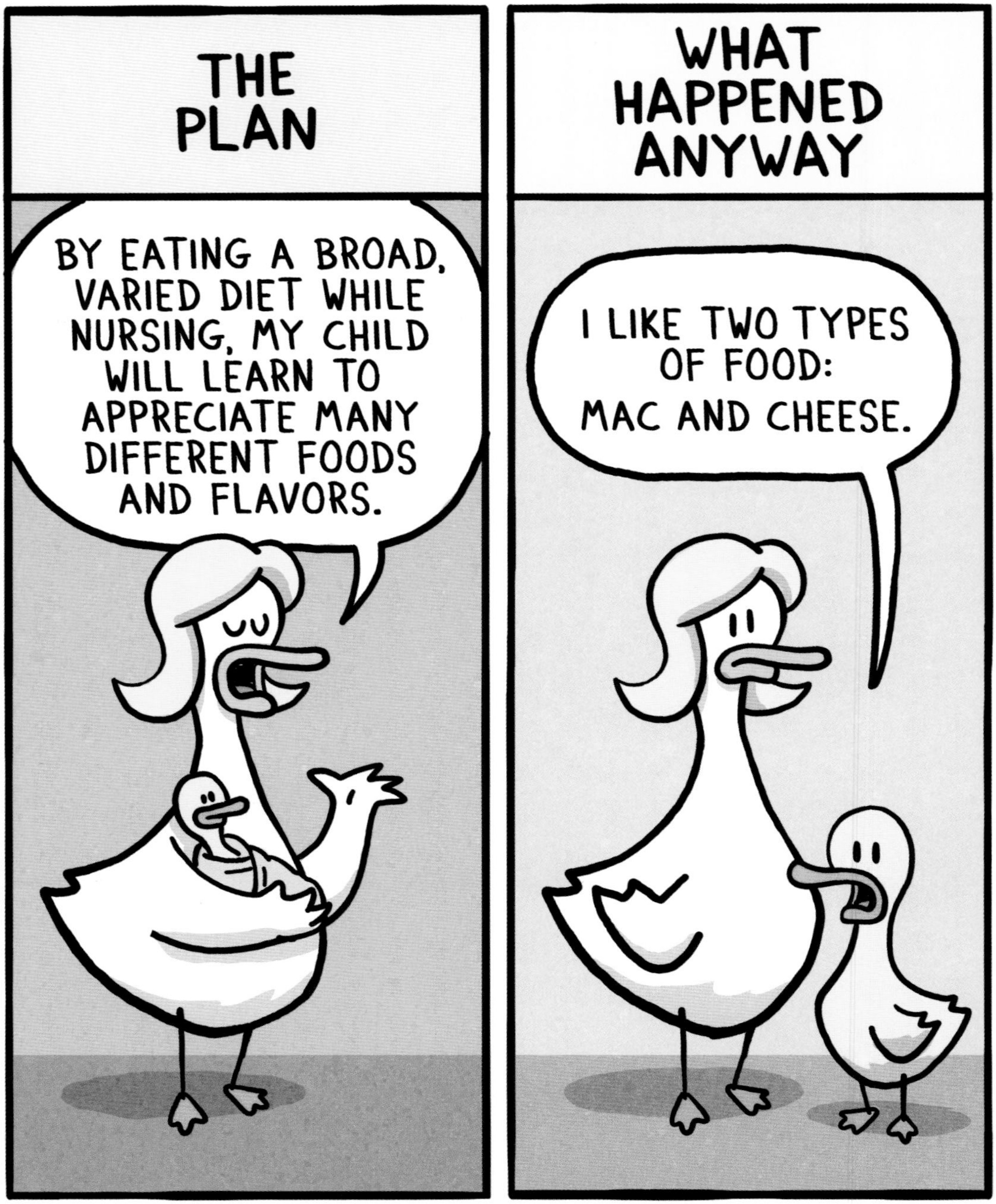
THE PLAN
BY EATING A BROAD, VARIED DIET WHILE NURSING, MY CHILD WILL LEARN TO APPRECIATE MANY DIFFERENT FOODS AND FLAVORS.
WHAT HAPPENED ANYWAY
I LIKE TWO TYPES OF FOOD: MAC AND CHEESE.

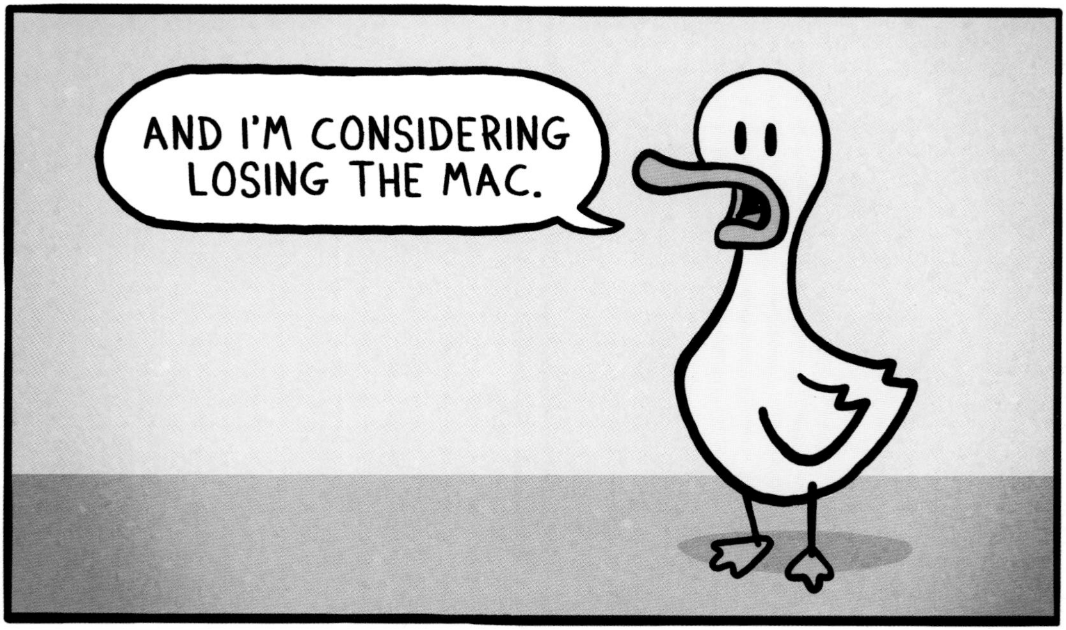
AND I'M CONSIDERING LOSING THE MAC.

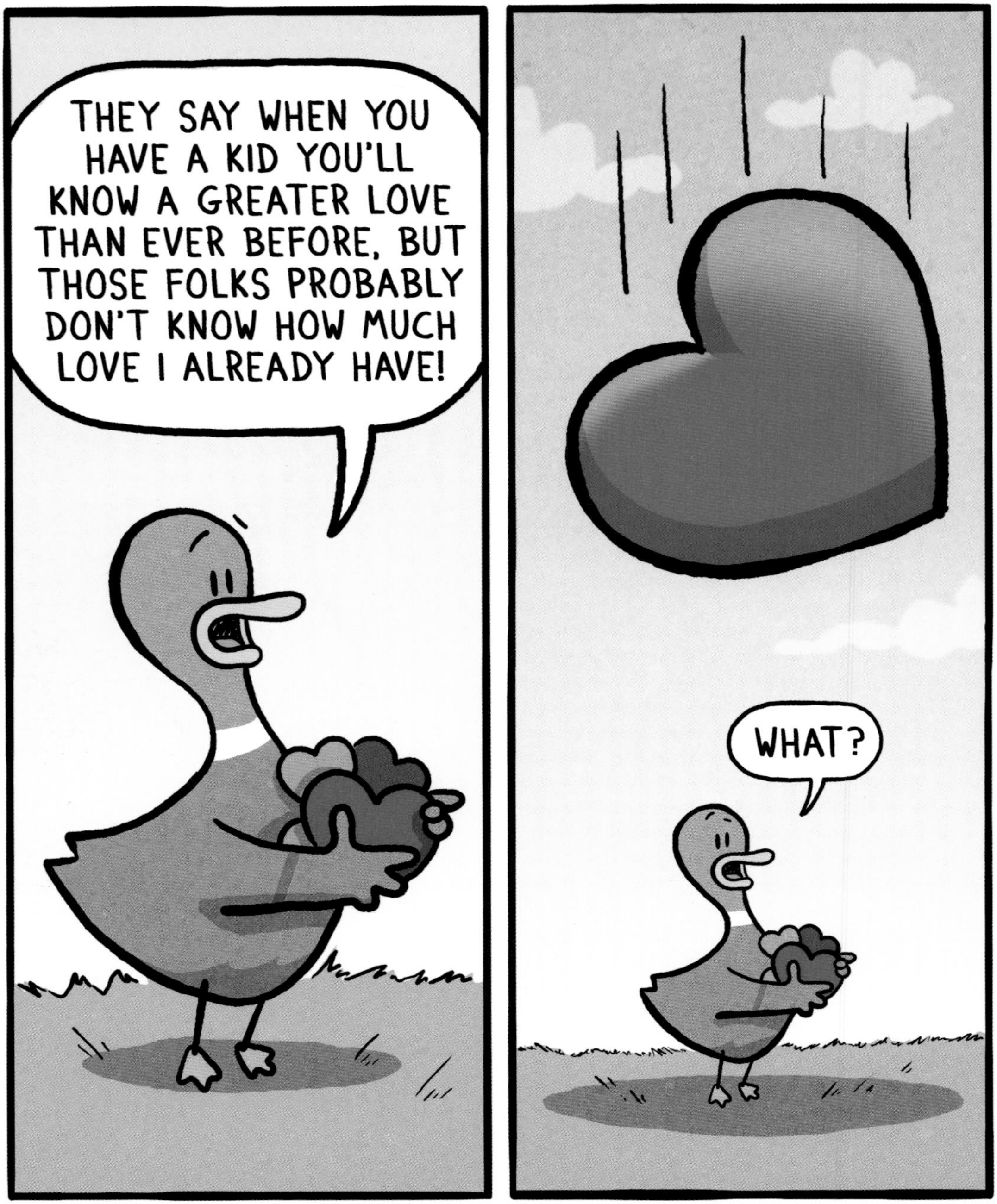
THEY SAY WHEN YOU HAVE A KID YOU'LL KNOW A GREATER LOVE THAN EVER BEFORE, BUT THOSE FOLKS PROBABLY DON'T KNOW HOW MUCH LOVE I ALREADY HAVE!
WHAT?

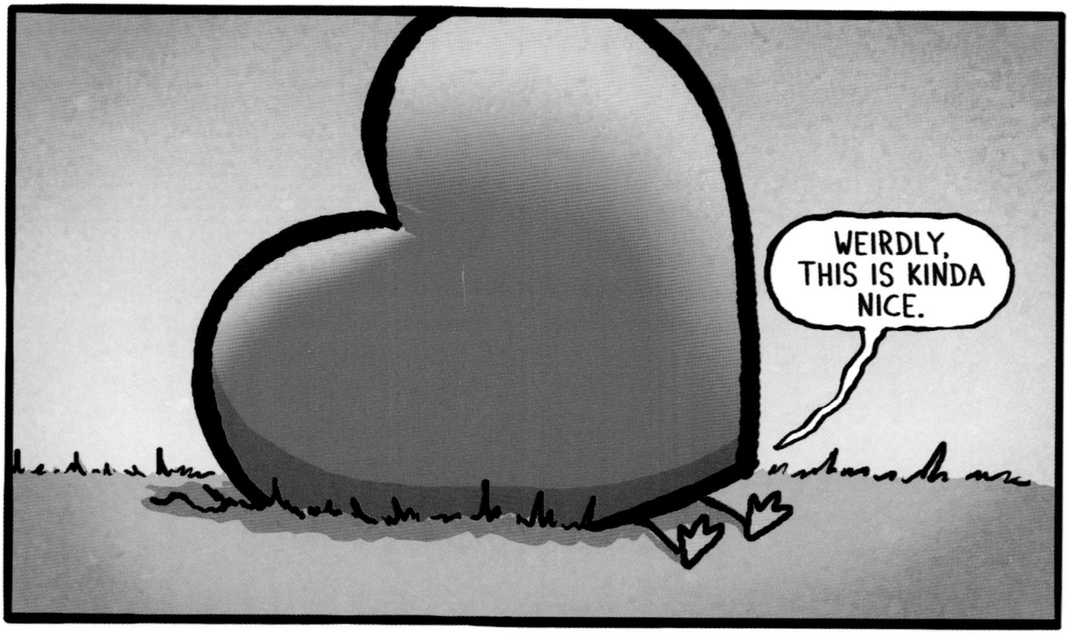
WEIRDLY, THIS IS KINDA NICE.

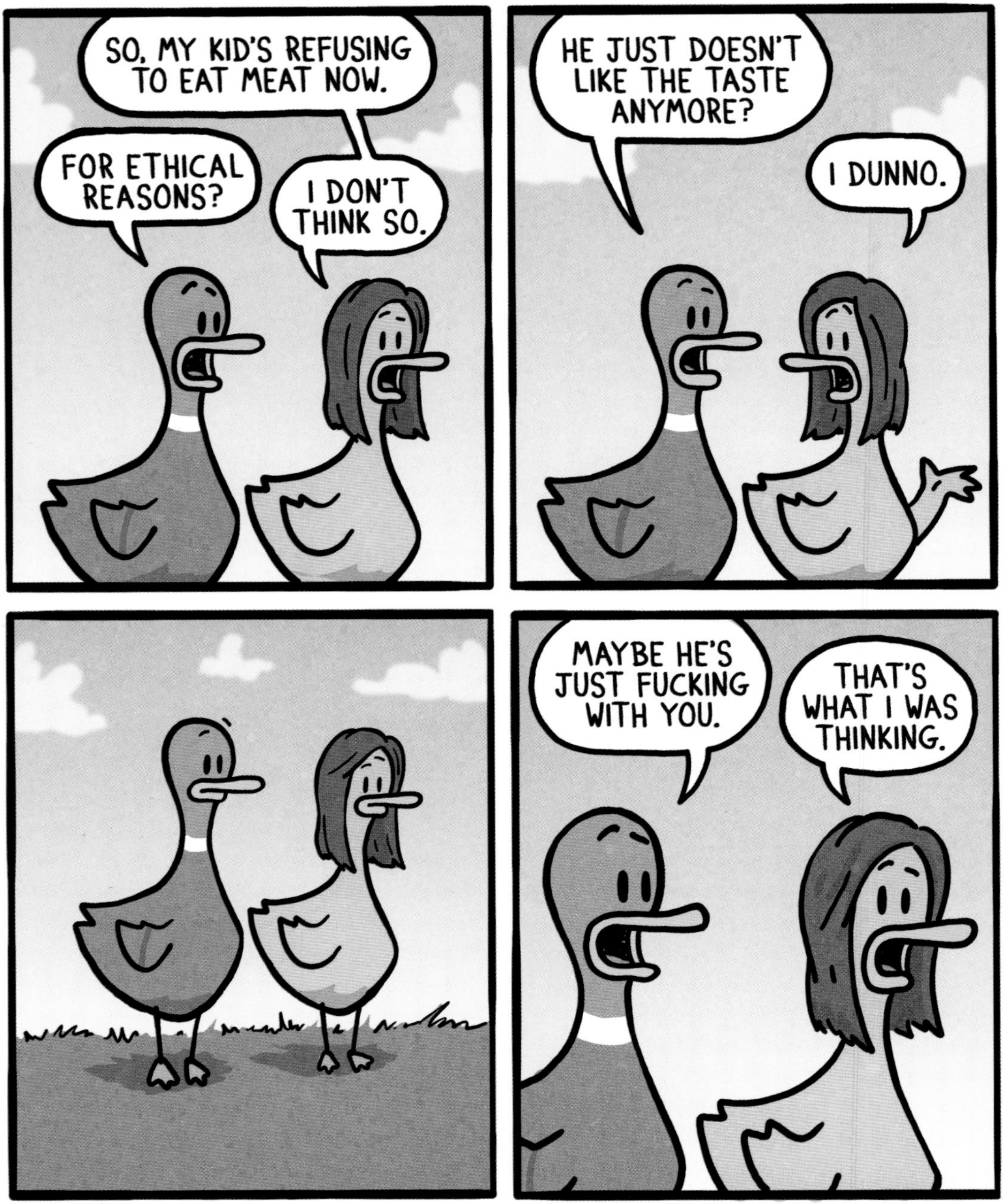
SO, MY KID'S REFUSING TO EAT MEAT NOW.
FOR ETHICAL REASONS?
I DON'T THINK SO.
HE JUST DOESN'T LIKE THE TASTE ANYMORE?
I DUNNO.
MAYBE HE'S JUST FUCKING WITH YOU.
THAT'S WHAT I WAS THINKING.

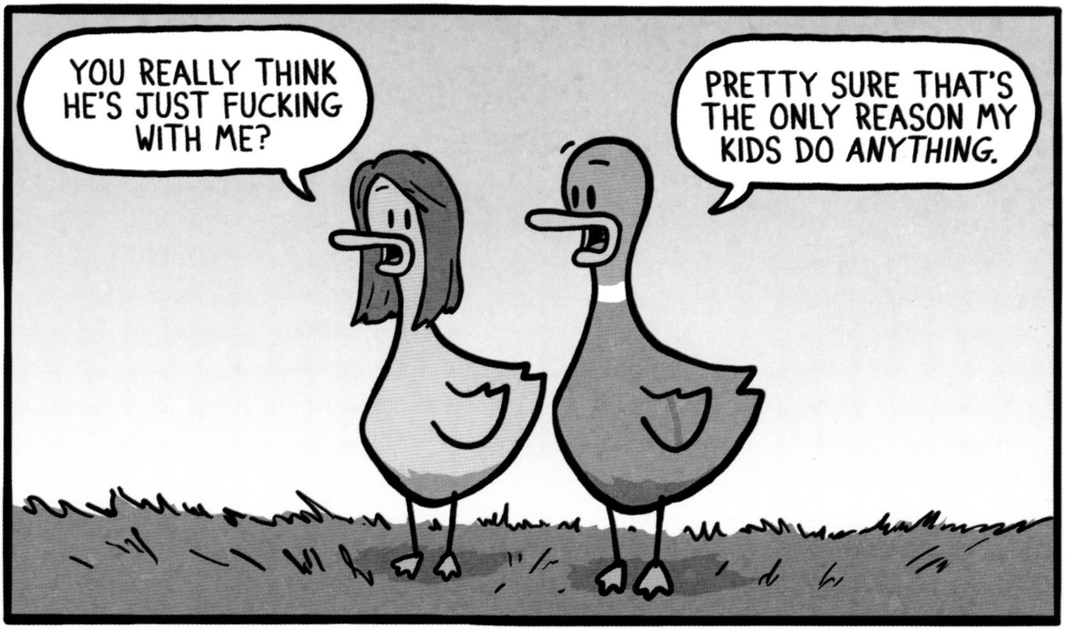
YOU REALLY THINK HE'S JUST FUCKING WITH ME?
PRETTY SURE THAT'S THE ONLY REASON MY KIDS DO *ANYTHING.*

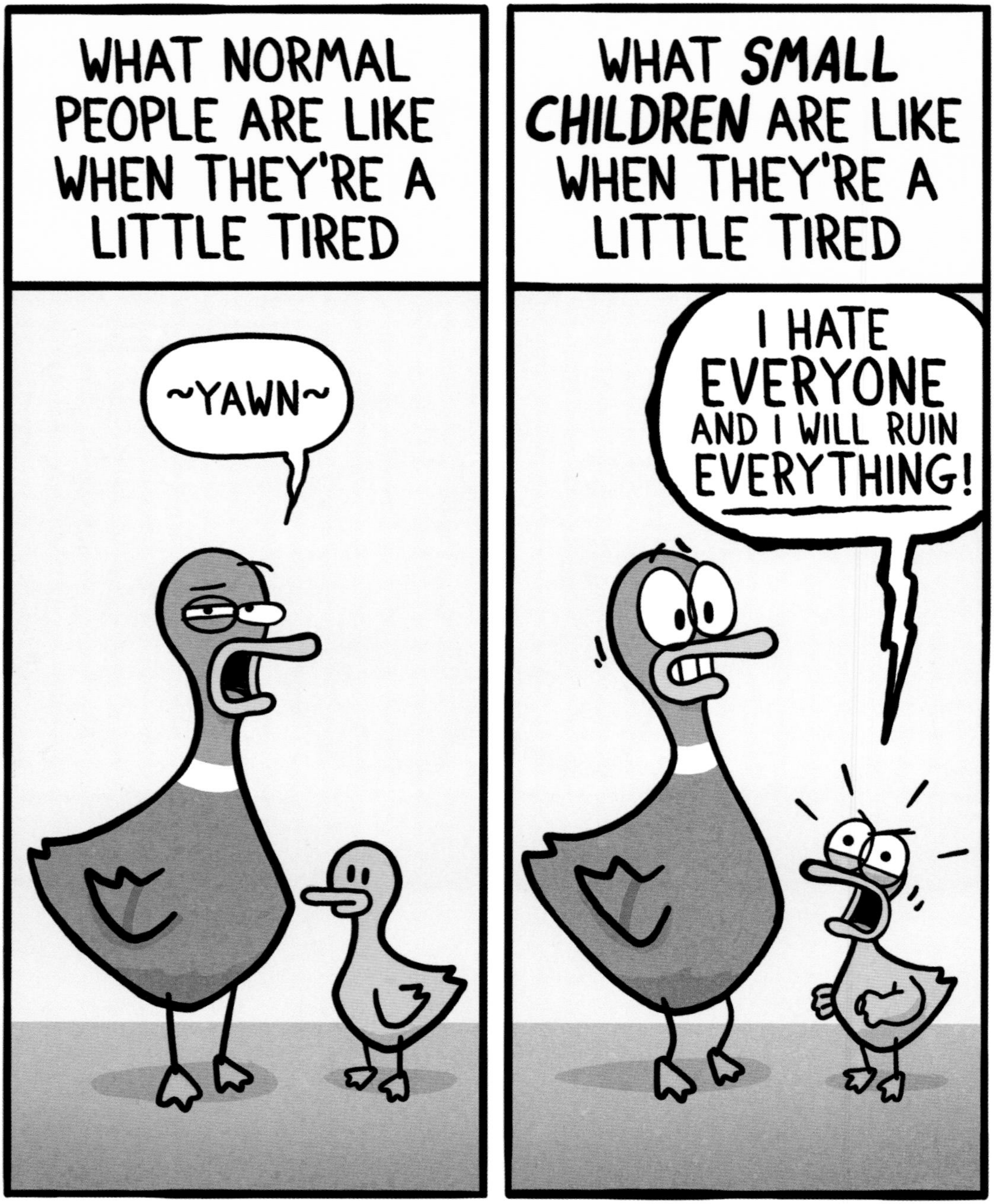

WHAT NORMAL PEOPLE ARE LIKE WHEN THEY'RE A LITTLE TIRED
~YAWN~
WHAT SMALL CHILDREN ARE LIKE WHEN THEY'RE A LITTLE TIRED
I HATE EVERYONE AND I WILL RUIN EVERYTHING!

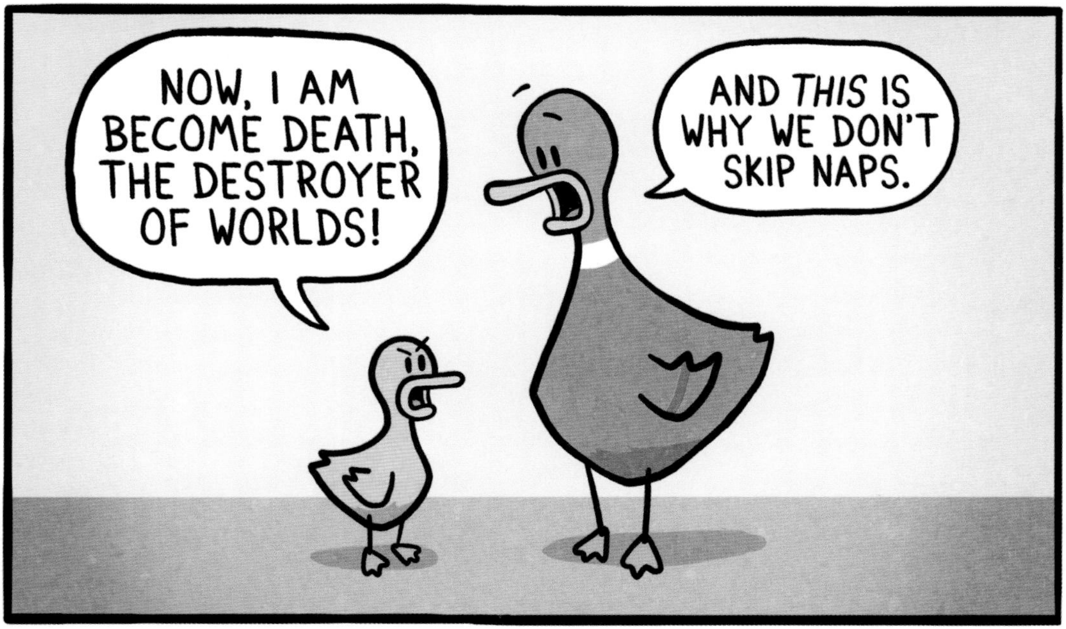
NOW, I AM BECOME DEATH, THE DESTROYER OF WORLDS!
AND *THIS* IS WHY WE DON'T SKIP NAPS.

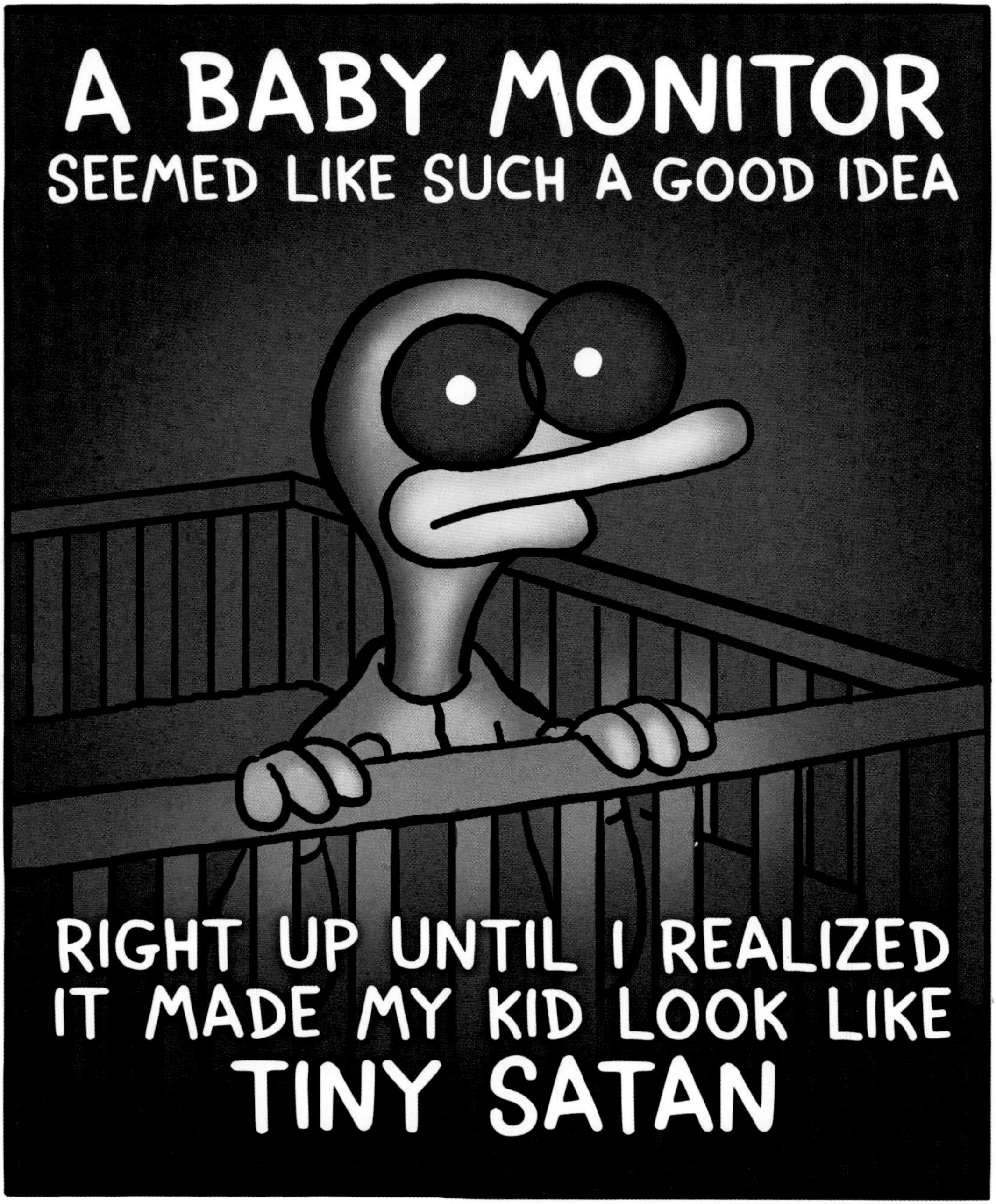
A BABY MONITOR
SEEMED LIKE SUCH A GOOD IDEA
RIGHT UP UNTIL I REALIZED
IT MADE MY KID LOOK LIKE
TINY SATAN

OH, CRAP.
LOOKS LIKE
BABY'S UP AGAIN–
ON THE CEILING.

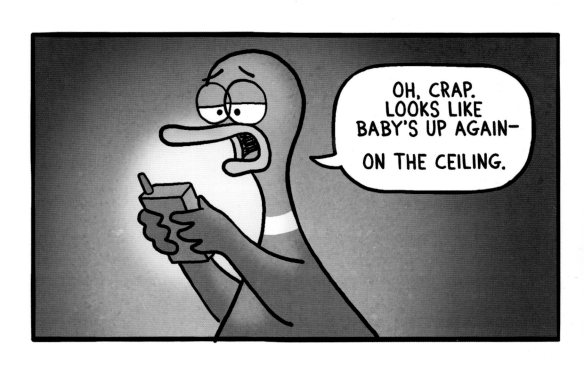

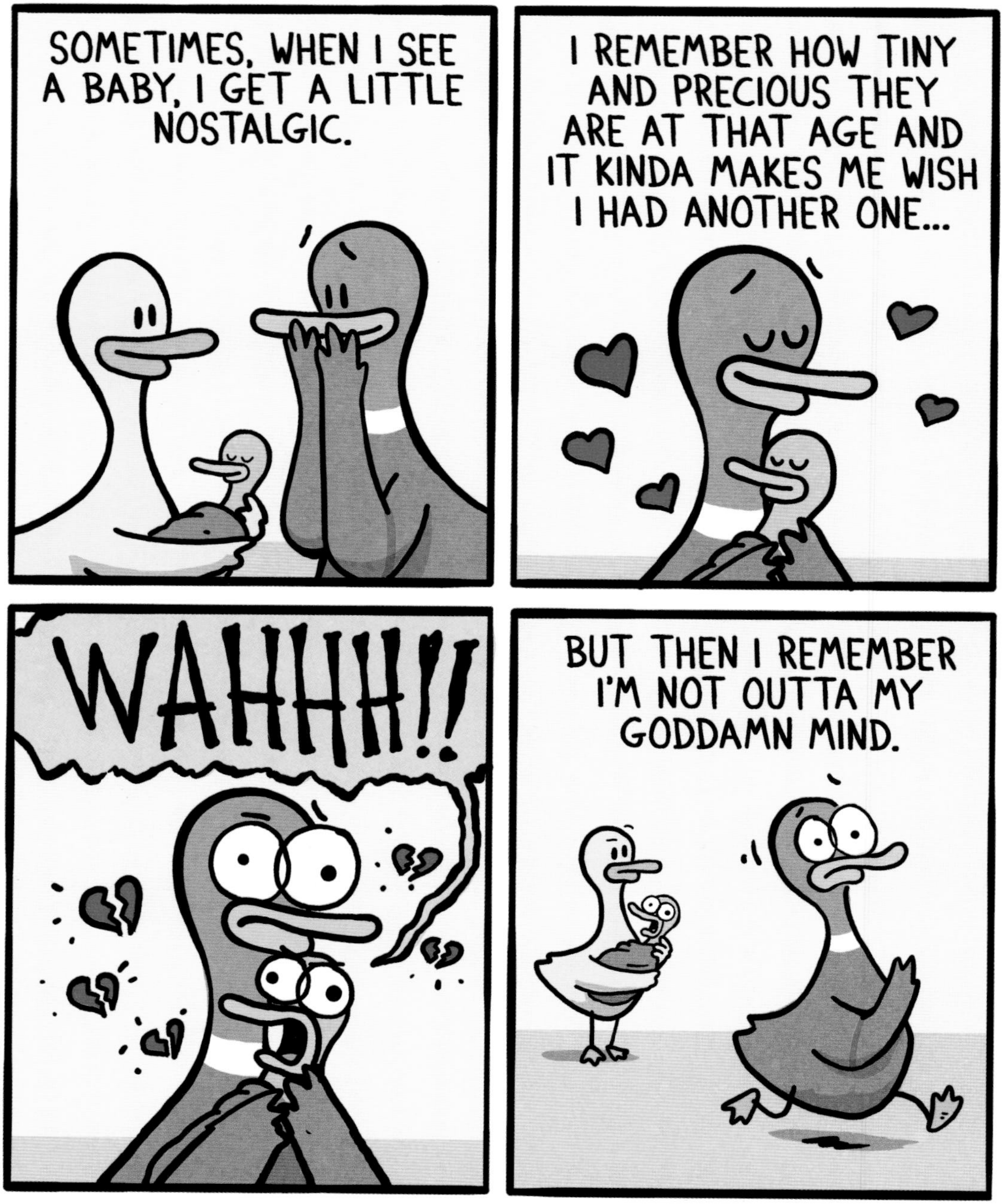
SOMETIMES, WHEN I SEE A BABY, I GET A LITTLE NOSTALGIC.
I REMEMBER HOW TINY AND PRECIOUS THEY ARE AT THAT AGE AND IT KINDA MAKES ME WISH I HAD ANOTHER ONE...
WAHHH!!
BUT THEN I REMEMBER I'M NOT OUTTA MY GODDAMN MIND.

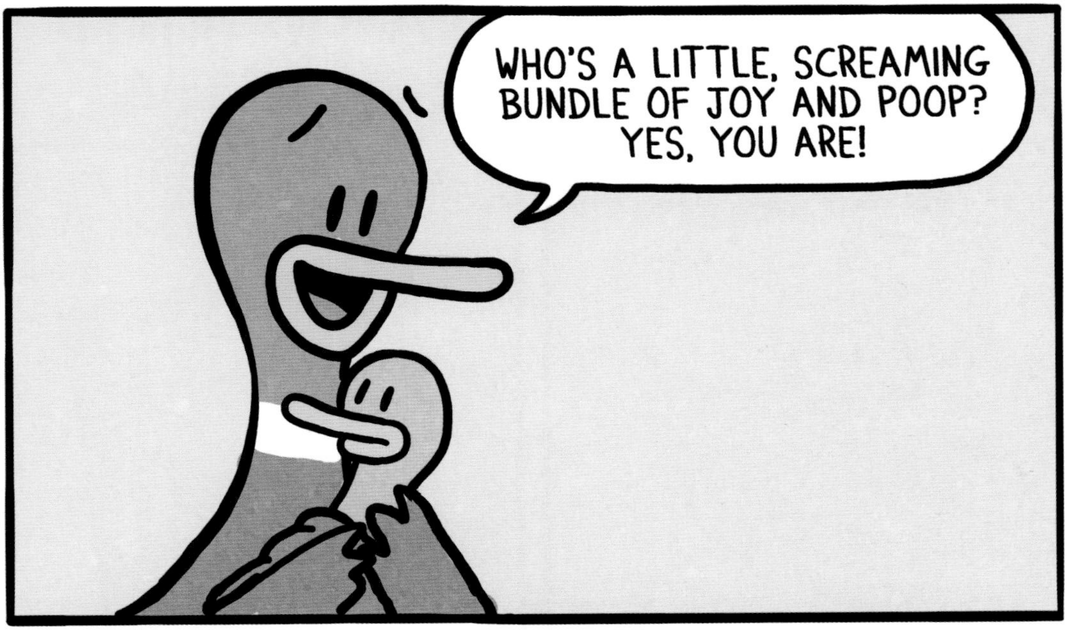
WHO'S A LITTLE, SCREAMING BUNDLE OF JOY AND POOP? YES, YOU ARE!

# HOW TO BABY PROOF YOUR HOME

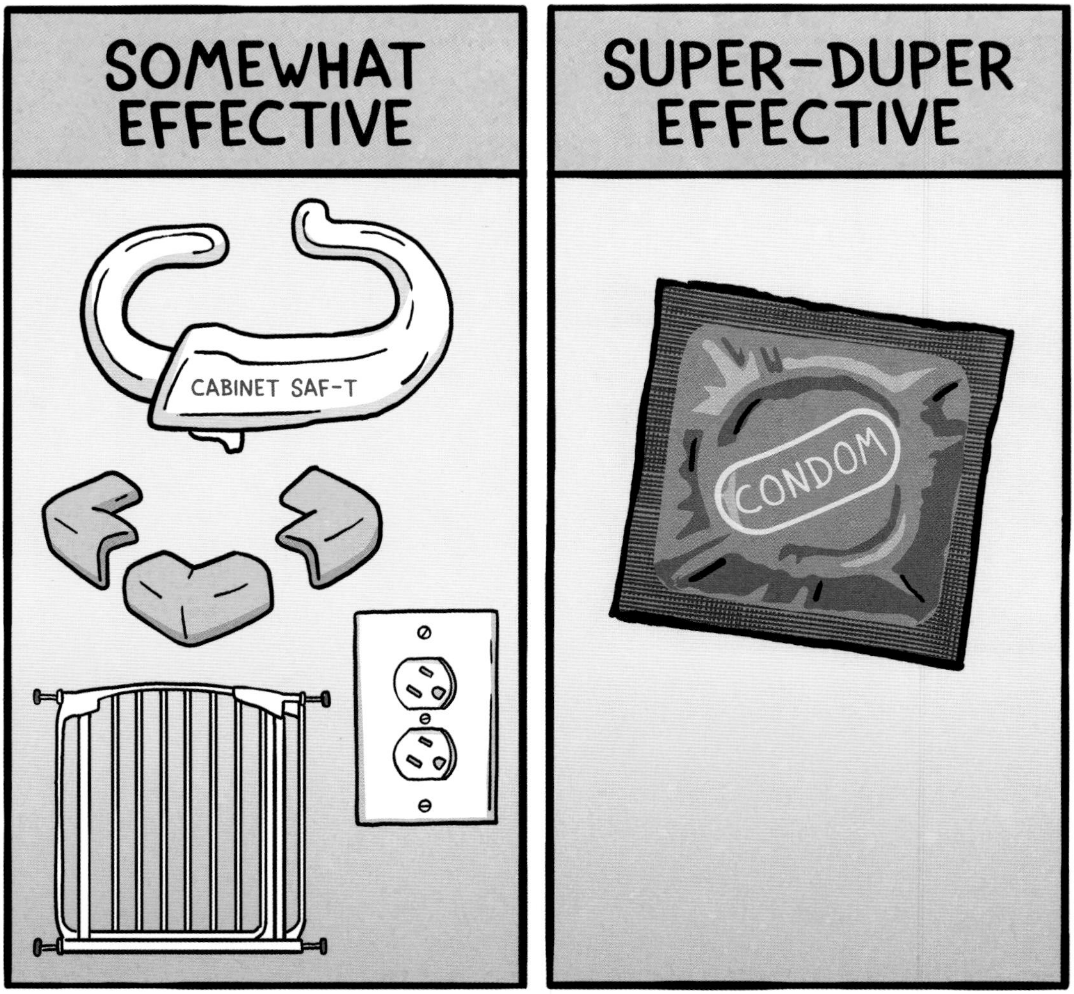
SOMEWHAT EFFECTIVE
CABINET SAF-T
SUPER-DUPER EFFECTIVE
CONDOM

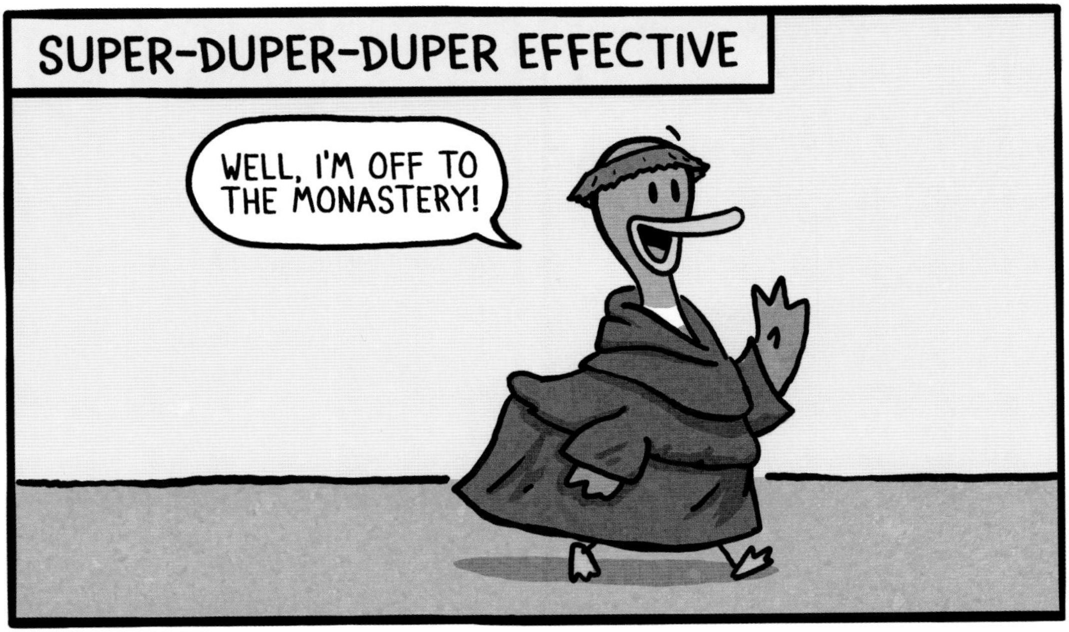
SUPER-DUPER-DUPER EFFECTIVE
WELL, I'M OFF TO THE MONASTERY!

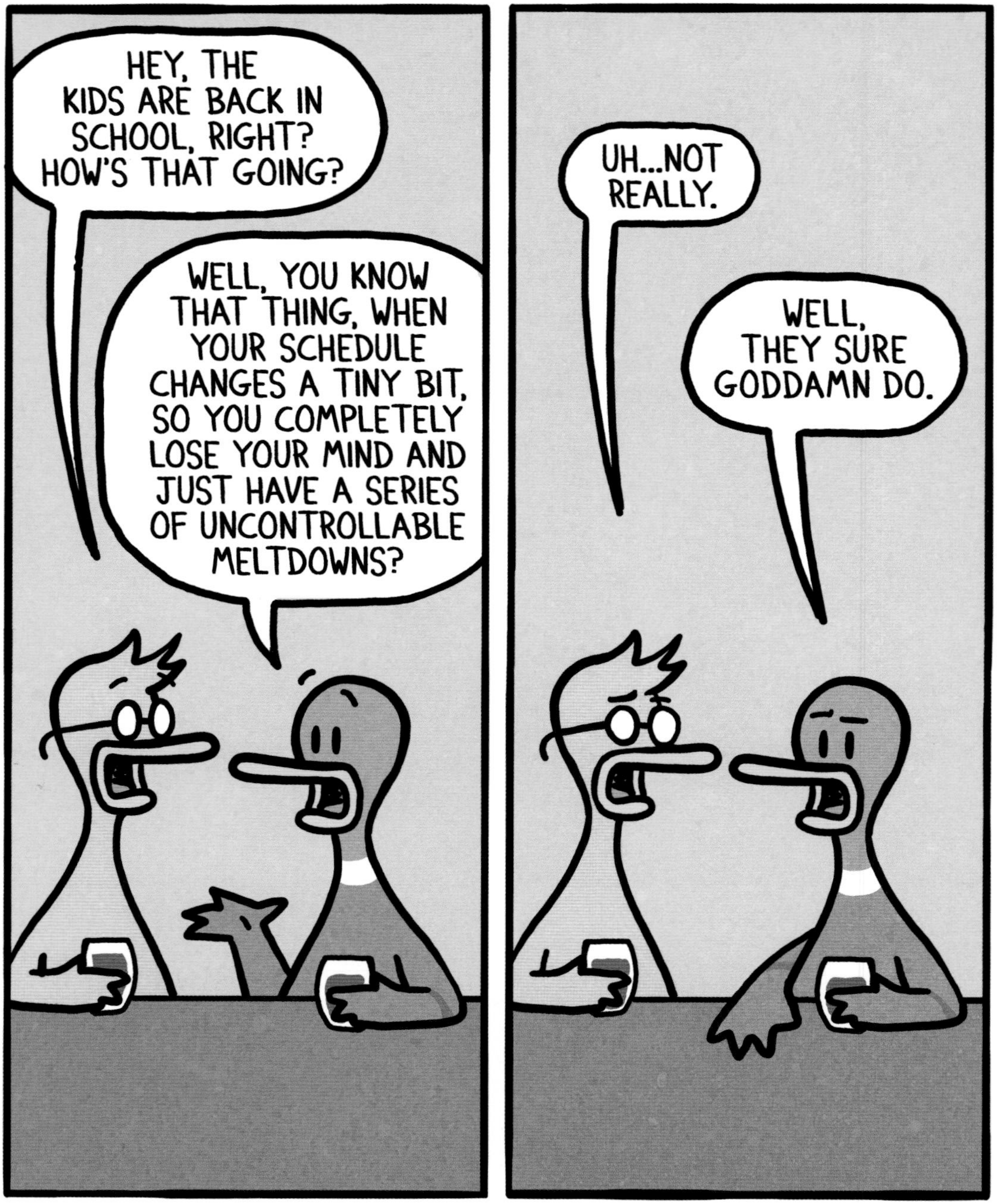
HEY, THE KIDS ARE BACK IN SCHOOL, RIGHT? HOW'S THAT GOING?
WELL, YOU KNOW THAT THING, WHEN YOUR SCHEDULE CHANGES A TINY BIT, SO YOU COMPLETELY LOSE YOUR MIND AND JUST HAVE A SERIES OF UNCONTROLLABLE MELTDOWNS?
UH...NOT REALLY.
WELL, THEY SURE GODDAMN DO.

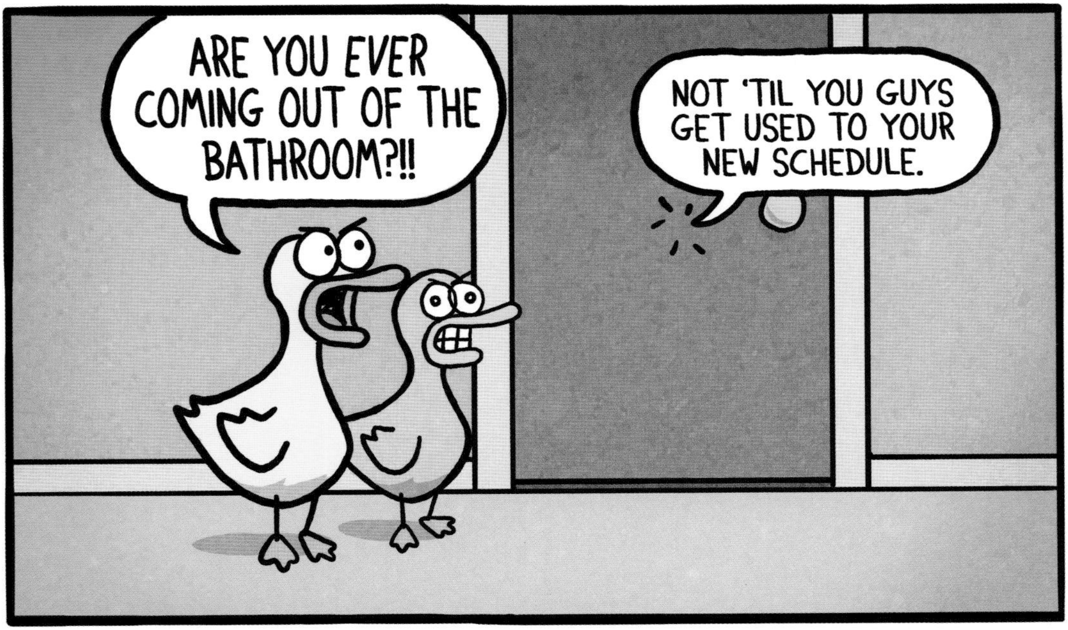
ARE YOU EVER COMING OUT OF THE BATHROOM?!!
NOT 'TIL YOU GUYS GET USED TO YOUR NEW SCHEDULE.

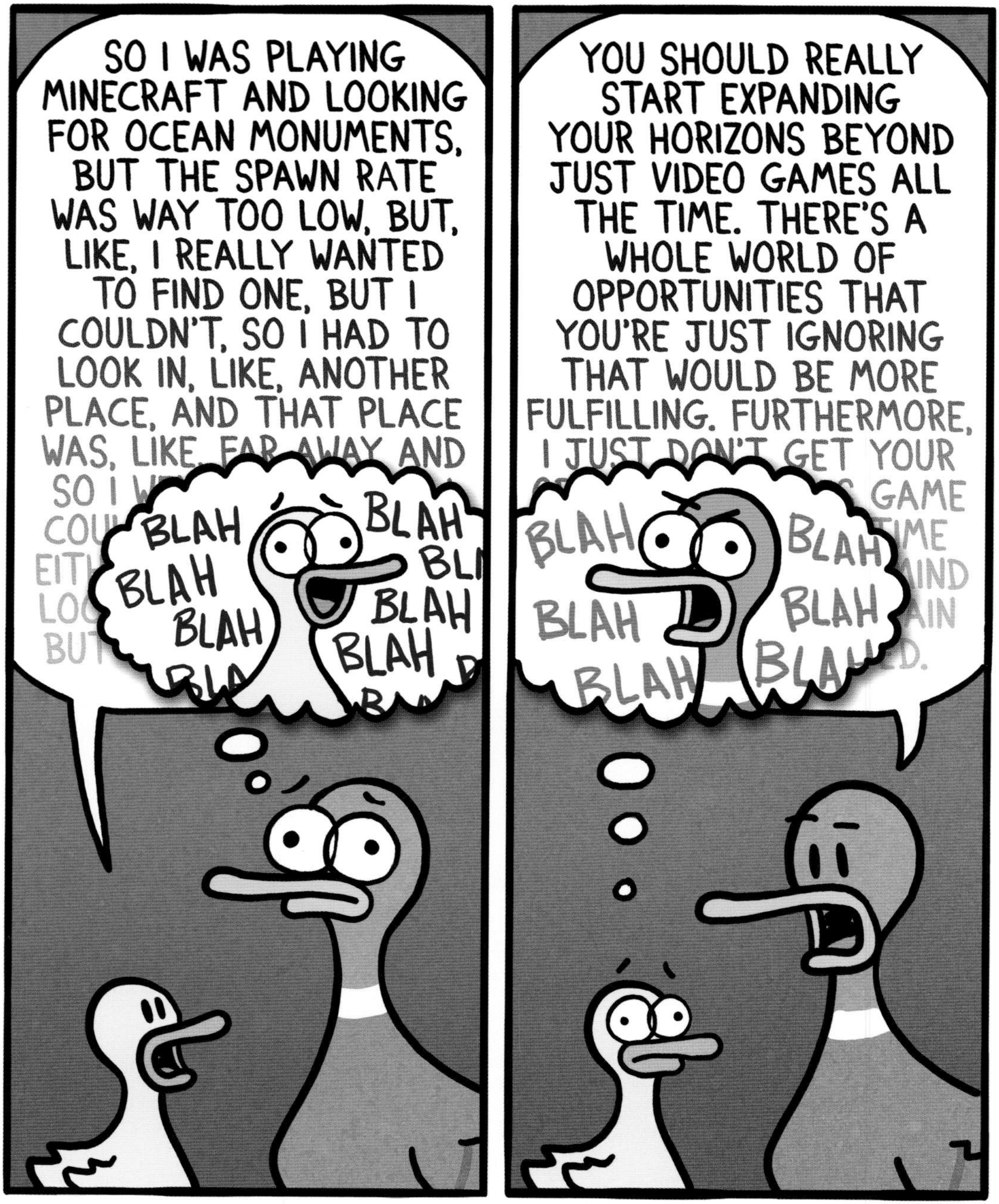
SO I WAS PLAYING MINECRAFT AND LOOKING FOR OCEAN MONUMENTS, BUT THE SPAWN RATE WAS WAY TOO LOW, BUT, LIKE, I REALLY WANTED TO FIND ONE, BUT I COULDN'T, SO I HAD TO LOOK IN, LIKE, ANOTHER PLACE, AND THAT PLACE
BLAH BLAH BLAH BLAH BLAH BLAH
YOU SHOULD REALLY START EXPANDING YOUR HORIZONS BEYOND JUST VIDEO GAMES ALL THE TIME. THERE'S A WHOLE WORLD OF OPPORTUNITIES THAT YOU'RE JUST IGNORING THAT WOULD BE MORE FULFILLING. FURTHERMORE,
BLAH BLAH BLAH BLAH BLAH

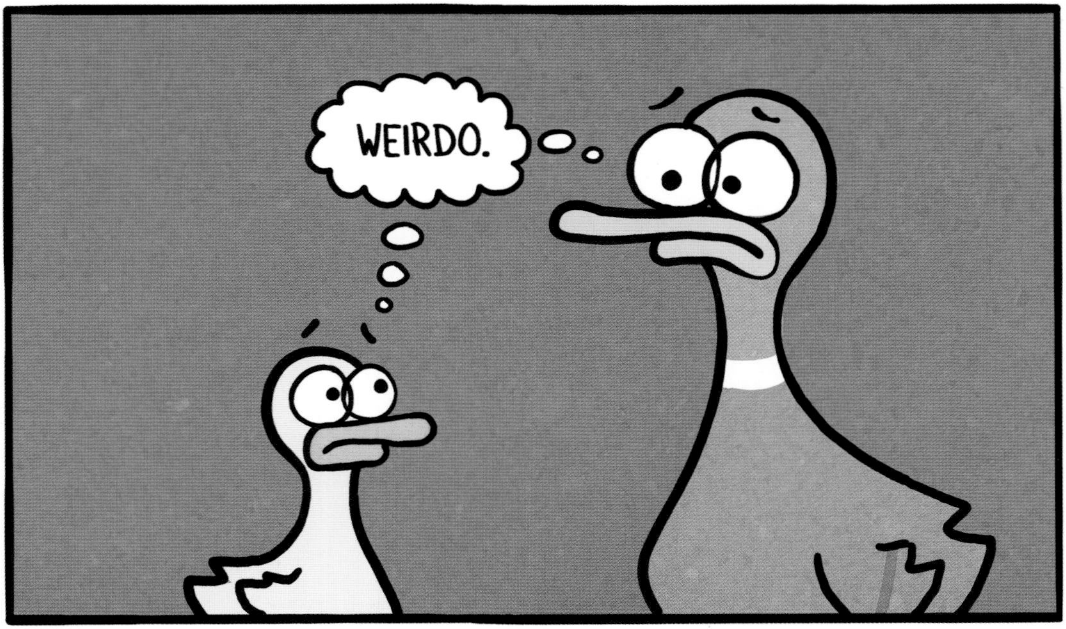
WEIRDO.

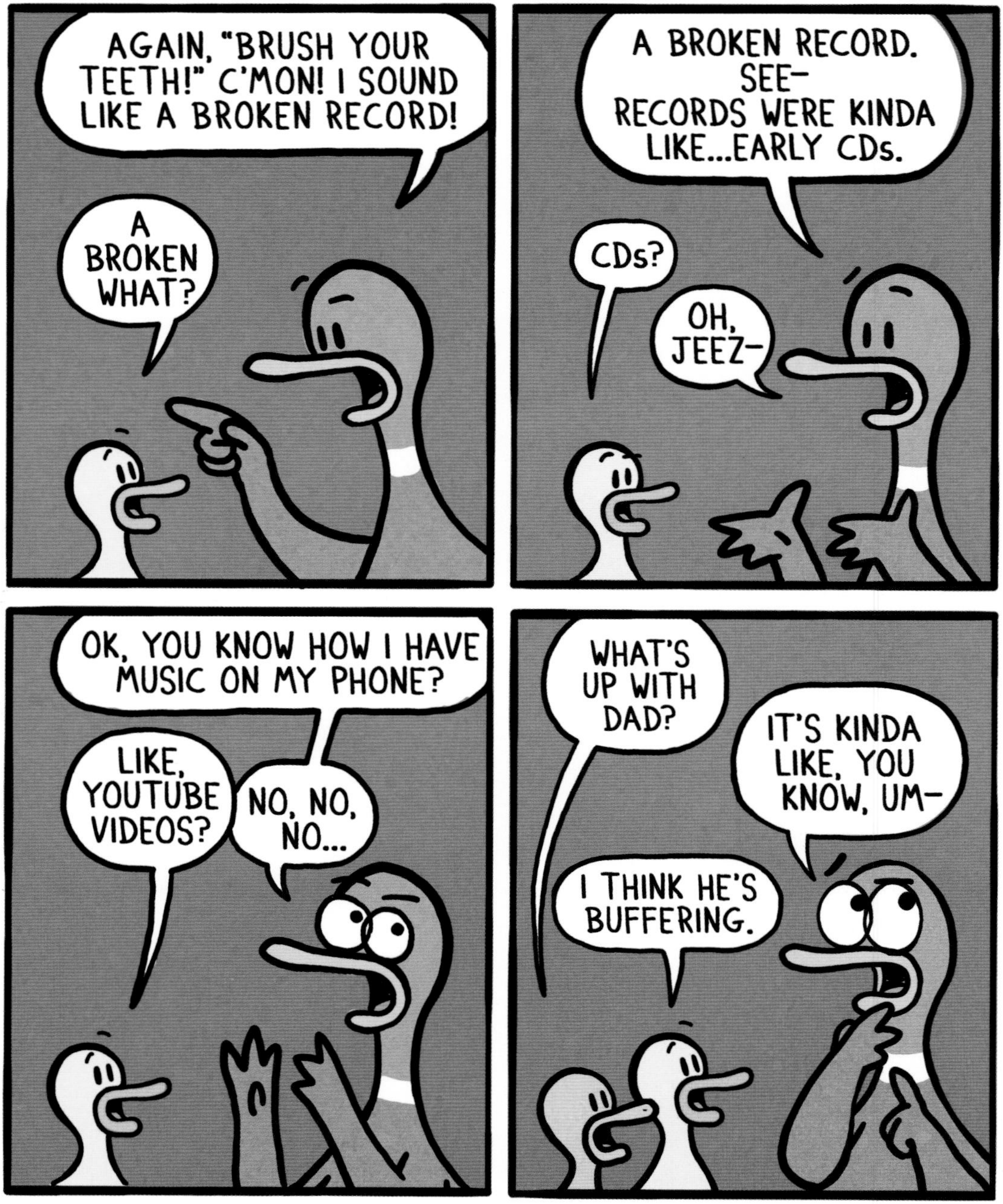
AGAIN, "BRUSH YOUR TEETH!" C'MON! I SOUND LIKE A BROKEN RECORD!
A BROKEN WHAT?
A BROKEN RECORD. SEE— RECORDS WERE KINDA LIKE...EARLY CDs.
CDs?
OH, JEEZ—
OK, YOU KNOW HOW I HAVE MUSIC ON MY PHONE?
LIKE, YOUTUBE VIDEOS?
NO, NO, NO...
WHAT'S UP WITH DAD?
IT'S KINDA LIKE, YOU KNOW, UM—
I THINK HE'S BUFFERING.

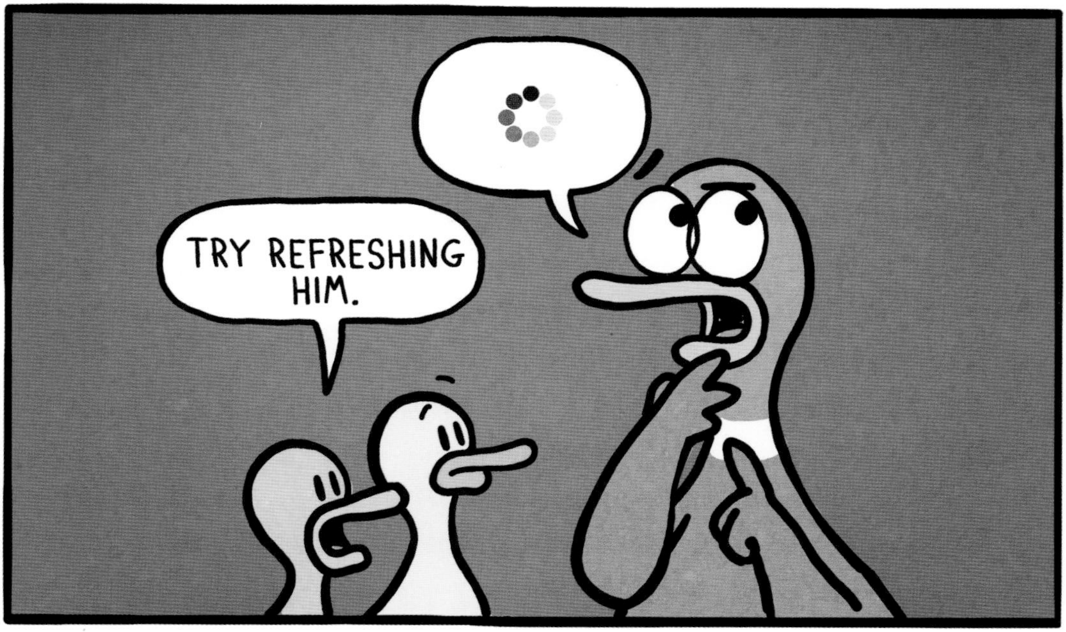
TRY REFRESHING HIM.

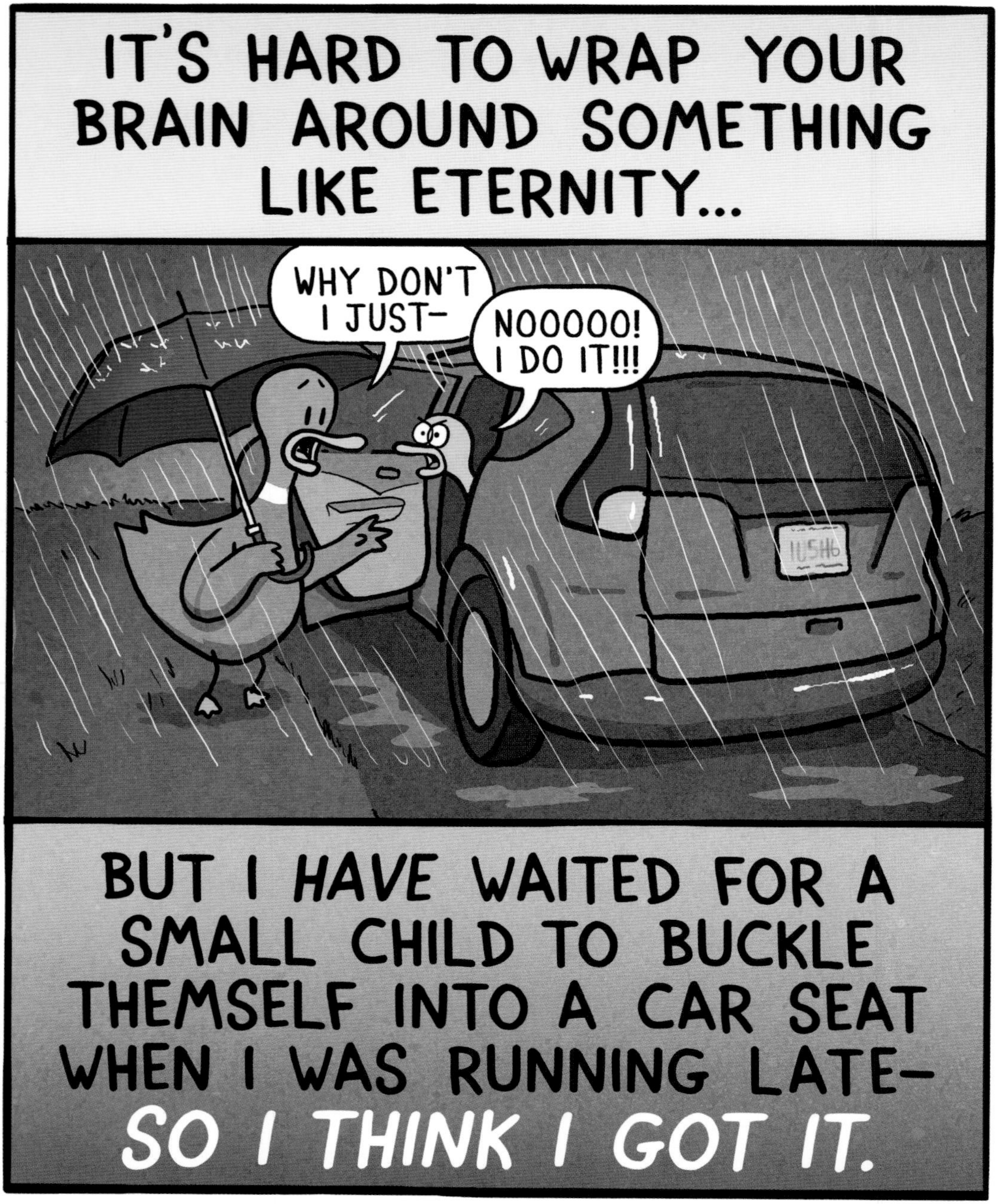
IT'S HARD TO WRAP YOUR BRAIN AROUND SOMETHING LIKE ETERNITY...
WHY DON'T I JUST–
NOOOOO! I DO IT!!!
BUT I *HAVE* WAITED FOR A SMALL CHILD TO BUCKLE THEMSELF INTO A CAR SEAT WHEN I WAS RUNNING LATE–
*SO I THINK I GOT IT.*

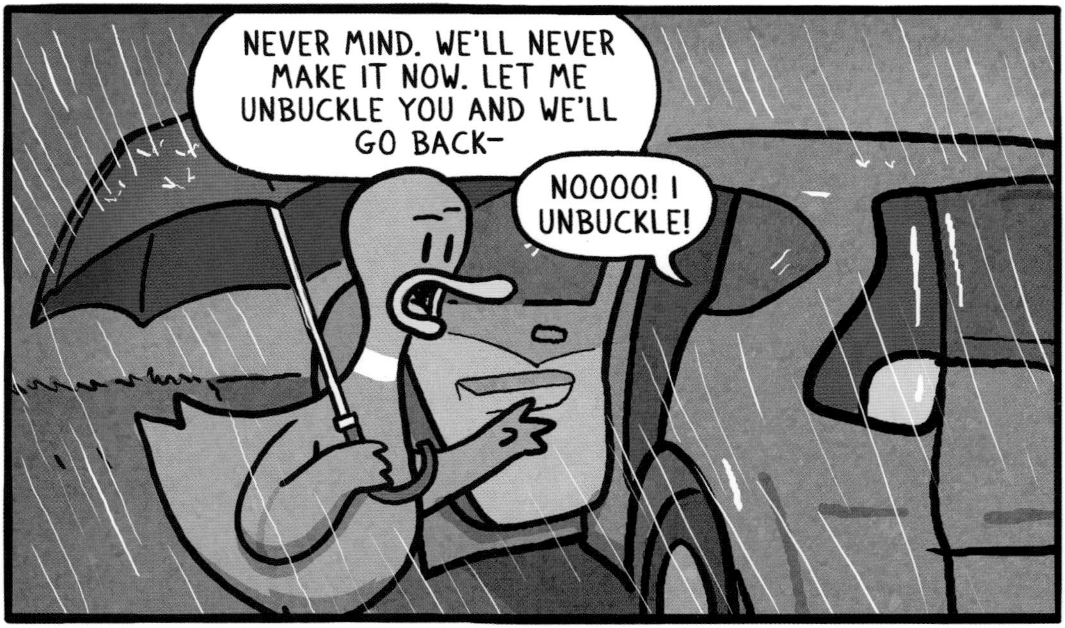
NEVER MIND. WE'LL NEVER MAKE IT NOW. LET ME UNBUCKLE YOU AND WE'LL GO BACK–
NOOOO! I UNBUCKLE!

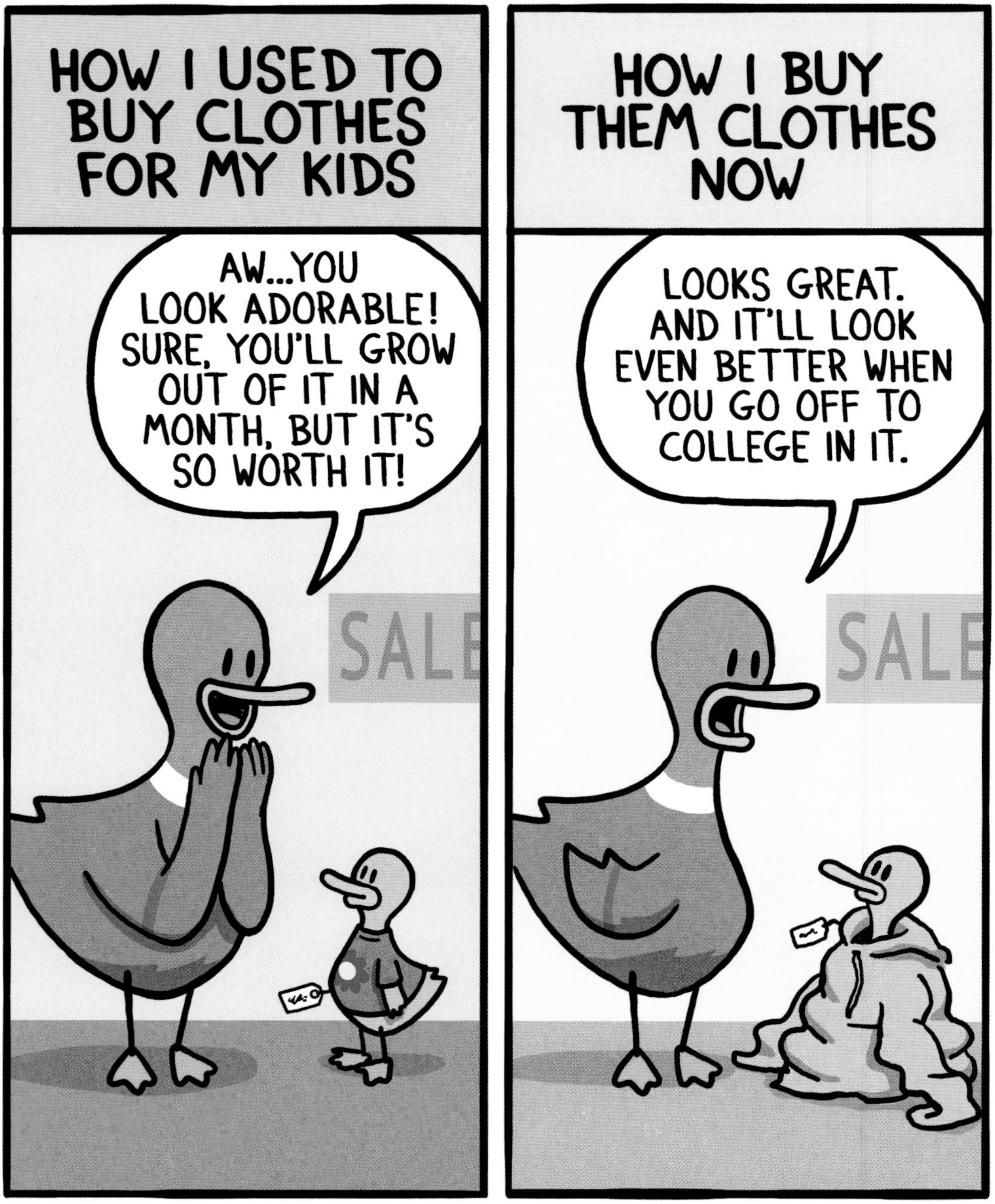
HOW I USED TO BUY CLOTHES FOR MY KIDS
AW...YOU LOOK ADORABLE! SURE, YOU'LL GROW OUT OF IT IN A MONTH, BUT IT'S SO WORTH IT!
SALE
HOW I BUY THEM CLOTHES NOW
LOOKS GREAT. AND IT'LL LOOK EVEN BETTER WHEN YOU GO OFF TO COLLEGE IN IT.
SALE

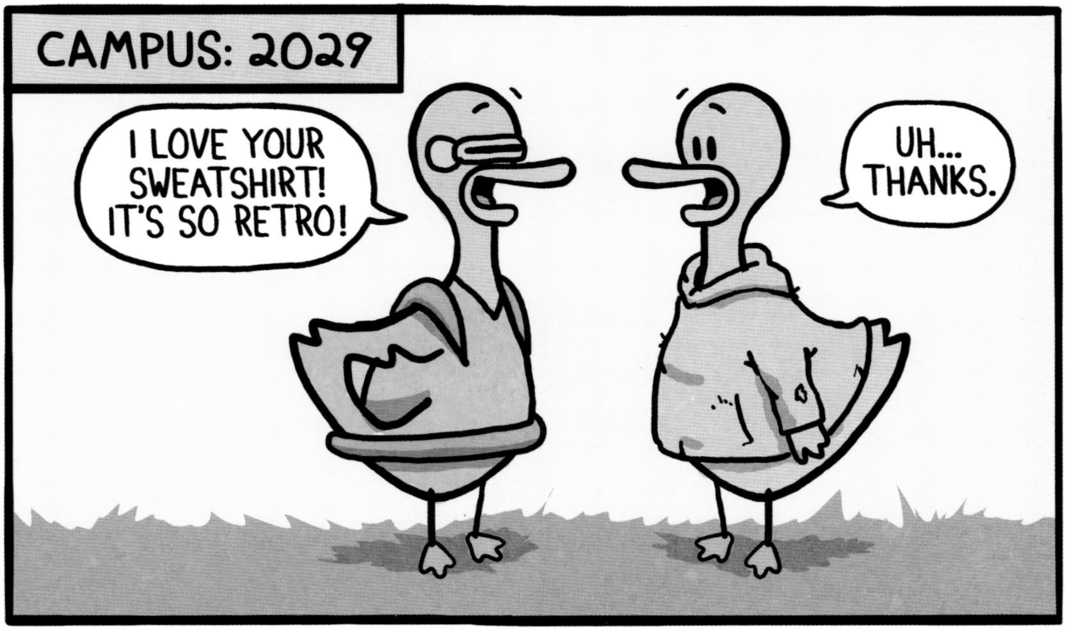
CAMPUS: 2029
I LOVE YOUR SWEATSHIRT! IT'S SO RETRO!
UH... THANKS.

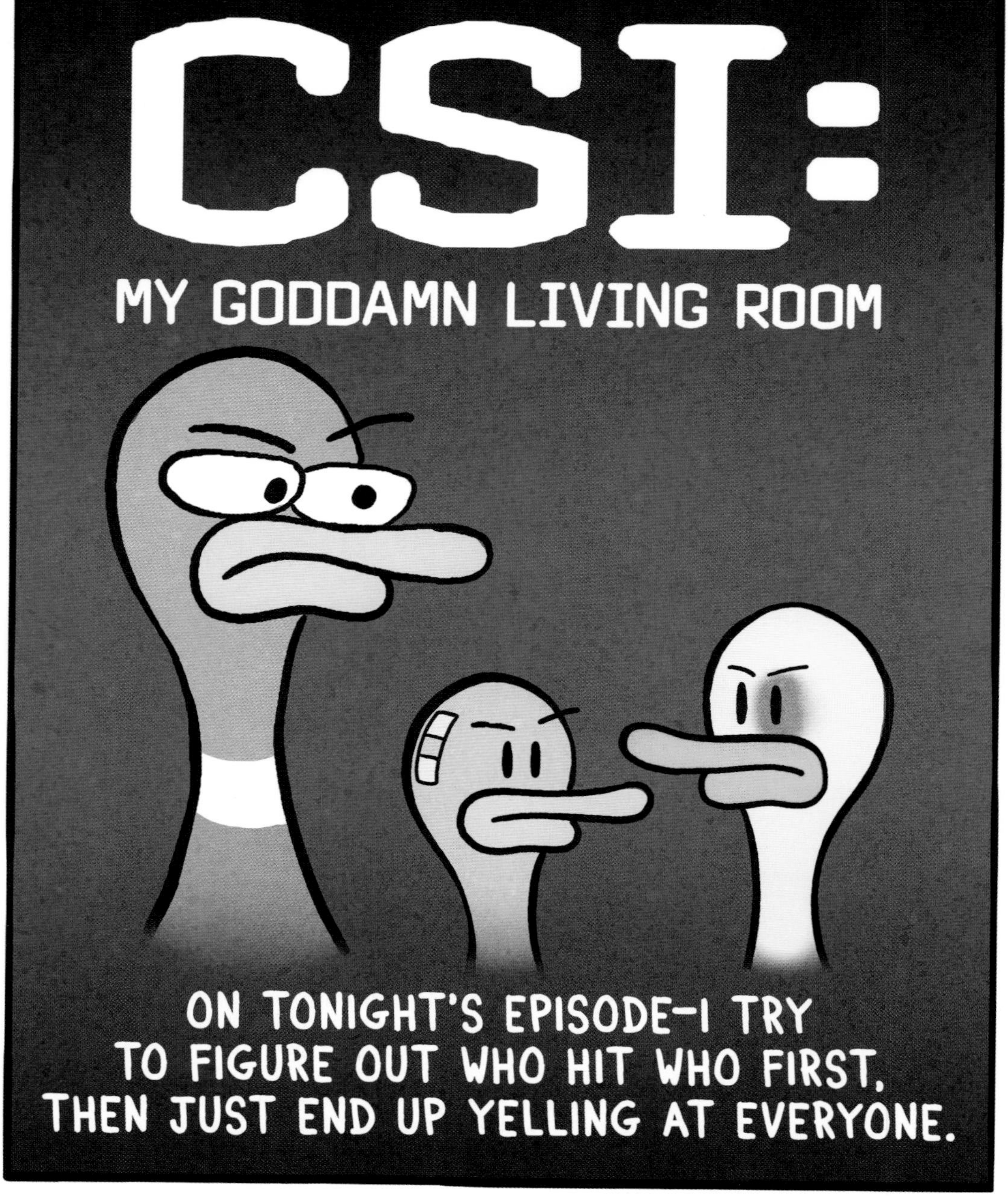
CSI:
MY GODDAMN LIVING ROOM
ON TONIGHT'S EPISODE—I TRY TO FIGURE OUT WHO HIT WHO FIRST, THEN JUST END UP YELLING AT EVERYONE.

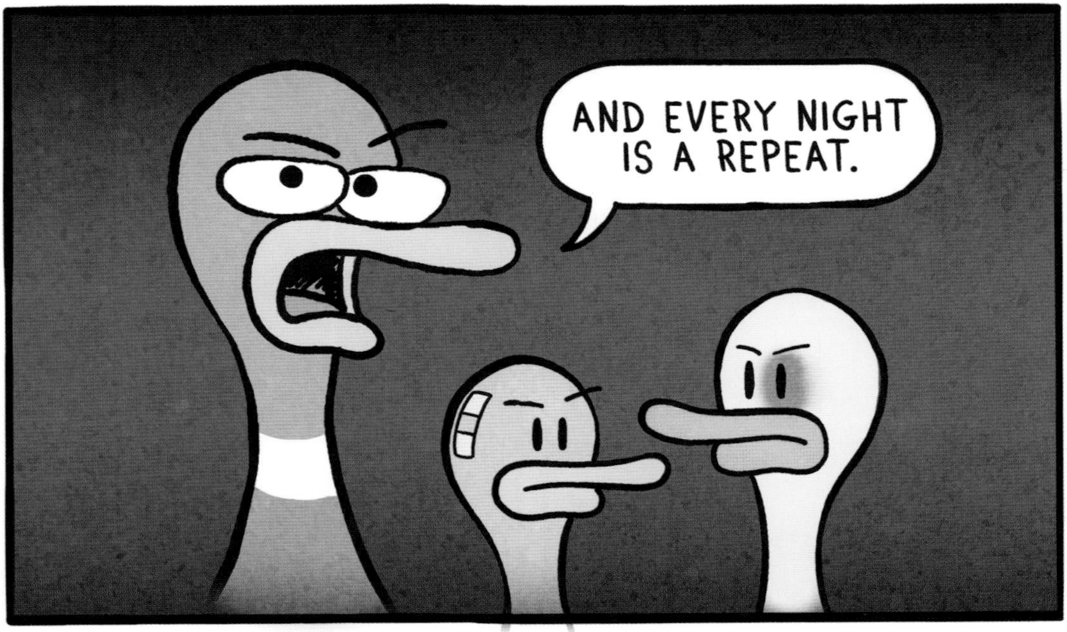
AND EVERY NIGHT IS A REPEAT.

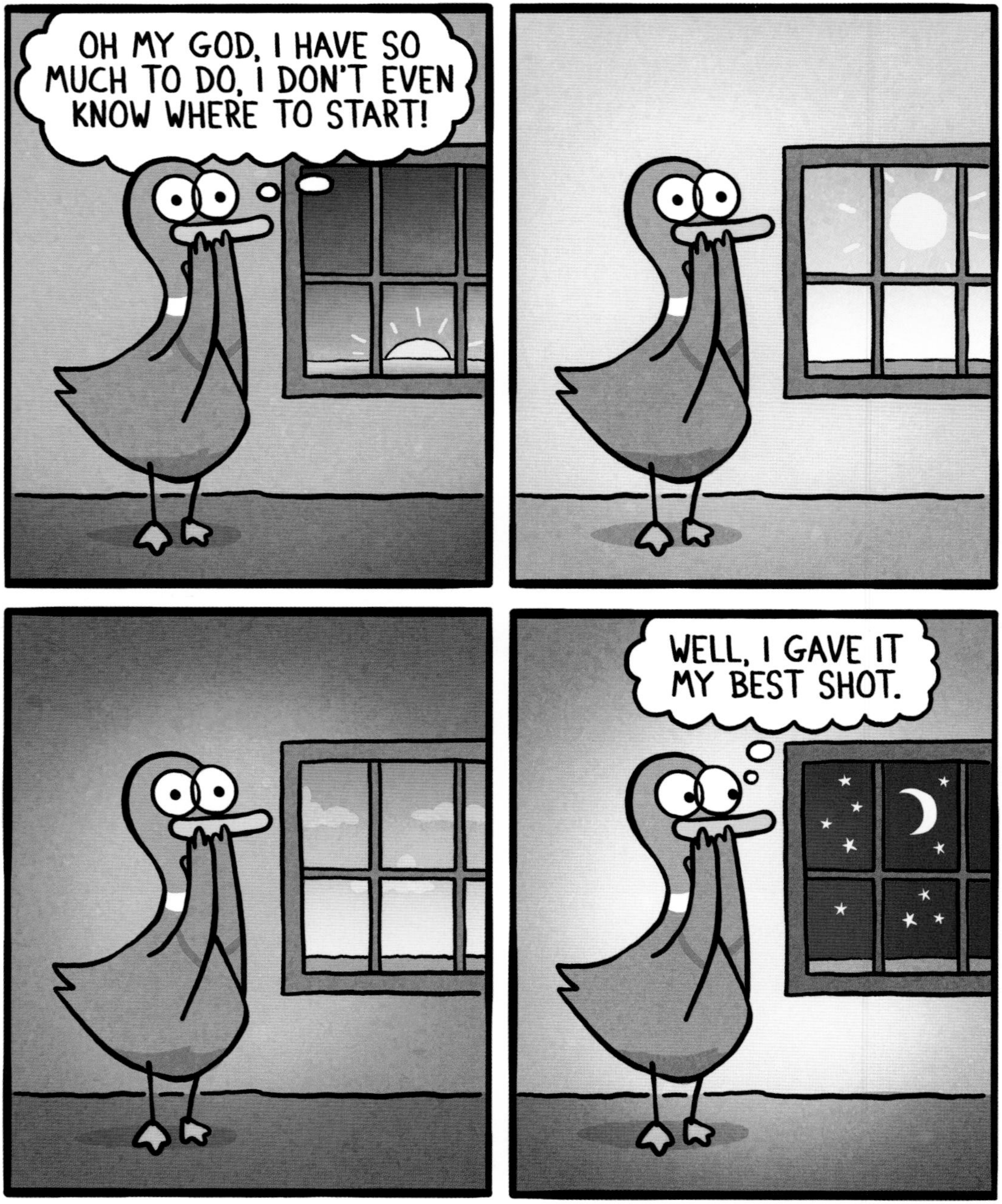
OH MY GOD, I HAVE SO MUCH TO DO, I DON'T EVEN KNOW WHERE TO START!
WELL, I GAVE IT MY BEST SHOT.

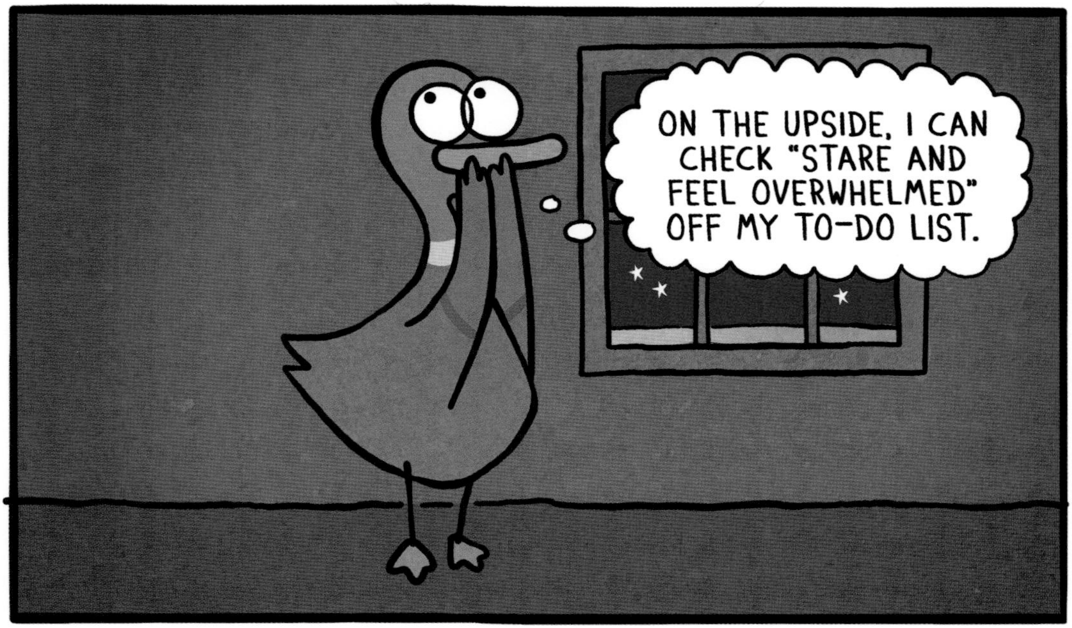
ON THE UPSIDE, I CAN CHECK "STARE AND FEEL OVERWHELMED" OFF MY TO-DO LIST.

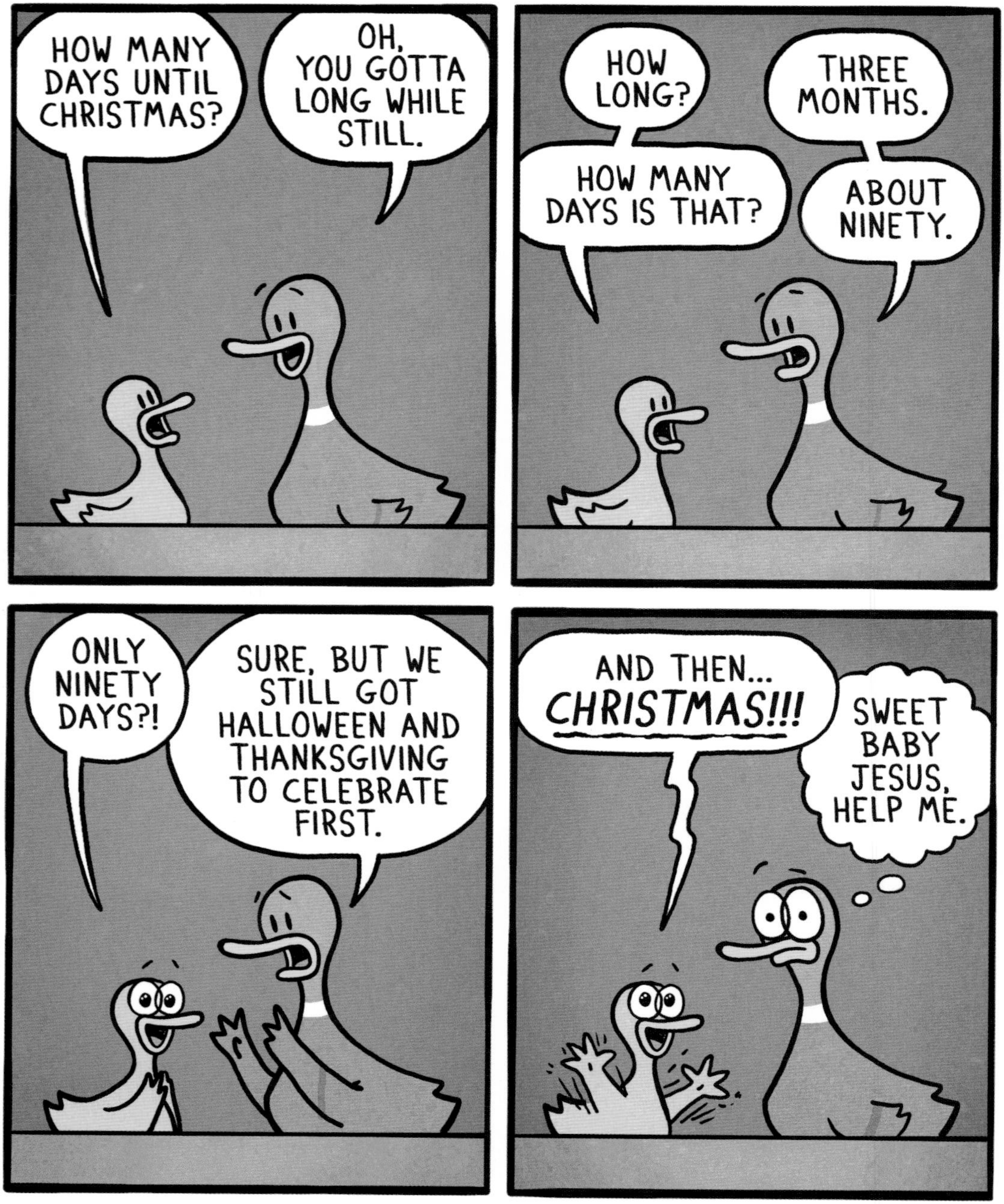
HOW MANY DAYS UNTIL CHRISTMAS?
OH, YOU GOTTA LONG WHILE STILL.
HOW LONG?
THREE MONTHS.
HOW MANY DAYS IS THAT?
ABOUT NINETY.
ONLY NINETY DAYS?!
SURE, BUT WE STILL GOT HALLOWEEN AND THANKSGIVING TO CELEBRATE FIRST.
AND THEN... CHRISTMAS!!!
SWEET BABY JESUS, HELP ME.

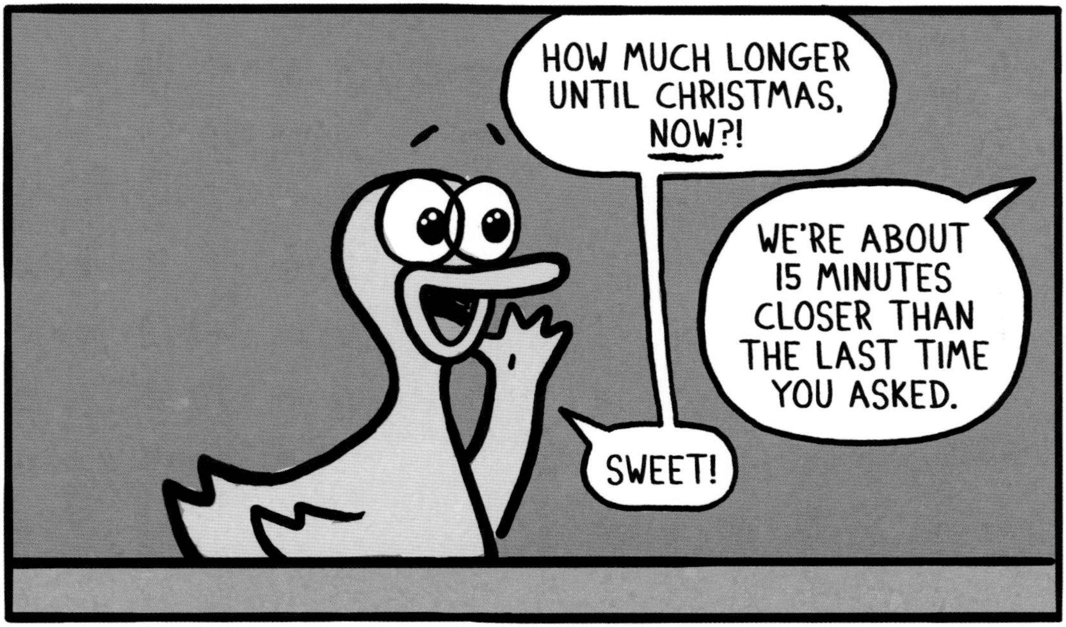
HOW MUCH LONGER UNTIL CHRISTMAS, NOW?!
WE'RE ABOUT 15 MINUTES CLOSER THAN THE LAST TIME YOU ASKED.
SWEET!

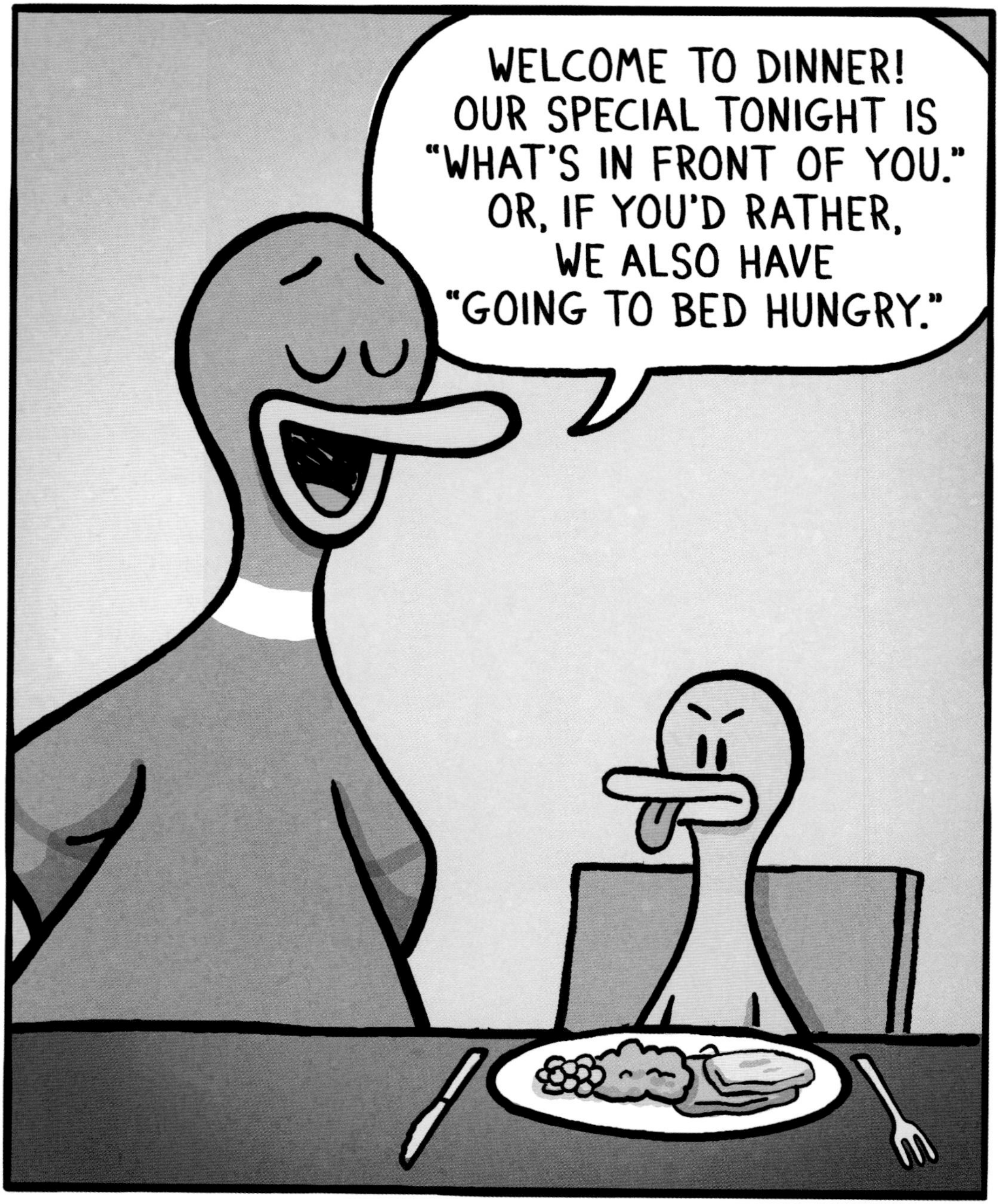
WELCOME TO DINNER! OUR SPECIAL TONIGHT IS "WHAT'S IN FRONT OF YOU." OR, IF YOU'D RATHER, WE ALSO HAVE "GOING TO BED HUNGRY."

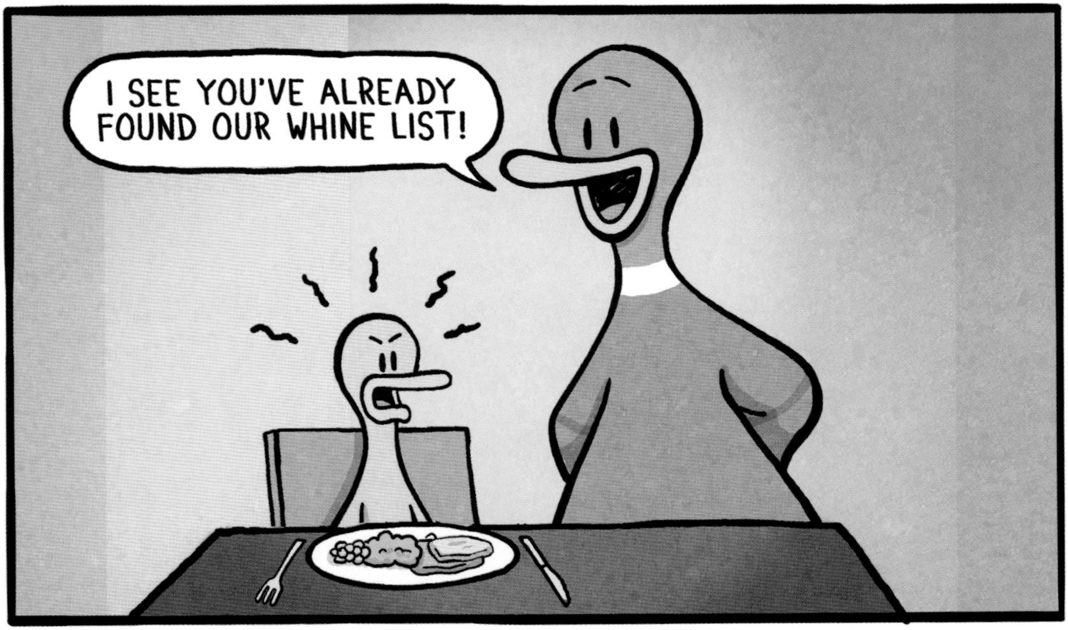
I SEE YOU'VE ALREADY FOUND OUR WHINE LIST!

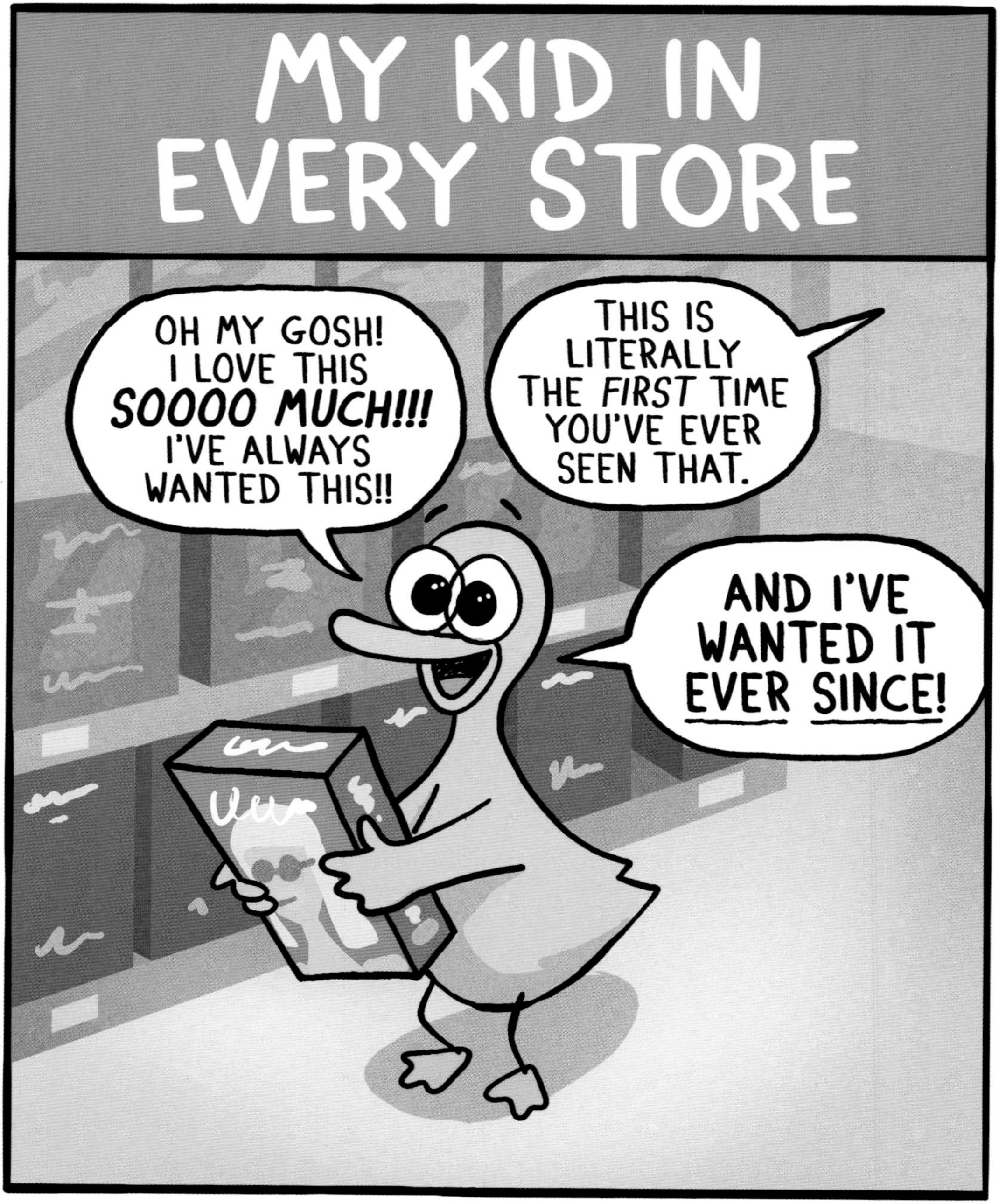
MY KID IN EVERY STORE
OH MY GOSH! I LOVE THIS SOOOO MUCH!!! I'VE ALWAYS WANTED THIS!!
THIS IS LITERALLY THE FIRST TIME YOU'VE EVER SEEN THAT.
AND I'VE WANTED IT EVER SINCE!

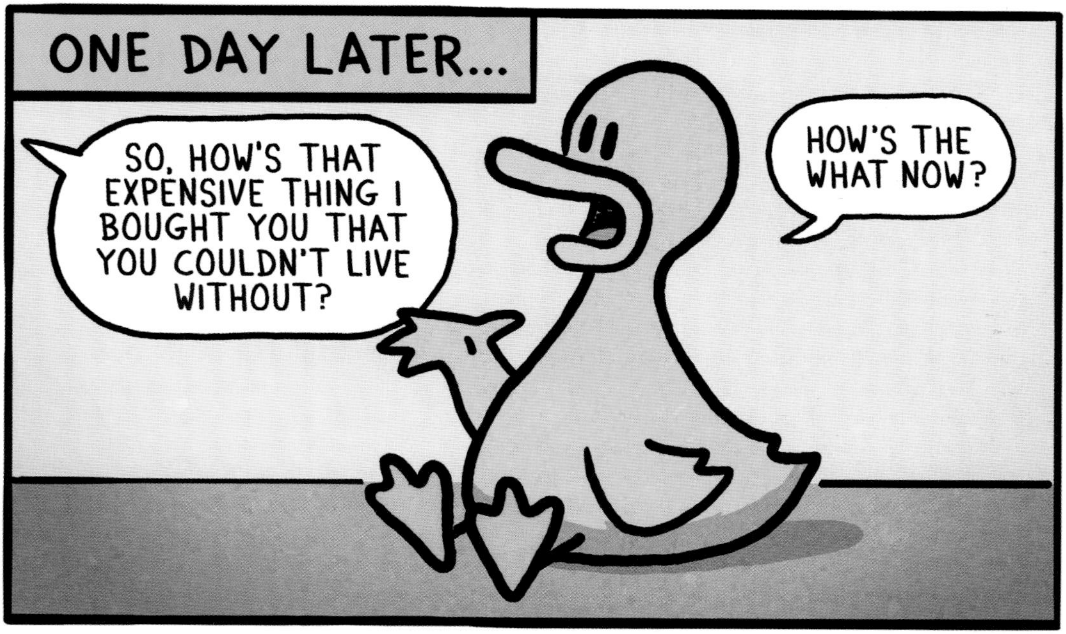
ONE DAY LATER...
SO, HOW'S THAT EXPENSIVE THING I BOUGHT YOU THAT YOU COULDN'T LIVE WITHOUT?
HOW'S THE WHAT NOW?

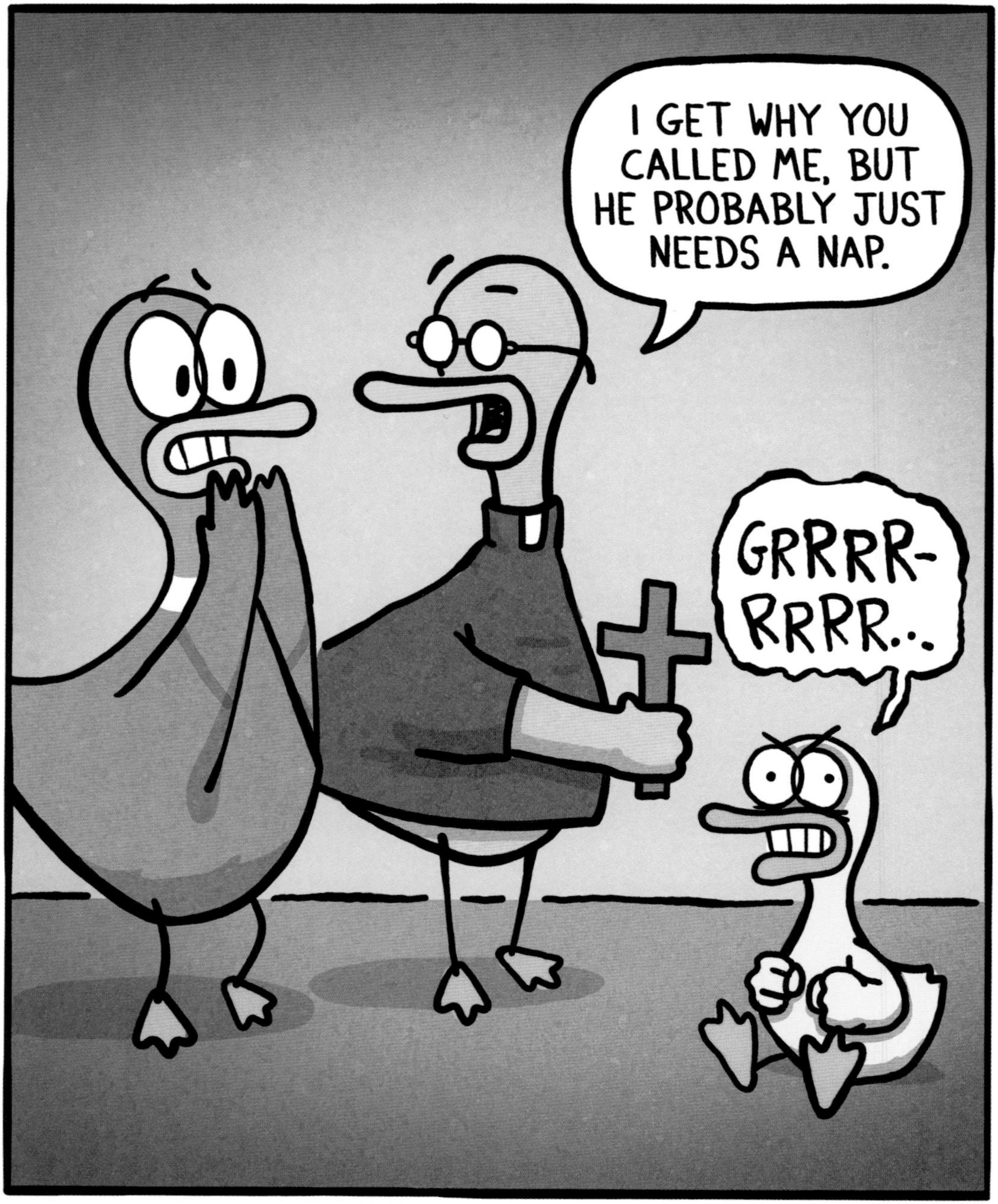
I GET WHY YOU CALLED ME, BUT HE PROBABLY JUST NEEDS A NAP.
GRRRR-RRRR...

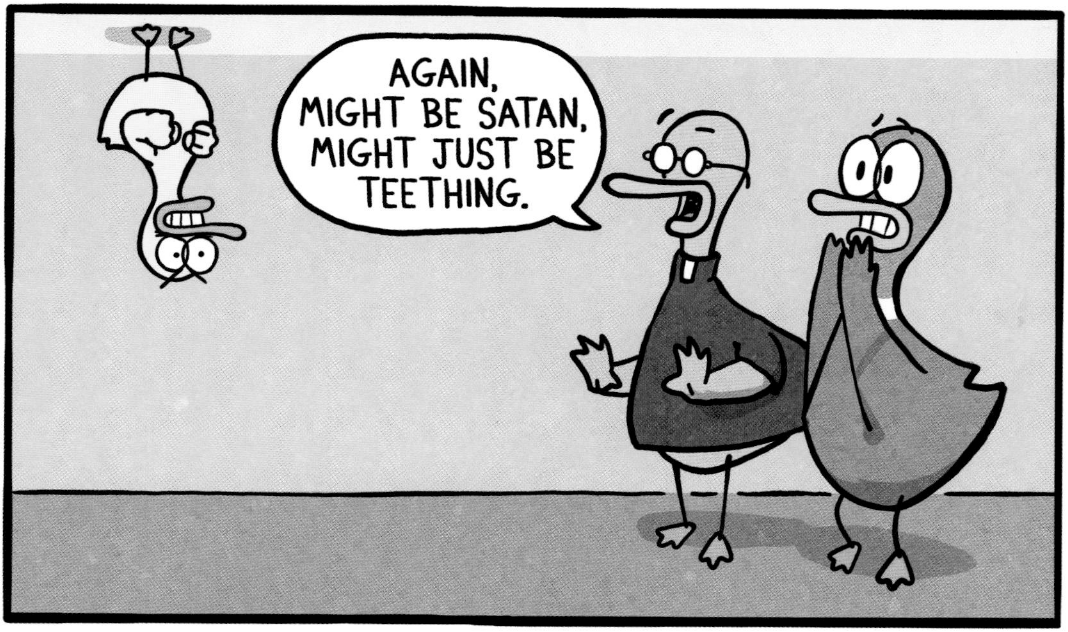
AGAIN, MIGHT BE SATAN, MIGHT JUST BE TEETHING.

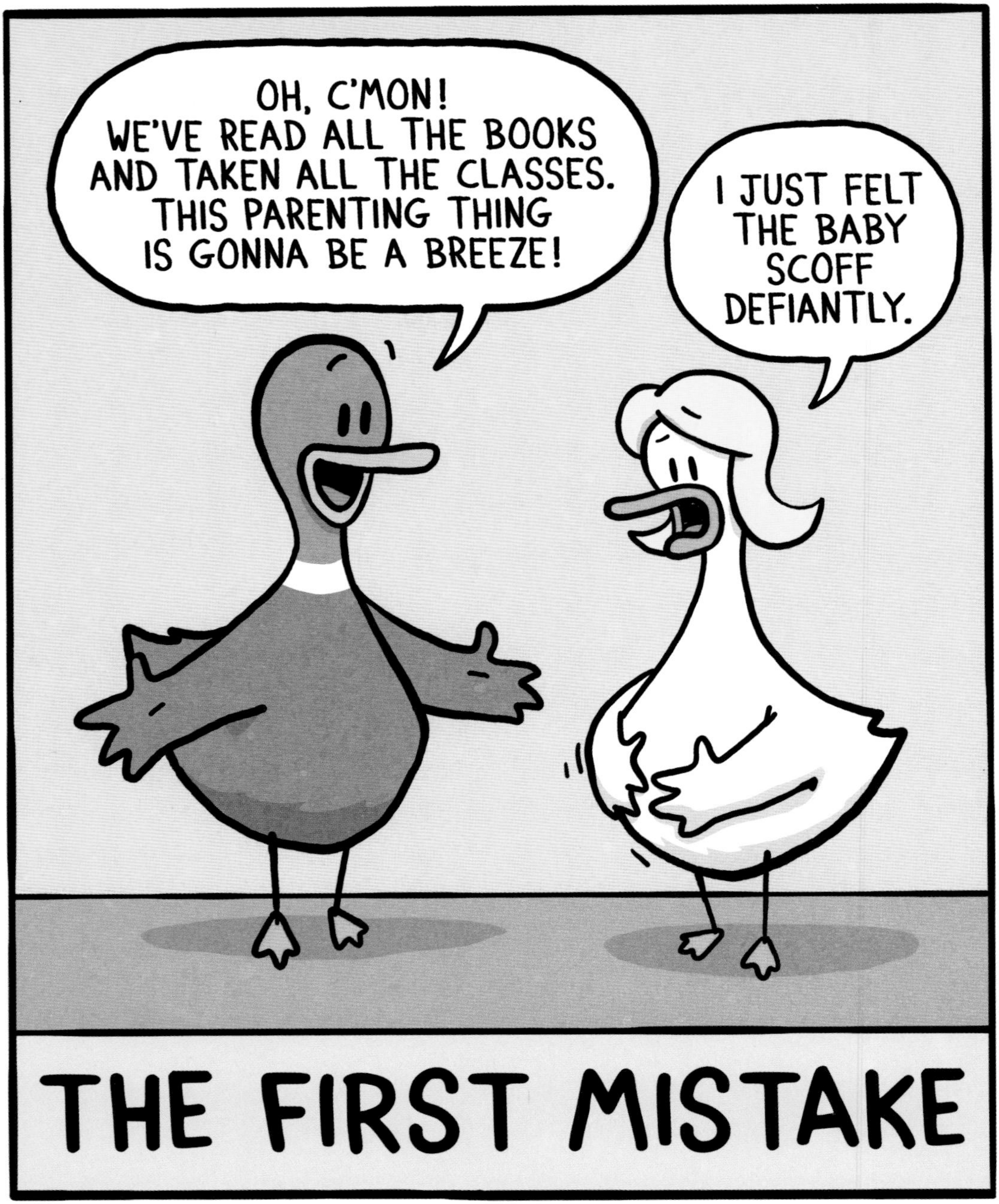
OH, C'MON! WE'VE READ ALL THE BOOKS AND TAKEN ALL THE CLASSES. THIS PARENTING THING IS GONNA BE A BREEZE!
I JUST FELT THE BABY SCOFF DEFIANTLY.
THE FIRST MISTAKE

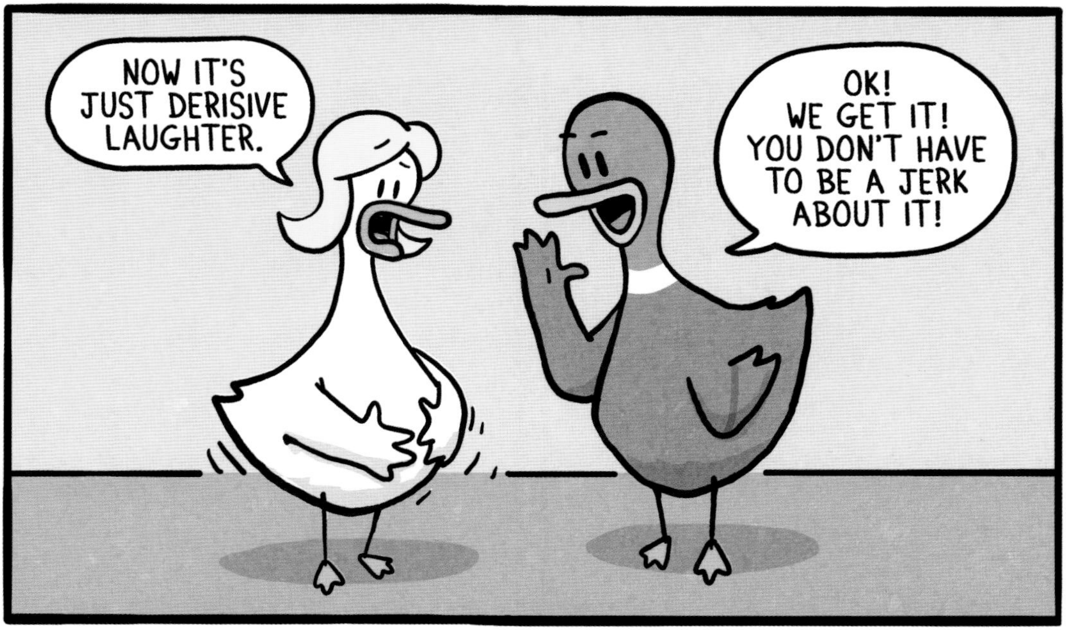
NOW IT'S JUST DERISIVE LAUGHTER.
OK! WE GET IT! YOU DON'T HAVE TO BE A JERK ABOUT IT!

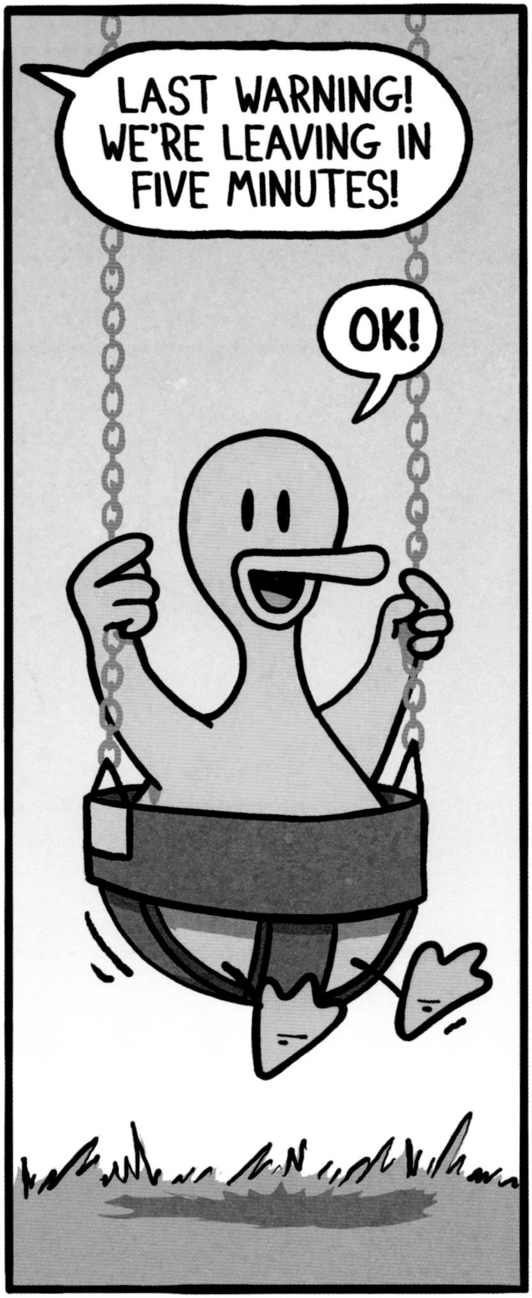
LAST WARNING! WE'RE LEAVING IN FIVE MINUTES!
OK!

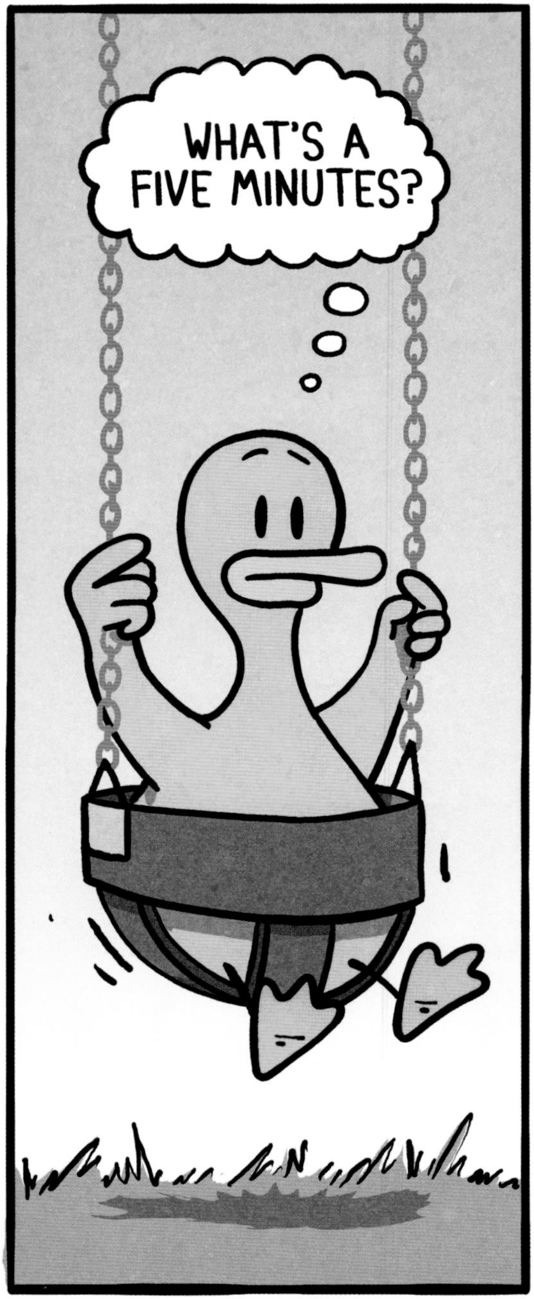
WHAT'S A FIVE MINUTES?

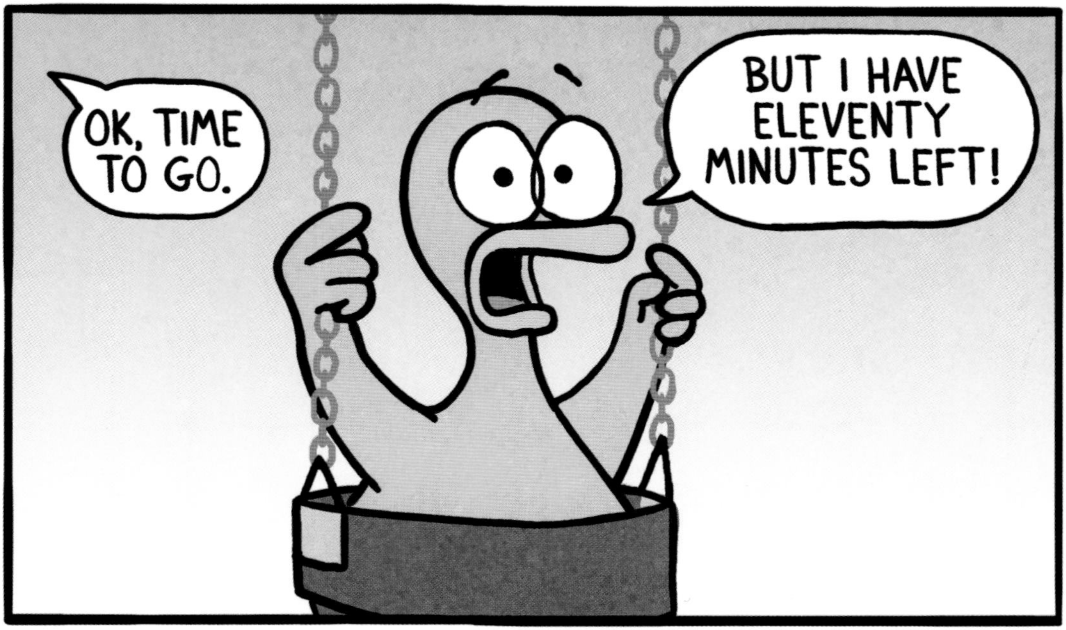
OK, TIME TO GO.
BUT I HAVE ELEVENTY MINUTES LEFT!

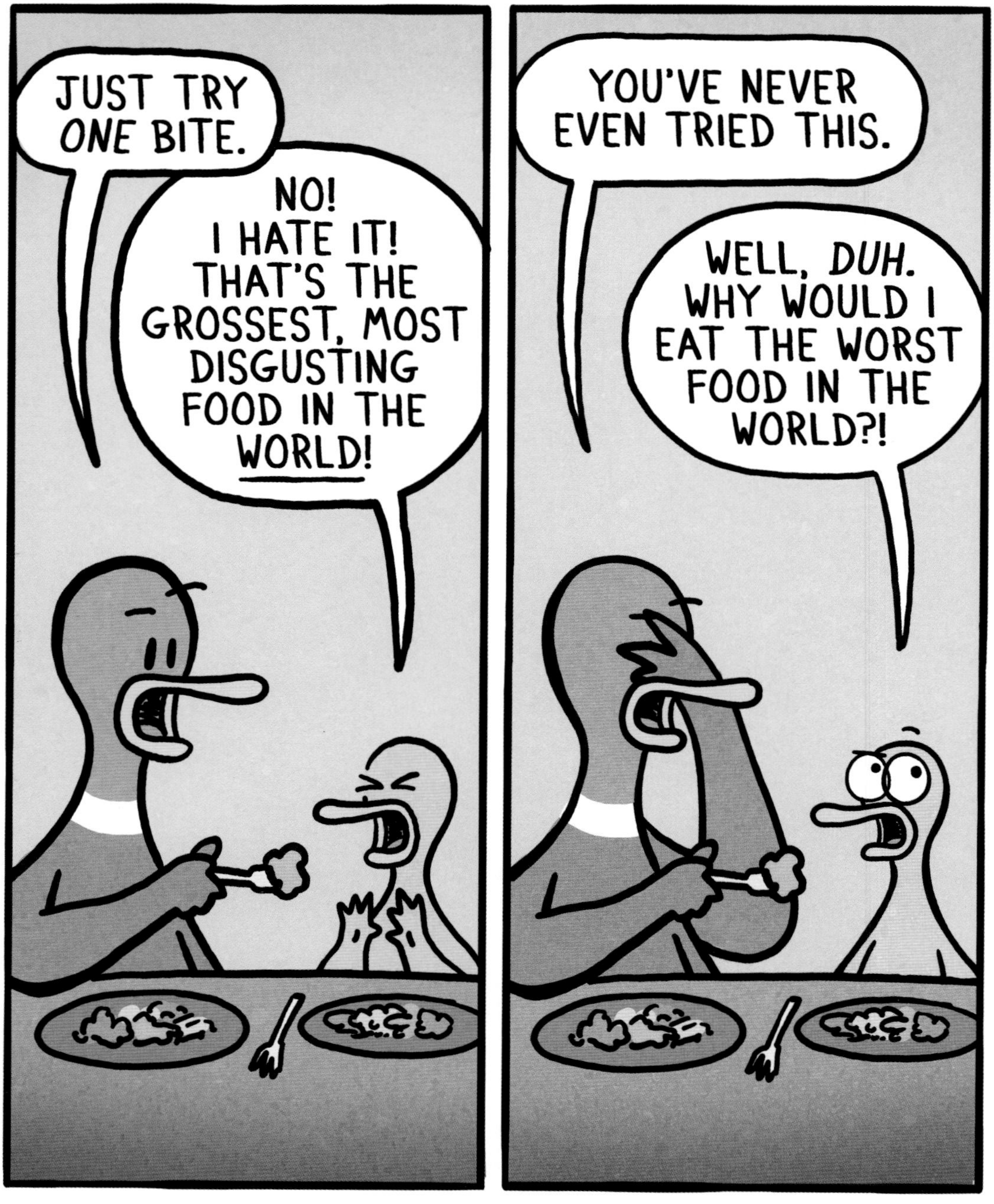
JUST TRY *ONE* BITE.
NO! I HATE IT! THAT'S THE GROSSEST, MOST DISGUSTING FOOD IN THE WORLD!
YOU'VE NEVER EVEN TRIED THIS.
WELL, *DUH.* WHY WOULD I EAT THE WORST FOOD IN THE WORLD?!

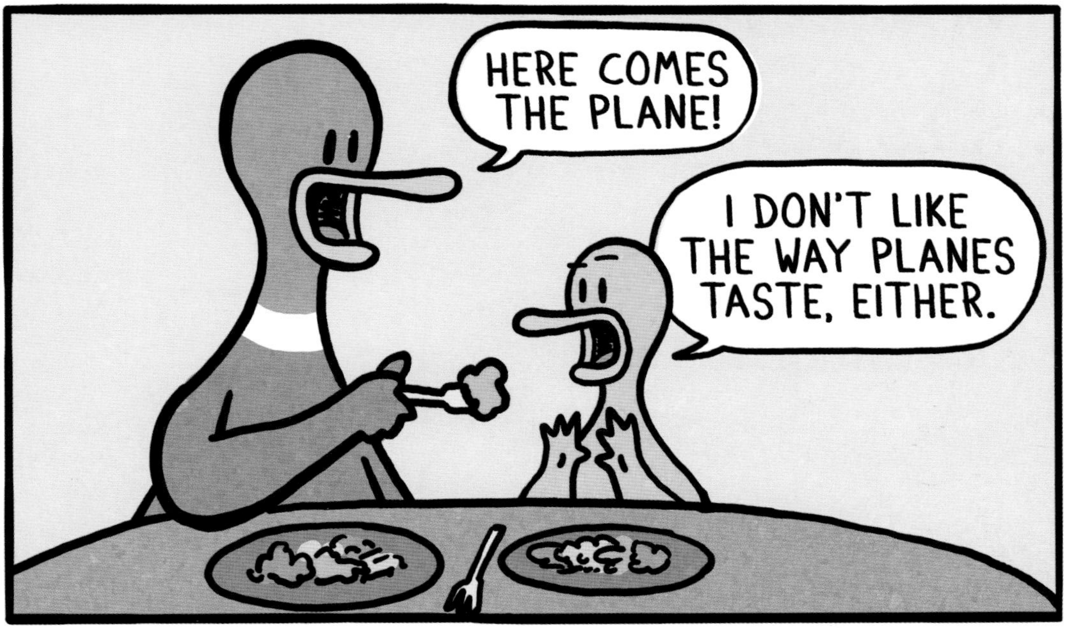
HERE COMES THE PLANE!
I DON'T LIKE THE WAY PLANES TASTE, EITHER.

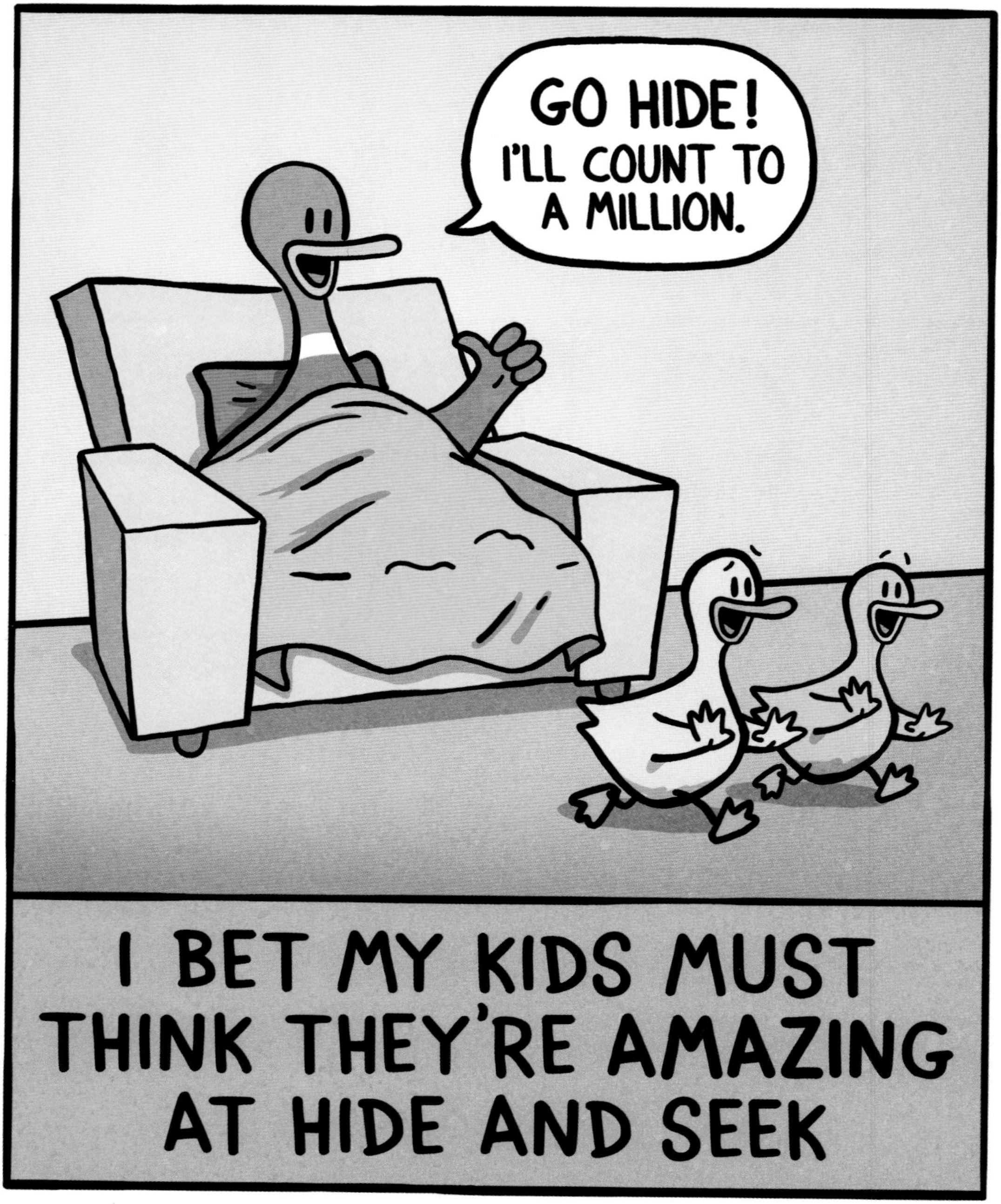
GO HIDE! I'LL COUNT TO A MILLION.
I BET MY KIDS MUST THINK THEY'RE AMAZING AT HIDE AND SEEK

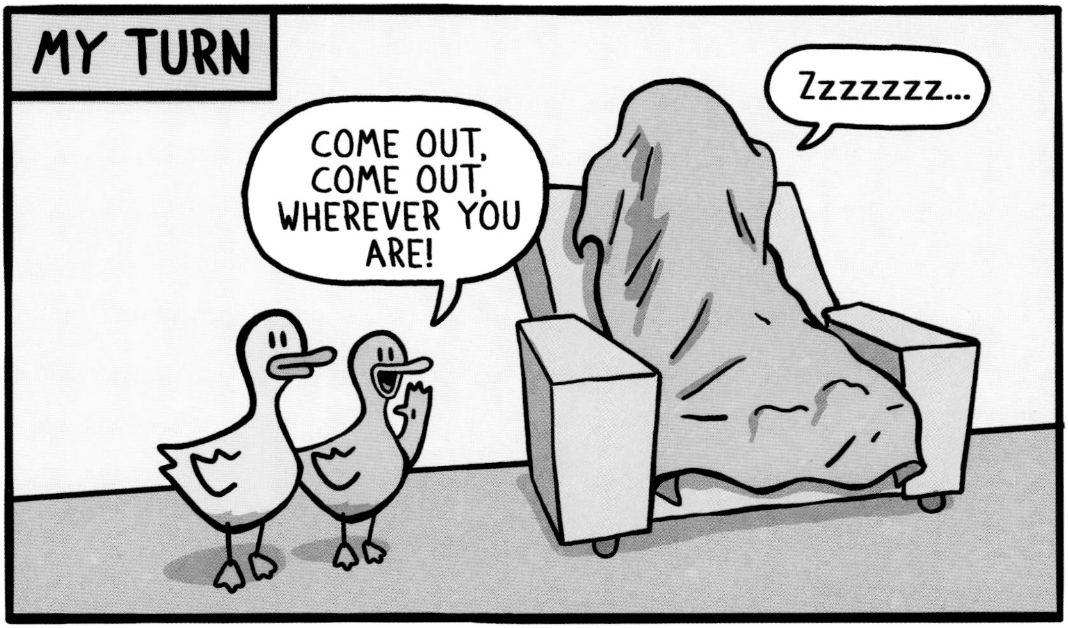
MY TURN
COME OUT, COME OUT, WHEREVER YOU ARE!
Zzzzzzz...

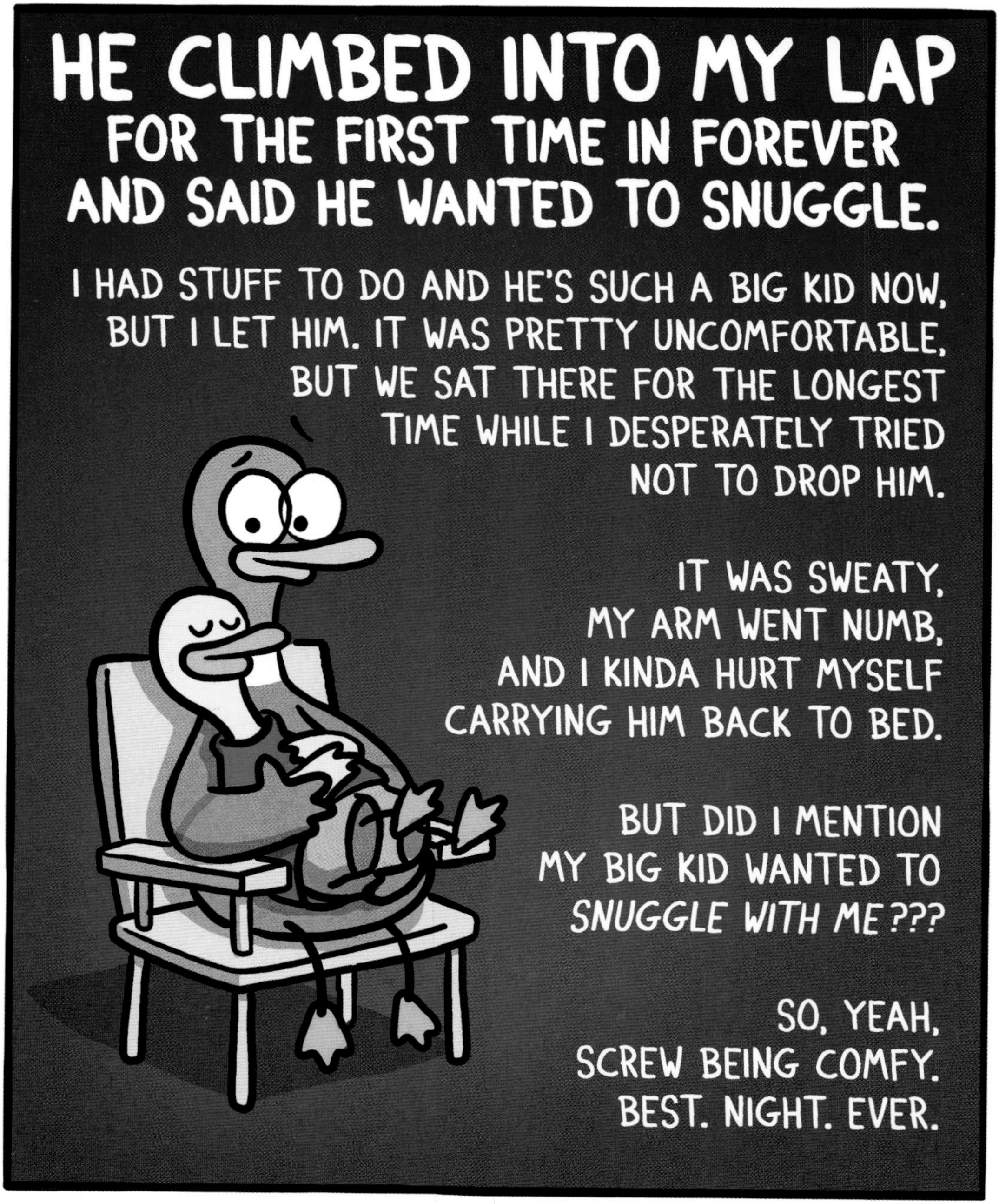

# HE CLIMBED INTO MY LAP
## FOR THE FIRST TIME IN FOREVER
## AND SAID HE WANTED TO SNUGGLE.

I HAD STUFF TO DO AND HE'S SUCH A BIG KID NOW,
BUT I LET HIM. IT WAS PRETTY UNCOMFORTABLE,
BUT WE SAT THERE FOR THE LONGEST
TIME WHILE I DESPERATELY TRIED
NOT TO DROP HIM.

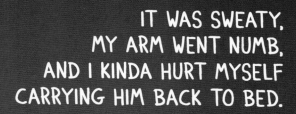

IT WAS SWEATY,
MY ARM WENT NUMB,
AND I KINDA HURT MYSELF
CARRYING HIM BACK TO BED.

BUT DID I MENTION
MY BIG KID WANTED TO
*SNUGGLE WITH ME ???*

SO, YEAH,
SCREW BEING COMFY.
BEST. NIGHT. EVER.

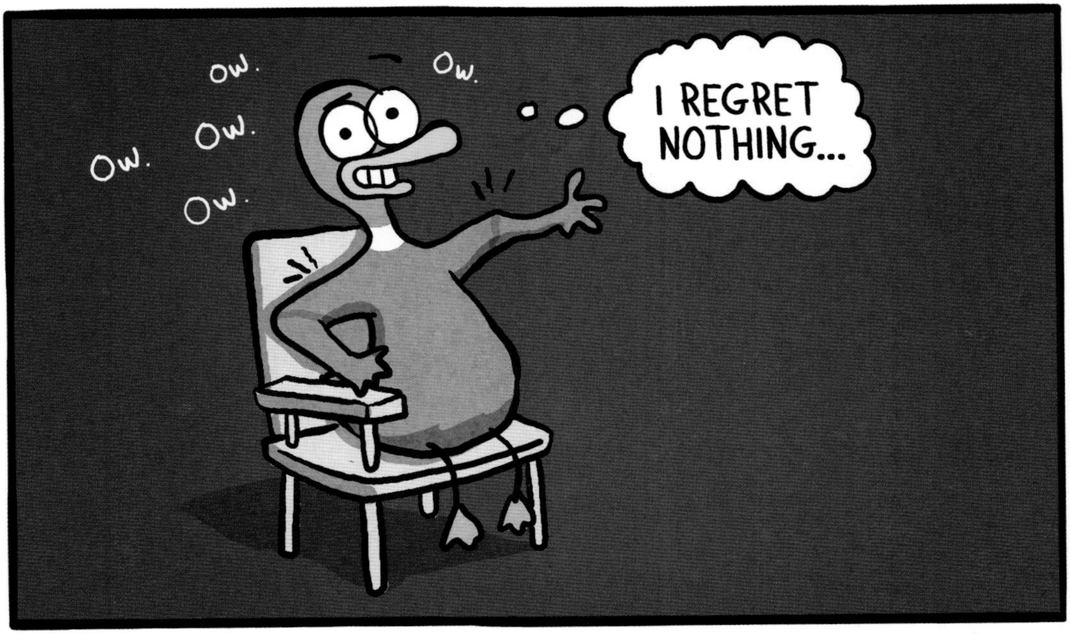
OW.
OW.
OW.
OW.
OW.
I REGRET NOTHING...

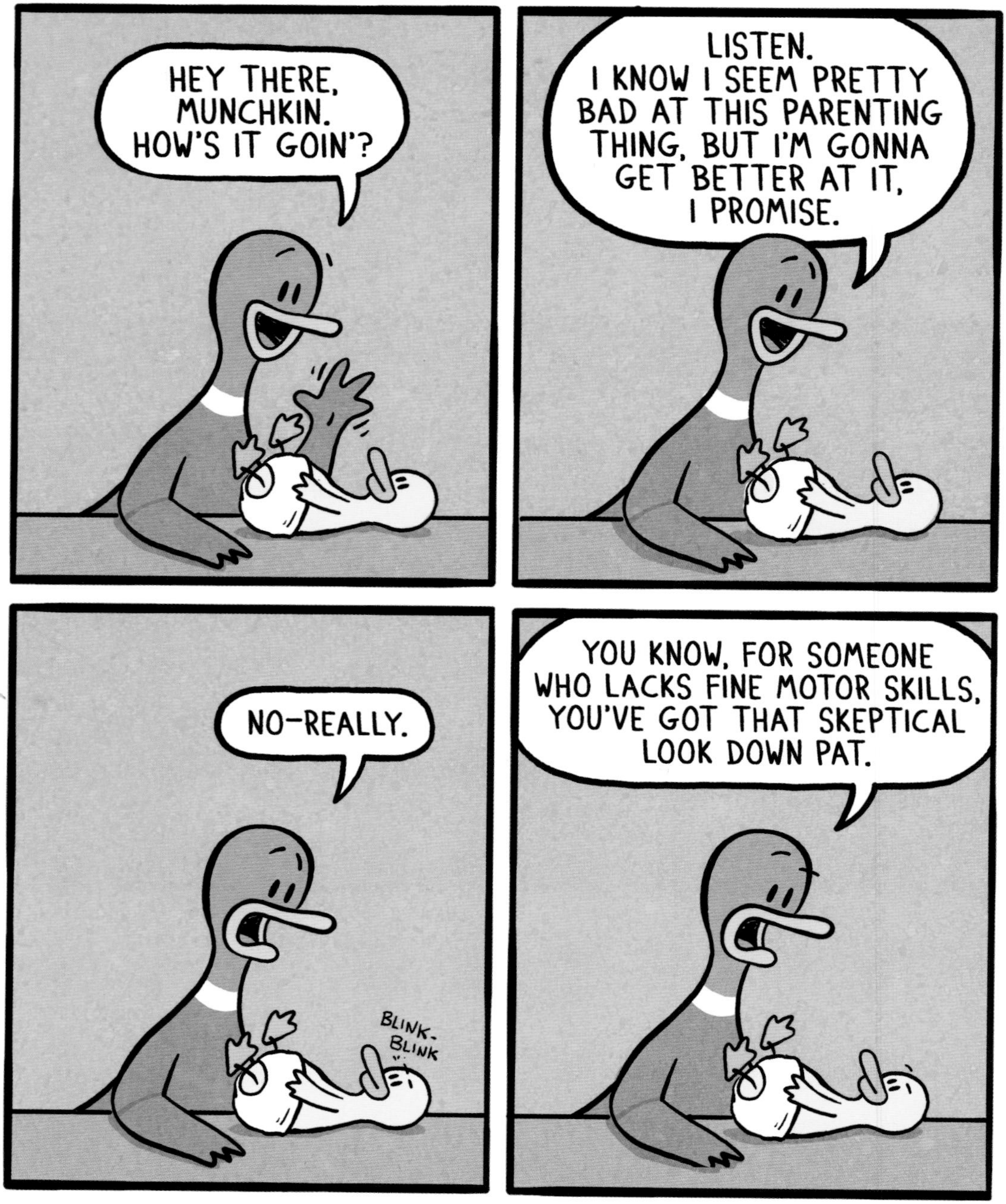
HEY THERE, MUNCHKIN. HOW'S IT GOIN'?
LISTEN. I KNOW I SEEM PRETTY BAD AT THIS PARENTING THING, BUT I'M GONNA GET BETTER AT IT, I PROMISE.
NO–REALLY.
BLINK-BLINK
YOU KNOW, FOR SOMEONE WHO LACKS FINE MOTOR SKILLS, YOU'VE GOT THAT SKEPTICAL LOOK DOWN PAT.

If it weren't for the kindness and generosity of my supporters on Patreon,
I wouldn't be able to keep making these comics (or feed my kids).
Thank you all from the bottom of my heart! XO Brian

JOSEPHINE MARCHES LEE NELSON AMY LYONS JIM PASTREICH BRIAN AND MEG CAREY
THE AWKWARD YETI PAUL NEUTRINO MICHELE NADA KIRKWOOD MICHAEL LACCETTI
NATHAN SINGER HELENA MCCABE DUSTY CARRILLO LIZ TEWS TIMOTHY CHRISMAN
TYLER MICHELLE SZETELA MR. X ELAINE MCKABA ANNE BARGUSS CINDY KEMPF
RICHARD STANFORD PETER MARTIN LENA CARDELL LISA SIMPSON NADIA FERNANDES MENDES
KAREN BROOMFIELD CAITLIN LOVETT GENISTA B. MARCUS HAVANEK NAOMI ANDERSON
TOM RICE RADIOACTIVE SCOOP SANDRA BUSO LUTZ WONG ANTHONY MUILENBURG
KRISTIAN BERNTZEN DON STEVENSON KATY COLBRY NICHOLAS BASSETT ELIANA BELÉN
CELIS ROJAS MARCY & EWEN CÉCILIA ADER ANDERSEN PAMELA DANIEL VICKIE CHANG
DANA BAKER TERRI BEHM DONNA DISTEFANO SINEAD QUEENBORG BORGERSEN
LAUREN NICOLE HEYES ANNE LERFORS VIVIAN LAKE JEN T. MICHAEL REDMOND
SARA W. DEAN JEAN LADENSACK DONNA S. JASON WRIGHT GIDON MOONT CHRISTIE STOUT
REBECCA HUBER BETH GERLACH STEVE THOMAS LAEL BRADDOCK ALICIA FREISNER
MORITZ KELLER SHEKHAR SRINIVASAN PIER HO MANUEL AZEVEDO BRYEN ZIMMERMAN
SANDRA WRIGHT H KRISHNAN COURTNEY LEE VALERIA HERSKOVIC SUSAN WARD
JACK BARNUM DEAH GULLEY NIKITA SHENOY KAREN FARLEY KELLY THOMPSON
ANDY CAPONE HOLLY KELLEY LISA JUAREZ CORI AGUILAR DEBBELLS CARYN MACKAY
BRENDA JACKELS FLORENCE JACQUET ED COLLADO MARK SMITH GARY SUGANO
SERENA THOMPSON JON GUIDRY BONNYE LAPENOTIERE SIRK HEATHER BELCHER
LISA WIDÉN IRIS HSU JENNIFER LARSON SHAWN CHANDLER THE LALLA FAMILY
ANDREA GOULET SAMUEL ALLEN KATHRYN PORTER JEANETTE AMANDA O'BRIEN
TAD MILLER S LIM SUSAN WATKINS SARA STRANG LAUREN HALL RYAN MOURA
MIKE BURNS CARLA BULMER RUPERT SU TROY RADFORD MELANIE & ALEXANDER SCHAAF
VIVIENNE PARISH SEAN MC JENNY REYNO SACHA MALIN BENJAMIN FOGARASI
TIM EKSTROM MEGAN ADAMIRE ROBERT MURRAY EMILY MCCALIB LINDSAY EVANS
NICOLAS CENDROWSKI ALEX ANN THOMPSON JEN PRIETO-AYRES SCOTT EMMONS
BARBARA LORI AND ANDREW BURNS RACHEL REESE ERICA STOLLMAN ALAN WRIGHT
GAIL NASTASI BOOKS TO BENEFIT BETH LAWLESS AMY FIELDS SHERRY STERRETT
GILL POTTS CHRISSY FLEMING ERIKA CHANG ROY PENNEY LOUISE TROEST
TRISH BERRONG RICHARD PENNELL NAYSHA RIVERA-SWANSON CAMILLE COOREMAN
NICOLE A. H. MCCLUNEY KERRI ABRAMS ERICA J. WHITAKER THOMAS RAUSCHER
LILIBEAN FLORIAN MUELLER ANTHONY Y. ELSA CADE ANJULIKA SHARMA ARNE
HELEN CLAYTON BEBE SUPREE RACHEL FUNK CHRIS NELSON VALENTINE KARL
CHRISTIAN NPEARSON JENICA ROGERS STEVE BRANGACCIO MICHELANN QUIMBY
DONALD YOUNG JESSICA COLLETT JARED LAW TIELA BLACK-LAW THE SCHERCK FAMILY
DANIEL TAP.NOS. MURRAY SAMPSON JONATHAN LONG ZEEZEE ELNIE LINARDI
VERONICA LAUREN BANKS AUBRY DZIAK KELLY OHLERT HOLLY WARREN NICKY MARIE
SUZANNE EATON CAMILLE GOOD ADAM KNIGHT ALEXANDRE PAULO LISA SALEHPOUR
THOMAS TA RUNE CHRISTIANSEN MARIANA SEGURA JENNIFER JHON FERNANDO DONATI
IGOR DRINCIC CATHERINE DELAGRANGE SHAWN SIMPSON RICHARD CINDY WINGERT
ANN LAWSON KELLY MITCHELL RM PRADEEP SATYAPRAKASH ANDREA ZACHER
GINA GOLDIE INEKE BAUWENS SAMI LAINE DEBORAH CUTLER KATE TESTERMAN
IAN ROTHMAN MARTYN DEWAR KARYN PHILLIPSON NOAH FANG MANDY RING ERIC HIND
THOMAS KELLER GNOUPI JARNAIL SINGH DHILLON ADAM BOVIE GRAEME ROSS
AUNTIESASH HAZLEWOOD KAI LUNDQUIST ANJELA BUGHER KNUT ANDRÉ HJORTH
AARON RENNER TOM DE BRUIJN ANNE BAGUETTE RYAN, TESSA, AND ANNABELLE BAXTER
SOPHIE LEVESQUE TERRY SUSANNA JANET WETMORE LUTHER RIEXINGER CHRISTOPHER
NESHA BENSTEAD STOOTZA KUNAL KP ASHLEY HELM NICOLAS BENORE WEENA DORE
HWAN-JOON KATHERINE PENNELL CLAY FISKE JOAN PETERS ROBIN GIESE LINDSAY
ANNE SCHLACK IRINA PALCZYNSKI TILGHMAN LESHER TAMMY VETTER POITRAS
ESTEBAN MAROTO KATY GREEN ART BRADY MICHAEL CARLSON MAMARI STEPHENS
ANNE-MARIE SCHULZ JEN GOSNELL LARA MARKS-NASH TAWANA TIM JOHNSON
CHANTAL PRISCILLA HETHERTON PAMELA J FOWLER ERICA HOWAT STEPHANIE BRADY
RAY MARÍA VERÓNICA LILLO JEN LIN PAT HULL DIANE THERIAULT ALISHA GALLANT
SARAH JO LORENZ SAMANTHA BROUWER SARAH ROBERT BOSTICK JENNY BRUCE
MARK F ALEX METCALF ANOUK WEHLI GAURAV GULATI NORAH DOOLEY NORINA JIMENO
ED MITCHELL BECKY SCOTT MARC DIAZ LIZZY DUNCAN YVONNE LEIALOHA HILL
AUNTIE HALLIE JON BALTOS SYLVIA DAVIDSON FOO CHOONG LIM SCOTT A. NEWTON
SARAH MCCALLUM RICHARD DANIEL HAGERTY JULIE WATT CHRIS WEIDNER MATT GIDNEY
FRIEND DOG STUDIOS PETE RZEMINSKI VENKATESH IYER JOE VASQUEZ SHARRIF BELWEIL
COLMAN JOERI PHEI STACIE SHAFFER ALIDA MYBURGH FRANCA SERRAU TOM VAN DER LEK
JULIE SAUBION RAMYA IYER KEAVEN HEVEL HOLLY HINTON EMMY CHANG MARIA PARRA
ANDY GARI STRAWN MAXIME CALLAERT CATHERINE RABOLD ERAN WEISS JENNIFER CHAU
LASSE LUND ELMER LINDA SIMPSON A SCHAFFAR DAVID ELLIOTT BRITTNEY VUJCICH
ELISE ROBINSON ELBA SCOTT WALLDREN SHONA MARTENS JACQUELINE MCCABE SANDY

Andrews McMeel Publishing
a division of Andrews McMeel Universal
1130 Walnut Street, Kansas City, Missouri 64106

www.andrewsmcmeel.com

17 18 19 20 21 SDB 10 9 8 7 6 5 4 3 2 1

ISBN: 978-1-4494-8675-4

Library of Congress Control Number: 2016959651

Editor: Dorothy O'Brien
Creative Director: Tim Lynch
Production Editor: Amy Strassner
Production Manager: Chuck Harper